UNIVERSITIES IN CRISIS: A MEDIAEVAL INSTITUTION IN THE TWENTY-FIRST CENTURY

UNIVERSITIES IN CRISIS: A MEDIAEVAL INSTITUTION IN THE TWENTY-FIRST CENTURY

Edited by
WILLIAM A.W. NEILSON
and **CHAD GAFFIELD**

The Institute for Research on Public Policy/
L'Institut de recherches politiques

Printed in Canada

Legal Deposit First Quarter
Bibliothèque nationale du Québec

Canadian Cataloguing in Publication Data

Main entry under title:
Universities in crisis

Prefatory material in English and French.
ISBN 0-88645-034-9

1. Universities and colleges — Philosophy —
Addresses, essays, lectures. I. Neilson,
William A.W. II. Gaffield, Chad, 1951-
III. Institute for Research on Public
Policy

LB2325.U55 1986 378'.001 C86-090125-4

The Institute for Research on Public Policy/
L'Institut de recherches politiques
2149 Mackay Street, Suite 102
Montreal, Quebec H3G 2J2

CONTENTS

FOREWORD

The University of Victoria celebrated its twenty-first anniversary as a degree-granting institution in 1984. A principal feature of its anniversary celebration was the hosting of a conference, The University into the Twenty-first Century, which attracted speakers and participants from around the world. The quality of the papers presented at the conference sessions prompted the interest of the Institute in stimulating broader debate and wider circulation of selected papers through publication of this volume.

Universities are in trouble. The pace of social and institutional change demands of all public institutions a difficult combination of resilience, adaptability, and stability amidst turmoil. As agents for and authors of research, training, and intellectual inquiry, universities and colleges are in the middle of the tempest. The papers in this volume provide a critical and balanced study of the pivotal issues of academic independence and the effect of technological change on North American universities. Their prognosis is for survival of the institution, but with difficulty and with a potential compromise of purpose.

The total social price of the resolution of these issues is of the utmost significance not only to academic, political, and business leaders but to all of us. Universities for the past thousand years and more have been the cultural centres of our society. The debate over their purpose and place as we prepare for the next century is illuminated by the papers presented in the following pages, and the Institute for Research on Public Policy is happy to encourage further discussion through their publication here. Only through such searching re-examination of current practices can we achieve the renewed broad support for the idea of the university that is, in my view, essential at this time.

Robert L. Stanfield
Chairman of the Board

November 1985

AVANT-PROPOS

L'université de Victoria célébrait en 1984 son vingt et unième anniversaire à titre d'établissement d'enseignement supérieur habilité à décerner des diplômes. L'un des événements marquants organisés par l'université dans le cadre de cette année anniversaire fut la conférence portant sur l'Université et le XXIe siècle, qui a accueilli des conférenciers et des participants du monde entier. Reconnaissant la qualité des propos livrés à cette occasion et désirant en favoriser la diffusion et la discussion sur une plus grande échelle, l'Institut a décidé de procéder à leur publication sélective, sous la forme du présent recueil.

L'Université est en difficulté. Le rythme des bouleversements sociaux et structurels exigent de toutes les institutions publiques une combinaison difficile de capacités de récupération, de souplesse et de stabilité. À titre de maîtres d'oeuvre en matière de recherche, de formation et d'élargissement des connaissances, les universités et collèges se trouvent au coeur de l'actuelle tourmente. Les exposés présentés ici constituent une étude critique et nuancée de deux questions névralgiques, soit l'autonomie du milieu de l'enseignement et l'incidence du virage technologique sur les universités nord-américaines. Leurs conclusions? L'Université survivra, mais avec difficulté, et devra peut-être accepter certains compromis quant au rôle qui lui a traditionnellement été dévolu.

Le prix social à payer pour la résolution de ces quesitons revêt une importance capitale non seulement pour les dirigeants pédagogiques, politiques et industriels, mais également pour l'ensemble de la population. Depuis plus de mille ans, les universités sont les foyers culturels de nos sociétés. Les propos ici regroupés présentent sous un éclairage pertinent le débat sur le rôle et la place de l'Université en cette fin de millénaire. L'Institut de recherches politiques est heureux d'en assurer la publication et d'encourager ainsi l'élargissement de la discussion.

Seul l'examen critique des pratiques actuelles nous permettra de renouveler le consensus autour de l'Université, consensus qui m'apparaît vital à l'époque que nous traversons.

Robert L. Stanfield
Président du Conseil

Novembre 1985

THE CONTRIBUTORS

Axelrod, Paul | Associate Professor, Division of Social Science, Faculty of Arts, York University

Bearman, Toni Carbo | Executive Director, National Commission on Libraries and Information Science, Washington, D.C.

Berman, Morris | Lansdowne Professor of the History of Science, University of Victoria

Cairns, Alan C. | Professor of Political Science, University of British Columbia

Cochrane, William A. | President and Chief Executive Officer, Connaught Laboratories Limited, Toronto

Cross, K. Patricia | Professor, Graduate School of Education, Harvard University

Fulton, E. Margaret | President, Mount St. Vincent University

Gaffield, Chad | Associate Professor of History, formerly University of Victoria, University of Ottawa

Katz, Michael B. | Professor, Urban Studies Program, University of Pennsylvania

Kornberg, Hans | Sir William Dunn Professor of Biochemistry and Master of Christ's College, Cambridge University

Meyerhoff, Albert H.   Attorney, Natural Resources Defense
                          Council, San Francisco

Michael, Donald A.   Professor Emeritus of Planning and
                          Public Policy, University of Michigan

Neilson, William A.W.   Dean and Professor of Law, Faculty of
                          Law, University of Victoria

Suppes, Patrick   Lucie Stern Professor of Philosophy,
                          Director of the Institute for Math-
                          ematical Studies in Social Sciences,
                          Stanford University

Vagianos, Louis   Special Assistant to the President,
                          Institute for Research on Public Policy,
                          Halifax

Winchester, Ian   Professor, Higher Education Group,
                          Ontario Institute for Studies and
                          Education, Toronto

SUMMARY

The late twentieth century will see a major social transformation affecting many aspects of individual, family, and community experience. The depth and duration of these shifts are yet unclear, but observers perceive fundamental changes at work in the theory and method of social organization. The arena for change includes the institutions, systems, and objectives of higher education. Not surprisingly, the very character and purpose of the university have become an important element in the current debate about the extent of change, its social implications, and our capacities to deal with it.

History teaches that the university is an exceedingly resilient institution, having survived wars, plagues, and social upheavals for centuries. Researchers for the U.S. Carnegie Commission on Higher Education identified only sixty-six organizations or institutions that have been in continuous existence in Europe since the Protestant Reformation of the sixteenth century. Listed were the Catholic and Lutheran churches, the parliaments of the Isle of Man and Iceland, and sixty-two universities.

This book is not about the demise of universities. Rather, it is about basic alterations that are, or need to be, under way in the university. Higher education is being significantly transformed in a proportion vastly exceeding the immediate controversies associated with an aging population, cutbacks in financing, and lifelong learning imperatives.

As the twenty-first century nears, two issues dominate the analysis of universities and social change. The first is the independence of universities from government and business. Has a "moral crisis" resulted from an assimilation of universities into the marketplace, or are universities simply "staying near the customer"? The second issue is the effect of technological development on intellectual inquiry. Can universities thrive in the Information Age, or is the "cybernetic dream" a nightmare from which all scholarly pursuit must be awakened?

These questions are explored thoughtfully and provocatively in the papers making up this collection. Two assumptions underlie the approach and form the framework within which the authors present their arguments. First, any consideration of the future of universities must be addressed in the context of worldwide social, economic, and intellectual environments. These papers explore the ways universities relate to governments, to the private sector, to research institutes, to different economic environments, and to other educational systems. Certainly it is difficult to view universities from such an integrated perspective, but the authors valiantly attempt to examine both the character of universities and their relations with their host societies. Second, the authors resist the tendency to concentrate on post-1945 developments. Several of the papers include a strong historical component, a perspective essential to any analysis of the university's capacity to cope with the influences of rapid social change on its educational purpose and integrity.

The papers in the first section explore the relations between government, business, and public universities. In the opening paper, **Michael B. Katz** draws upon his considerable scholarship in Canadian and American educational history to examine the coupling of the marketplace and higher education. The accelerated pace of the university's integration with the market model and the state, in his view, is directly related to a growing moral degeneration that threatens the community of learning, which has historically distinguished the university from other public institutions. The integrity of university programs, both in teaching and in research, must be openly questioned in the face of a growing abdication of moral leadership by university faculty and administrators. Their entanglement with external constituencies and providers has developed over many decades and at a very high price.

According to **William A. Cochrane**, distinguished medical dean and president of Connaught Laboratories, legitimacy has much to do, however, with the relevance and utility of services provided by universities to their local communities, with the needs of employers, and with national economic goals. Cochrane sets out the arguments for a thoughtful adaptation of the market model to university research priorities, faculty evaluation and retraining, and curriculum planning. He presses the case for the detailed co-ordination of government, business, and university planning, particularly in scientific research, use of personnel, and high technology investments. Without an intelligent application of the market model to significant activities in higher education, Cochrane despairs for Canada's competitiveness in global trading relations, upon which the country's well-being depends so heavily.

York University social scientist **Paul Axelrod** traces the relations between business and universities in the twentieth century. In recent years, he observes, the interests of politicians and business in the activities of universities have become selective and increasingly conditional as they favour "the pragmatic disciplines at the expense of arts and general education." The necessary shift to increased private sector funding, according to Axelrod, will favour applied research to the prejudice of theoretical research, will stifle the dissemination of results adverse to the interests of funding sponsors, will depress the humanities, and will tie the universities to the erratic and self-serving interests of powerful entrepreneurs. He abhors the coming of the "brave new university" of the twenty-first century.

Some of Axelrod's concerns acquire a riveting immediacy in lawyer **Albert Meyerhoff's** paper, a tough and unyielding commentary on the ethical implications confronting American universities in their dependence on the private funding of research projects, facilities, and personnel. In several respects, the "commercialization" of university research in the United States had imperiled the integrity of the institutions and their faculty and programs, particularly at the graduate and post-graduate levels. His review of the University of California's experience with conflict of interest legislation crystallizes the clash between scholarship and self-interest in the merging worlds of university and commercial scientific laboratories. Meyerhoff's paper graphically raises profound concerns about the implications for society if present trends continue. His case studies return us easily to the tempest of moral crisis analyzed in the book's opening paper by Michael Katz.

Sir Hans Kornberg, distinguished U.K. scientist, by comparison feels cautiously sanguine about the price of greater involvement by business in the research activities and priorities of universities. An appropriate balance can be struck, and must be achieved in the wake of declining government funding, "provided that the universities remain alive to the needs for maintaining their basic research capability."

This will not be easy, for great patience and forbearance are required to permit scientists to "follow their bent without coercion" in their pursuit of the "type of free inquiry on which unpredicted, and as yet unpredictable, advances in the future will undoubtedly rest." Several case studies posed by Kornberg suggest that the discipline-based organization of universities must undergo significant changes for efficient and productive links with business and industry to be forged.

The papers in the second section address the debate over machines and minds. This debate challenges the conventional assumption that science and technology can be used for either good or evil, that computers, for example, are value-free. Moreover, the authors suggest that the increasing importance of access to information will engender a new definition of the have/have not dichotomy. Just as the fading Industrial Age was characterized by a division between property owners and proletarians, the emerging Information Age threatens to divide the information rich from the information poor.

The university is at the centre of debate about these issues, and three distinct perspectives are offered by Morris Berman, Patrick Suppes, and Toni Carbo Bearman. **Morris Berman**, Lansdowne historian of science at the University of Victoria, argues that society in general and the university in particular are now at a crucial crossroads. The choice is to continue our attachment to mechanistic science and thus to welcome uncritically the computerization of society, including teaching and research in universities, or to work toward a new paradigm "grounded in the real behaviour of man in the environment" and thus perhaps to reject technological "advances." Berman describes the historical origins of what he terms the cybernetic dream and relates these origins to diverse contemporary phenomena such as Pac-Man and artificial intelligence. In this way, his chapter challenges directly the optimistic vision of the future that characterizes most discussion about recent developments in computerization and their implications for higher learning.

Patrick Suppes of Stanford also refers to historical traditions but, in contrast to Berman, articulates an optimistic view of the new integration of computers and education. Suppes sees the current technological revolution as a further advance over the great educational innovations of the past. Computerization follows upon five major developments: the introduction of written records in ancient times; the founding of libraries, as in Alexandria in 300 B.C.; the introduction of printing in the fifteenth century; the establishment of mass schooling in the nineteenth century; and the refinement of testing for defining aptitudes and skills in modern decades. In his view, computers build upon this tradition by individualizing rather than alienating, by decentralizing rather than standardizing, and by liberating rather than confining the intellectual activities of their users.

Suppes argues that computers have the capacity to renew the classic pattern of learning by allowing students to be tutored individually. Moreover, such instruction can take place in a variety of locations, and Suppes predicts that large universities and large lecture courses will wither together. Increasingly, education at all levels will take place in the home, which itself will recapture its historic role as the basic unit of all social organization. Suppes concludes that the use of computers can be "a key element in creating a better world than we have ever known before."

Toni Carbo Bearman, acclaimed information scientist, is similarly optimistic about the entry of the university into the Information Age. She suggests that basic questions remain unanswered about computerized information and the role of government, the economy, ethics, and professional training. Bearman uses the experience of the United States to discuss the wide-ranging implications of information storage and retrieval for the relations between universities and their host societies. She identifies basic concerns and suggests an agenda for reform. Bearman emphasizes that the university must not leave the resolution of information-related problems to leaders in government or industry; rather, the academic community must join in renewed partnerships with such leaders to meet the challenges of tomorrow's world.

The papers in the third section concentrate on the responsibility and capacity of today's university to prepare for tomorrow's changes. How are colleges and universities preparing for the future? What ought to be their priorities? What other communities are involved in the exercise? In the opening paper, **Louis Vagianos**, of the Institute for Research on Public Policy, strongly doubts that the university can prepare for tomorrow within its present institutional framework. The ultimate responsibility of higher education is to produce leaders who can cope with a high technology society and are also well schooled in the humanities.

Unfortunately, in Vagianos' analysis, universities are hindered by aging faculty and facilities. Faculty unions on some campuses have added "an institutionalization of suspicion toward those who advocate change." A strong social inertia within colleges has combined with public scepticism about the worth of university degrees to raise serious concerns about the ability of the university to discharge its educational obligations. "Sitting still," says Vagianos, "will not help solve our paradox. . . . Action is required, but action to be effective must be planned. We have to get down to specifics now. This means effective, constructive planning soundly based on the realities of the present."

Donald A. Michael, distinguished critic of social planning and change, regards the university as a learning system whose organizational culture appears drastically unfit to deal with the turbulence of uncertainty and rapid change facing higher education as we move toward the twenty-first century. "A key determinant of an organization's ability to engage its circumstances effectively is the characteristics of its culture: its norms of conduct; styles of personal relationships; reward systems; structures; modes of intercourse with its internal and external stakeholders; and its expectations and beliefs about its purposes and reasons for existence."

The university's culture, like other social organizations, is the residue of *past* learned successes and suppressed failures. Not surprisingly, it is badly equipped to deal with tomorrow's challenges. The only way for the university to turn the corner will be consciously to adopt a "learning approach" to organizational development. The task sounds simple, but, in fact, preparing for tomorrow will require a fundamental restructuring of organization, attitudes, and personal relationships. University administrators and faculty must continuously address questions about the direction, pace, and objectives of change. Michael's paper challenges universities to stop wallowing and take action. The world will not settle down. Neither withdrawal nor muddling through are viable options.

K. Patricia Cross, a leading U.S. educator, agreed that the university must alter its structure and purpose if it is to respond appropriately to the changing demands of social and technological change. In her view, the university must make a place for itself in an emerging learning society where formal education is a lifelong process. Cross defines this society as one in which most individuals are engaged in organized learning throughout their lives rather than primarily as young adults. Universities will therefore have an almost permanent student body rather than one that changes dramatically from year to year.

Cross pursues this assessment by emphasizing six elements of change now apparent in higher education: the proliferation of organized instruction for adults outside universities; the blurring of roles among various educational providers; the increasingly part-time commitment of both university students and faculty; the growing necessity that learning become a lifelong activity in a rapidly changing society; the new demand for broad intellectual skills; and the changing role of education itself within the

Information Age. These factors are transforming the university as a centre of teaching and research. Cross remains optimistic that the university can meet this challenge, but, she warns, the required alternatives will substantially redefine the established pattern of higher education.

Current claims that the university may soon be sacrificed in the name of restraint or relevancy miss the mark, according to **E. Margaret Fulton**, president of Mount St. Vincent University in Nova Scotia. In her view, the university is *already* dying. Fulton not only shares the concerns of Katz about the influence of the marketplace and of Berman about the popularity of a cybernetic dream but also emphasizes the loss of a "spiritual component" within higher education. She condemns Canadian universities, which are "so constrained by the classical scientific and educational paradigm that they cannot accommodate the spiritual and recognize the visionary."

In this way, Fulton argues that the real challenge to the university is internal rather than external. The university must not simply devise ways to respond to the pressures of government, business, or technology but, more significantly, must recapture a fundamental meaning and purpose that have been lost in modern society. Fulton perceives that the university has forgotten the meaning of true learning, which, as Robertson Davies said, is "to save the soul and enlarge the mind." The crisis of higher education, therefore, extends to the heart of the academy and goes well beyond issues of enrolments, budgets, and curricula. If the university does not realize that the current reality is divorced from the traditional rhetoric of higher education, Fulton warns, the challenges of external interests will have no meaningful effect; the real damage will have already been done. For this reason, the university must first heal itself through restructuring and reorientation. Only then will it be able to address the external challenges.

Alan C. Cairns, an eminent Canadian political scientist, explores the relation between scholarship and the subtleties of tradition, process, community, and identity. For him, it is impossible to understand the university without comprehending the "subtle context of cues, values, and ambitions that motivates individual researchers" and the complementary regime of "norms, understandings, and constraints" that leads to the co-ordination of superior scholarship. Cairns discusses the high degree of social instability within university structures, the effect of external influences on the social sciences and humanities, and the incompatibilities between the institution and the academic disciplines. His findings and prognosis, at first blush, would tend to soften some of the alarms raised in this section's preceding papers but careful reflection by the reader is advised.

The final selection brings together many themes within a sweeping vision of the past, present, and future. **Ian Winchester** draws upon his wide-ranging background in the arts and sciences to analyze the fundamental characteristics of the university as it has evolved in Western society. Winchester approaches the controversies over higher education as a philosopher with a keen sense of history. For him, the profound issue is not enrolments or budgets. Rather, it is the role of the university as the "cultural centre," which should pursue "knowledge of the good and the beautiful." Winchester's complex argument integrates insights from other authors, including Katz, Berman, Suppes, and Fulton, and, in the end, leads to a fascinating discussion of how the university can best adjust in the coming decades.

This discussion not only shows why the hope for a return to the "lost liberal education" is wrongheaded but also why other similar proposals would not be effective strategies for the renewal of higher education. Winchester does not, however, only criticize. He offers what appears at first to be a startling suggestion for how the university can best fulfil its position as the cultural centre of society. Upon reflection, this suggestion becomes increasingly persuasive and, in fact, provides a focus for continuing the debate joined in the chapters of this book. The future of higher education is at stake; the crisis is upon us.

ABRÉGÉ

La fin du XXe siècle constituera un tournant social important, qui touchera un grand nombre d'aspects de la vie individuelle, familiale et collective. Si l'ampleur et la durée des mutations prévues sont encore vagues, les observateurs en perçoivent dès à présent les conséquences tant pour ce qui est de la théorie que de la méthode d'organisation sociale. Le théâtre de ces changements englobe les établissements, les systèmes ainsi que les objectifs de l'enseignement supérieur. Il n'est donc pas surprenant que le caractère et le rôle mêmes de l'Université soient devenus un élément important du débat actuel sur l'étendue de la transformation, ses conséquences sociales et notre capacité d'y faire face.

L'histoire nous enseigne que l'Université est dotée d'une faculté de récupération tout à fait exceptionnelle, celle-ci ayant survécu aux guerres, aux fléaux et aux bouleversements sociaux séculaires. Des chercheurs de la commission américaine Carnegie sur l'enseignement supérieur ont pu recenser soixante-six organisations ou institutions européennes existant de façon ininterrompue depuis la Réforme, au XVIe siècle. Celles-ci regroupent l'Église catholique, l'Église luthérienne, les parlements de l'île de Man et de l'Islande ainsi que soixante-deux universités.

Le présent ouvrage n'annonce pas la disparition prochaine de l'Université, mais tente plutôt de circonscrire les principaux changements amorcés et à entreprendre dans le milieu universitaire. L'enseignement supérieur fait actuellement l'objet de mutations profondes, qui vont bien au delà des controverses à portée plus immédiate ayant trait au vieillissement de la population, aux compressions budgétaires et à la place à accorder à l'éducation permanente.

À l'approche du XXIe siècle, deux questions principales dominent l'analyse des changements sociaux et pédagogiques qui s'annoncent. La première porte sur l'autonomie de l'Université par rapport à l'État et à l'entreprise. L'apparente soumission de l'Université aux lois du marché est-elle symptômatique d'une crise morale de cette dernière ou simplement l'indice de son désir de demeurer près de sa clientèle? La seconde question qui se pose est l'incidence du progrès technologique sur la recherche intellectuelle. En d'autres mots, l'Université peut-elle se développer dans cette nouvelle ère de l'information, ou le "grand rêve cybernétique" ne serait-il qu'un cauchemar dont le milieu de l'enseignement supérieur aurait intérêt à se réveiller?

Les exposés ici présentés examinent ces questions de façon à la fois réfléchie et audacieuse. Deux prémisses sous-tendent la démarche adoptée par leurs auteurs ainsi que la structure de leur argumentation. Le premier principe posé est que toute réflexion sur l'avenir de l'Université doit s'effectuer en tenant compte des environnements sociaux, économiques et intellectuels de l'ensemble de la planète. On trouvera ainsi des analyses sur les rapports que l'Université entretient avec les pouvoirs publics, le secteur privé, les établissements de recherche, les différents milieux économiques ainsi que les autres structures d'enseignement. L'établissement d'une telle perspective n'est pas chose facile, mais les auteurs ont su relever ce défi avec brio, en se penchant attentivement sur ce qui fait le caractère de l'Université et sur ses relations avec la société. En second lieu, les auteurs refusent de confiner leur analyse à la seule période suivant la Deuxième Guerre mondiale. À ce titre, plusieurs des exposés offrent une solide perspective historique, jugée essentielle à l'analyse de la capacité de l'Université de maîtriser l'influence exercée par une transformation social accélérée sur son intégrité et son rôle pédagogiques.

Les propos regroupés dans la première section étudient les relations entre l'État, l'entreprise et les universités publiques. Puisant dans sa connaissance approfondie du Canada et de l'histoire de l'enseignement aux États-Unis, **Michael B. Katz**, auteur du premier exposé, se penche sur les nouveaux rapports unissant l'Université au marché. L'adaptation accélérée de l'Université au modèle imposé par le marché et par l'État est, selon lui, directement liée à la dégénérescence morale menaçant de plus en plus le milieu de l'enseignement, qui historiquement a toujours su établir l'autonomie de l'Université face aux pouvoirs publics. Il convient de remettre sérieusement en question l'intégrité des programmes offerts par l'Université, tant sur le plan de l'enseignement que sur celui de la recherche, en raison, précise-t-il, du renoncement croissant des facultés et de leurs administrateurs à exercer leurs responsabilités en matière de direction et d'orientation. Pour Katz, l'Université paie très cher les rapports étroits qu'elle a noués au fil des dernières décennies avec les organes externes ainsi qu'avec ses "pourvoyeurs".

Selon **William A. Cochrane**, doyen distingué de la faculté de médecine et président des laboratoires Connaught, la légitimité de l'Université se fonde en grande partie sur la pertinence et l'utilité des services qu'elle fournit à son milieu ainsi que sur les besoins des employeurs et les grands objectifs économiques de la nation. Cochrane est d'avis que l'Université aurait intérêt à s'inspirer du modèle fourni par le marché pour procéder à l'établissement des priorités en matière de recherche, à l'évaluation et au recyclage des facultés ainsi qu'à la planification des programmes d'études. Il énonce des arguments en faveur de la coordination étroite des efforts de planification déployés par l'État, l'entreprise et l'Université, particulièrement en ce qui a trait à la recherche scientifique, à l'encadrement des ressources humaines et au financement de l'effort technologique. À défaut de l'application intelligente des lois du marché aux principaux secteurs d'activité caractérisant l'enseignement supérieur, Cochrane craint que le Canada ne fasse qu'affaiblir sa compétitivité commerciale globale, si déterminante pour le bien-être de ses citoyens.

Paul Axelrod, spécialiste en sciences sociales de l'Université York, retrace l'évolution des rapports entre l'entreprise et l'Université au XXe siècle. Il fait observer que l'appui de l'État et de l'entreprise à cette dernière est devenu, au cours des dernières années, de plus en plus sélectif et conditionnel, favorisant les disciplines pragmatiques au détriment des lettres et d'une formation générale. Selon Axelrod, le recours accru aux capitaux privés entravera la recherche fondamentale au profit de la recherche appliquée, réprimera la diffusion par l'Université d'études contraires aux intérêts de ses bailleurs de fonds, réduira l'importance des humanités et se traduira par son asservissement aux besoins immédiats d'entrepreneurs puissants. Il trouve particulièrement désolant l'avènement de l'université-usine, à l'image de ce "meilleur des mondes" que semble nous réserver le XXIe siècle.

Certaines des préoccupations d'Axelrod trouvent un écho retentissant dans l'exposé du juriste **Albert Meyerhoff**, qui livre ici un réquisitoire impitoyable sur les conséquences éthiques de la dépendance des universités américaines à l'égard du financement privé en matière de projets, d'installations et de personnel de recherche. Sous plusieurs aspects, la "commercialisation" de la recherche universitaire aux États-Unis remettrait en question l'intégrité de l'Université ainsi que celle de ses facultés et programmes, particulièrement pour ce qui est des études de 2ᵉ et de 3ᵉ cycles. Son analyse des démêlés de l'université de la Californie en regard de la législation concernant les conflits d'intérêts fait bien ressortir le point de rupture entre l'activité d'élargissement des connaissances et l'égoïsme des bailleurs de fonds, dans le cadre d'un rapprochement croissant entre l'Université et les laboratoires scientifiques commerciaux. Ses études de cas nous renvoient directement à l'importante crise morale analysée auparavant par Michael Katz.

Sir Hans Kornberg, éminent scientifique britannique, affiche, pour sa part, un optimisme prudent face à l'influence croissante exercée par l'entreprise sur l'exécution des travaux de recherche et la définition des priorités au sein des universités. Selon lui, ces dernières peuvent et doivent prendre des mesures réfléchies pour compenser la réduction des subventions que l'État leur accorde, sans toutefois renier leur rôle en matière de recherche fondamentale.

Il s'agit là d'un défi de taille, car la recherche scientifique doit s'effectuer avec le minimum de contrainte et bénéficier d'une bonne dose de patience et de tolérance pour mener à terme, les travaux souvent théoriques dont dépendent certainement les progrès encore imprévisibles de demain. À partir de plusieurs études de cas, Kornberg laisse entendre que la structure modulaire actuelle de l'Université doit être révisée en profondeur si l'on désire établir un lien efficace et productif entre cette dernière et le monde des affaires et de l'industrie.

Les exposés regroupés dans la seconde partie de cet ouvrage relèvent de la polémique sur l'Homme et la machine. On y remet en question le postulat guère contesté selon lequel la science et la technologie seraient libres de toute finalité et l'ordinateur, pour prendre un exemple concret, ne créerait pas de nouveaux déterminismes. Qui plus est, les auteurs font valoir que l'importance sans cesse accrue de l'accès à l'information pourrait engendrer une nouvelle catégorie de possédants et de démunis, articulée non plus sur la propriété privée, comme en cette fin d'ère industrielle, mais plutôt sur la facilité d'accès à l'information.

L'Université est sans nul doute au coeur de cette controverse, et Morris Berman, Patrick Suppes et Toni Carbo Bearman nous offrent ici trois perspectives différentes. **Morris Berman**, spécialiste en histoire de la Science de l'Université de Victoria, soutient que la société, y compris l'Université, sont actuellement devant une alternative, dont les termes pourraient s'exprimer ainsi : ou bien nous maintenons notre attachement à l'égard de la science mécaniste et assistons ainsi béatement à l'informatistation des différentes sphères d'activité de la société, y compris l'enseignement et la recherche universitaires, ou bien nous élaborons un nouveau modèle social inspiré du comportement réel de l'Homme dans son milieu, ce qui pourrait nous conduire à rejeter certains "progrès" technologiques. Berman retrace les origines de ce qu'il appelle le rêve cybernétique et fait ressortir les liens entre ces dernières et divers phénomènes contemporains, comme les jeux de type Pac-Man et ce qu'on appelle l'intelligence artificielle. Son exposé se trouve ainsi à remettre directement en question la vision optimiste de l'avenir qui caractérise la plupart des discussons sur les récents progrès en informatique et leurs conséquences pour l'enseignement supérieur.

Patrick Suppes, de l'Université Stanford, se réfère également à L'Histoire, mais, contrairement à Berman, compose un tableau optimiste de l'intégration de l'informatique au milieu de l'enseignement. Pour ce dernier, le virage technologique actuel est dans la lignée des grandes innovations technologiques qui ont marqué l'histoire de l'enseignement. Selon Suppes, l'informatisation constitue la sixième innovation déterminante pour l'éducation en général, les cinq premières étant, par ordre d'ancienneté, l'avènement de l'écriture, qui remonte à la haute antiquité, la création des bibliothèques, comme celles d'Alexandrie au IVe siècle avant Jésus-Christ, la découverte de l'imprimerie, au XVe siècle, la généralisation de la scolarisation, au XIXe siècle, et le perfectionnement des méthodes d'évaluation des aptitudes et des connaissances, au cours des dernières décennies. Suppes est d'avis que l'ordinateur favorise l'individualisation plutôt que l'aliénation, la décentralisation plutôt que la standardisation et entraîne la libération de l'activité intellectuelle de ses utilisateurs, et non sa limitation.

Il exprime l'avis que l'avènement de l'ordinateur est l'occasion de renouveler le modèle classique de l'apprentissage en instaurant un type d'enseignement individualisé, pouvant de surcoît être donné dans une grande diversité de lieux, tandis qu'il condamne à la caducité les méga-universités et les vastes salles de cours. De plus en plus, prédit-il, l'enseignement à tous les niveaux se fera au foyer, qui sera ainsi appelé à reprendre son rôle historique d'unité de base au sein de la structure sociale. Suppes conclut son exposé en affirmant que l'ordinateur peut se révéler un élément clé dans l'édification d'un monde meilleur.

Spécialiste de renom en sciences de l'information, **Toni Carbo Bearman** se montre tout aussi optimiste quant à l'entrée de l'Université dans l'ère de l'information. Elle fait cependant remarquer qu'un certain nombre de questions

demeurent sans réponse quant au rôle que doit jouer l'État dans
le processus d'informatisation et quant aux conséquences de cette
dernière sur l'économie, l'éthique et la formation professionnelle.
Se référant à l'expérience vécue aux États-Unis, elle traite
ensuite des innombrables répercussions du stockage et de la
recherche d'information, que permet l'ordinateur, sur les
relations entre l'Université et son milieu. Elle identifie· par
ailleurs un certain nombre de lacunes, tout en proposant un
programme de réforme. Bearman insiste sur le fait que
l'Université ne doit pas laisser aux seuls gouvernants et
industriels la responsabilité de résoudre les problèmes
concernant l'information; pour le milieu de l'enseignement,
affirme-t-elle, le moment est venu de conclure avec ces derniers
une nouvelle alliance, de façon à relever les défis de demain.

Les exposés regroupés dans la troisième section portent sur
la responsabilité de l'Université d'aujourd'hui à titre d'agent de
transformation ainsi que sur son aptitude à tenir pareil rôle.
Comment les collèges et les universités préparent-ils l'avenir?
Quelles devraient être leurs priorités? Quels sont les autres
milieux intéressés? Dans le premier exposé sur ce thème, **Louis
Vagianos**, de l'Institut de recherches politiques, doute fortement
de la capacité de l'Université actuelle de collaborer à
l'aménagement de la société de demain. Selon lui, la
responsabilité ultime de l'enseignement supérieur actuel doit
être de produire des chefs et des dirigeants qui pourront faire face
à un monde à forte composante technologique, tout en faisant
preuve d'une vaste culture générale.

Malheureusement, poursuit Vagianos, les universités
doivent composer avec des facultés et des installations
vieillissantes. En outre, les syndicats de professeurs ont parfois
institutionnalisé la méfiance à l'endroit des partisans du
changement. Une forte dose d'inertie sociale dans les collèges
combinée au scepticisme du public quant à la valeur des diplômes
universitaires laissent planer de sérieux doutes sur l'aptitude de
l'Université à assumer ses responsabilités pédagogiques.
L'immobilisme, ajoute Vagianos, n'aidera sûrement pas à
résoudre le paradoxe auquel nous sommes confrontés. Il faut
agir, mais de façon réfléchie et planifiée. L'Université doit se
fixer sans délai des objectifs bien précis et, pour ce faire, elle doit
procéder à une planification efficace et constructive, solidement
ancrée dans la réalité contemporaine.

Donald A. Michael, critique reconnu en matière de
planification et de transformation sociales, voit l'Université
comme une structure d'enseignement dont la philosophie en
matière d'organisation souffre d'un défaut total d'adaptation au

tumulte d'incertitudes et de bouleversements auquel l'enseignement supérieur doit faire face en cette fin de siècle. "L'un des éléments déterminants," soutient-il, "de la capacité d'une organisation de mobiliser ses diverses composantes réside dans les caractéristiques de sa philosophie, ses normes de conduite, le style des relations interpersonnelles de ses membres, son système de gratification, sa structure, ses rapports avec ceux qu'il est convenu d'appeler les dépositaires d'enjeux, tant internes qu'externes, ainsi que ses attentes et ses convictions quant à son rôle et à sa raison d'être."

Comme c'est le cas pour tout milieu, la philosophie universitaire est le résultat du rappel des réussites et de l'étouffement, pourrait-on dire, des échecs qui ont marqué le *passé*. Dans ces conditions, se demande Michael, comment se surprendre que l'Université soit mal préparée à affronter les défis de demain? La seule façon pour l'Université de se mettre au diapason de son époque est d'adopter une démarche didactique en matière de développement organisationnel. Si pareille tâche semble simple, la préparation effective à la société de demain nécessite néanmoins une restructuration fondamentale sur les plans de l'organisation, des attitudes et des relations personnelles. Les administrateurs et les professeurs de faculté doivent jauger en permanence l'orientation, le rythme et les objectifs du changement à effectuer. Enfin, il importe, selon Michael, que l'Université abandonne toute complaisance et se mette au travail. Le monde ne pouvant arrêter d'évoluer, ni la démission, ni l'improvisation ne sauraient se révéler acceptables.

Pédagogue américaine de premier plan, **K. Patricia Cross**, convient de la nécessité pour l'Université de repenser son rôle et sa structure afin de pouvoir réagir de façon appropriée aux exigences sans cesse renouvelées imposées par les changements sociaux et technologiques. Selon elle, l'Université doit se tailler une place dans cette nouvelle société où l'apprentissage constituera un processus non plus temporaire, mais à vie. Elle est d'avis que la plupart des individus seront bientôt intégrés en permanence, et non plus durant leur seule jeunesse, à un processus de formation structuré. En conséquence, la population étudiante de chaque établissement sera beaucoup plus stable, composée pour l'essentiel d'étudiants permanents, et les changements d'effectif seront réduits à leur plus simple expression.

Elle fonde cette hypothèse sur six éléments de mutation ressentis dès à présent dans l'enseignement supérieur, soit la prolifération des maisons d'enseignement et écoles spécialisées parallèles à l'Université, la confusion des rôles au sein du corps professoral, l'accroissement du nombre d'étudiants à temps partiel et l'augmentation des ressources que l'Université leur consacre, la place de plus en plus importante de l'éducation permanente dictée par l'évoluation rapide de la société, l'exigence renouvelée en matière d'aptitudes intellectuelles générales et enfin la modification du rôle de l'enseignement lui-même en cette ère de l'information. Ces différents facteurs contribuent à transformer l'Université comme centre d'enseignement et de recherche. Elle demeure optimiste quant à l'aptitude de l'Université à relever ce défi même si les solutions de rechange qui devront être adoptées redéfiniront radicalement le modèle classique de l'enseignement supérieur.

Pour **E. Margaret Fulton**, présidente de l'Université Mount St. Vincent en Nouvelle-Écosse, les allégations actuelles selon lesquelles l'Université se verrait bientôt sacrifiée au nom des contraintes extérieures ou de son inadaptation ne sont pas pertinentes. Selon elle en effet, l'Université est *déjà* parvenue au stade terminal. En plus de partager les vues de Katz sur l'influence du marché et celles de Berman sur la popularité du mythe cybernétique, elle insiste sur le fait que l'enseignement a été vidé de toute dimension spirituelle. Elle condamne l'Université pour ne pas être en mesure de faire une place à cette importante composante ni de reconnaître les apports visionnaires, toute enfermée qu'elle est dans le modèle scientifique et pédagogique classique.

Fulton fait valoir que le défi réel qui se pose à l'Université est intérieur, et non extérieur. L'Université ne doit pas se contenter de répondre aux pressions exercées par l'État, l'entreprise ou la technologie, elle doit plutôt s'efforcer de retrouver une raison d'être et un sens, qui font si cruellement défaut à la société moderne. Elle constate que l'Université semble avoir oublié l'objectif premier de la formation, qui, comme le soulignait Robertson Davies, est de sauver l'âme et d'ouvrir l'esprit. La crise de l'Université atteint donc le coeur du milieu enseignant et dépasse de beaucoup des considérations telles que le recrutement, les budgets et les programmes d'études. À défaut de se rendre compte du divorce actuel entre la réalité et la rhétorique de l'enseignement supérieur, l'Université, soutient Fulton, ne pourra vraiment bénéficier des défis présentés par les intervenants externes; le mal sera trop profond. Pour cette raison, l'Université doit d'abord se réhabiliter par un exercice rigoureux de restructuration et de réorientation, au terme duquel elle pourra penser à relever les défis qui lui viennent de l'extérieur.

Alan C. Cairns, éminent spécialiste Canadien en sciences politiques, examine le lien entre le savoir et les subtilités propres à la tradition, aux processus, à la collectivité et à l'identité universitaires. Selon lui, on ne peut comprendre l'Université à moins de saisir le contexte subtil des signaux, des valeurs et des ambitions qui motivent les différents chercheurs et le régime complémentaire de normes, d'ententes et de contraintes, qui sont les instruments de coordination de l'enseignement supérieur. Cairns traite du haut degré d'instabilité sociale caractérisant les structures universitaires, de l'incidence des influences extérieures sur les sciences sociales et les humanités ainsi que des incompatibilités entre l'institution que représente l'Université et les disciplines qui y sont enseignées. D'abord quelque peu vagues, ses conclusions et son pronostic méritent une réflexion attentive du lecteur, malgré leur apparente modération comparativement aux propos, plus alarmistes, des exposés antérieurs.

Enfin, le dernier exposé de ce recueil aborde toute une gamme de thèmes dans une vision englobante du passé, du présent et de l'avenir. Son auteur, **Ian Winchester**, y analyse les traits distinctifs fondamentaux de l'Université aux différentes étapes qui ont marqué son évolution dans la société occidentale, en puisant dans ses connaissances étendues dans les domaines des lettres et des sciences. Il aborde la controverse concernant l'enseignement supérieur en philosophe possédant un sens aigu de l'Histoire. Pour lui les enjeux importants ne résident pas tant dans les questions de recrutement et de budget que dans le rôle joué par l'Université à titre de foyer culturel de nos sociétés, dont l'objectif suprême doit être de cultiver la connaissance du beau et du bon. L'argumentation complexe de Winchester intègre les intuitions présentes dans d'autres exposés, notamment ceux de Katz, de Berman, de Suppes et de Fulton, et se termine par une discussion fascinante sur la meilleure façon pour l'Université de s'adapter aux changements qui l'attendent dans les prochaines décennies.

Ses propos démontrent que tout espoir d'un retour à l'éducation libérale d'antan est vain et qu'aucune proposition en ce sens ne saurait constituer une stratégie efficace pour le renouvellement de l'enseignement supérieur. Winchester ne se contente pas de critiquer; il nous livre une suggestion a priori étonnante sur la façon dont l'Université pourrait remplir, dans les meilleures conditions possibles, son rôle de foyer culturel. À la réflexion, cette suggestion s'avère des plus sensées et offre une perspective intéressante pour la poursuite du débat auquel se livrent les auteurs des exposés réunis dans le présent document.

L'avenir de l'enseignement supérieur est en jeu; la crise ne fait que commencer.

PART I

GOVERNMENT, BUSINESS, AND
THE INDEPENDENCE OF THE UNIVERSITY

THE MORAL CRISIS OF THE UNIVERSITY, OR, THE TENSION BETWEEN MARKETPLACE AND COMMUNITY IN HIGHER LEARNING

MICHAEL B. KATZ

Prologue

On Tuesday, February 22, 1983, an undergraduate woman at the University of Pennsylvania reported that she had been raped by a group of fraternity students early on the previous Friday morning after a party at their house. After more than a month of hesitation, the university's administration decided to charge the individual men with a violation of the university's code of conduct (a brief statement requiring students to behave in a mature and responsible fashion) and to prepare for hearings before the university court, composed solely of students. Before any hearing took place, however, the university reached settlements with the men. Although the terms are secret, it is known that the settlements required the men to undergo a process of re-education through reading, essay writing, discussion, and community service. Because settlements reached under the university's judicial charter preclude expulsion or suspension as sentences, these sanctions were not invoked.

The settlements were reached in May, just before graduation, when it is virtually impossible to mobilize opinion around any issue. The grumbling among many faculty, staff, and students about the secrecy and apparent leniency of the sanctions therefore dissipated. However, when the Philadelphia *Inquirer*'s Sunday magazine carried an extensive and, as it turned out, reasonably accurate account of the event, the issue exploded again. Because of concern on campus, the executive committee of the faculty senate voted early in the fall to establish a committee of senior faculty to investigate the administration's handling of the case against the individual men and its treatment of the young woman.

The senate executive asked me to chair the committee, and the task consumed my life and the committee's for the fall semester. Our report deliberately did not speculate on the motives for administrative actions. Instead, we concerned ourselves only with what had been done and with evaluating

3

those choices and outcomes. Although there are several plausible, if sometimes contradictory, theories about the issues, one of them seems to me clearly wrong: that this event was an isolated, if tragic, occurrence, epiphenomenal, divorced from the mainstream of campus life, and of no general significance. To the contrary, I believe the incident raises fundamental issues about the character of universities in the late twentieth century. It illustrates a powerful and disturbing trend that has robbed universities of the capacity to answer questions critical to their own future. I refer to the assimilation of universities to the marketplace and to the state.

Origins of the Multiversity

In his 1963 Godkin lectures at Harvard, Clark Kerr, then president of the University of California, announced the birth of the multiversity. "The basic reality for the university," he said, "is the widespread recognition that new knowledge is the most important factor in economic and social growth." Because they were "called upon to produce knowledge as never before," universities had assumed a "new role with few precedents to fall back on, with little but platitudes to mask the nakedness of change."[1] In the 1960s, public recognition that knowledge had become a new and vital form of capital also shaped the development of Canadian higher education. In both countries one result was to accelerate the assimilation of universities to the marketplace and to the state.[2]

To Kerr, the structure of the multiversity reflected "competing visions of true purpose, each relating to a different layer of history, a different web of forces. . . . The university is so many things to so many different people that it must, of necessity, be partially at war with itself." Kerr celebrated this lack of a common centre as an expression of a healthy, vital pluralism that enhanced both creativity and freedom. "A university anywhere," he wrote, "can aim to be no higher than to be as British as possible for the sake of the undergraduates, as German as possible for the sake of the graduates and research personnel, as American as possible for the sake of the public at large – and as confused as possible for the sake of the preservation of the whole uneasy balance." Universities, he said, might be defined "as a series of individual faculty entrepreneurs held together by a common grievance over parking."[3]

Kerr stressed the massive increase in federal financing of universities since World War II; the multiversity could also be called the "federal grant university." As early as 1960, he pointed out, federal support constituted 75 per cent of all university research expenses and 15 per cent of total university budgets. The emergence of the federal grant university, he observed, had been eased because it took place without "conscious design." Because universities had no coherent view of the changes affecting them, they had made "piecemeal adjustments." As a consequence, "the federal government and the leading universities entered into a common-law marriage unblessed by predetermined policies and self-surveys — but nonetheless they formed a very productive union." The paradox, as Kerr pointed out, was that the "federal colossus had the power to influence the most ruggedly individual universities." "The better the university," he commented wryly, "the greater its chances of succumbing to the federal embrace." Even as it snuggled up to the federal government, the university managed to keep at least one arm around the corporate world. "The university and segments of industry are becoming more alike," wrote Kerr. The professor has assumed "the character of an entrepreneur. Industry, with its scientists and technicians, learns an uncomfortable bit about academic freedom and the handling of intellectual personnel. The two worlds are merging physically and psychologically."[4]

One lesson was clear. The dynamic forces shaping universities have come from outside their walls. "The location of power has generally moved from inside to outside the original community of masters and students. The nature of the multiversity makes it inevitable that this historical transfer will not be reversed . . . ." Those faculty who longed for a quiet, self-contained world were guilty of a "guild" mentality; they were romantics, unaware of, or unwilling to accept, the transformation of higher learning. To be sure, faculty still exercised authority "over admissions, approval of courses, examinations, and granting of degrees . . . ," and they had achieved "considerable influence over faculty appointments and academic freedom . . . "; but "organized faculty control or influence over the general direction of the growth of the American multiversity" had been "quite small," and it would not grow larger. Whether or not faculty approve of the multiversity is therefore beside the point; its emergence was inevitable. To oppose it would be to stand in the way of history. The legitimacy of the multiversity rests, in the final analysis, not on its worth but on its necessity.[5]

Kerr intended his remarks as an analysis and celebration of the multiversity. Although he did not try to mask its internal tensions, he viewed its evolution as a great triumph. Its loosely coupled structure, internal diversity, human and financial resources, and protection of academic freedom released an unprecedented burst of intellectual energy and creativity that spread beyond the boundaries of the university to invigorate, instruct, and improve the world around it. "The campus and society," according to Kerr, "are undergoing a somewhat reluctant and cautious merger, already well advanced."[6] Implicit and unanswered in Kerr's account is a critical question: Where are the boundaries of the university? Are there any principles that distinguish the conduct and development of universities from other social institutions? Are they anything more than sites of advanced teaching and research? What principles and criteria guide their activities?

In Kerr's account, the principles and criteria underlying the recent development of universities reveal a process that a less sanguine observer can term the assimilation of the university to the marketplace and to the state. Although this process stretches far back in time, it always has met resistance from those who believed that neither the needs of the state nor the criteria of the marketplace should be allowed unmediated power to shape the organization and conduct of higher learning. Universities have been "contested terrain" where the forces of resistance have won important, if partial, victories. There is nothing inevitable about the shape of higher learning. It is the result, if not of planning, of human agency. It is the product of compromise, of conflict, and, above all, of choice.

The conflict between what, to be concise, I will call the forces of the marketplace and of the community in higher education echoes an old struggle. For centuries, faculty argued that universities should be self-governing communities of scholars and tried to resist the pull of church or state, which sought the inculcation of orthodoxy and the training of loyal servants. The ascendancy of liberal economics in the nineteenth century, however, reshaped the ancient tensions within higher education. Liberal economics substituted the demands of an impersonal marketplace for the intrusive authority of church or crown. Under the mantle of service to the whole community and of relevance to contemporary life, some university reformers attempted to apply the principles of supply and demand to the evaluation of academic institutions. A clear example was Francis Wayland's argument in the mid-nineteenth century that colleges were suffering a decline in popularity because they remained aloof from popular desires and changing tastes. He proposed their transformation into educational supermarkets governed by laws of supply and demand where students would come and go at will, choosing as many or as few courses as they wished.[7]

Even in the heady days of liberal economics in the early nineteenth century, some faculty resisted the application of a market model to higher education, and, for several reasons, Wayland failed to implement his vision of a free-market university.[8] Indeed, although nineteenth-century liberal economics made the laws of supply and demand enduring arbiters of academic life, the great attempt to press higher education into the service of the market and the secular state began with the creation of modern universities in the late nineteenth and early twentieth centuries. The process took only twenty or thirty years in the United States and somewhat longer in Canada. The major, new features in universities were: graduate and professional schools; lectures and seminars; the elective system; a strong, non-clerical president; an emphasis on public service; internal bureaucracy; specialized academic departments; a commitment to research; and expanded size. By the early twentieth century, commentators pointed to the presence of a new and distinctive institution. American universities, wrote Edward Slosson, a professor of chemistry, in 1910, "are very much alike; more alike, doubtless, than they claim to be.... The American university tends to be a specific type, very different from that of England, Germany or France."[9]

In a recent book, Colin Burke contends that historians have overstated the extent of the "university revolution." He finds, first, that enrolment increased much less than has usually been imagined. Second, most students chose traditional curricula over the newer, more innovative ones. The factors affecting enrolment, he argues, were the increasing incorporation of college education into the training of lawyers, ministers, and educators and the entrance of a much larger number of women. At the same time, the range in ages of new students narrowed and assumed a much more — by our standards — modern pattern. Still, outside forces, including the cost of college, apprenticeship, and patterns of entry to many occupations, retarded the pace of growth in enrolment.[10]

Despite the continuities Burke and others have found between the higher education of the early and late nineteenth century, no one denies that great changes occurred. They were centred, however, in a relatively few institutions, which, over time, transformed academic life. The process, it is important to remember, did not happen easily or automatically. As Laurence Veysey has pointed out, in the late nineteenth and early twentieth centuries the ideals of utility, service, culture, and research competed for dominance in American universities. Yet, according to Clark Kerr, no one of these four ever triumphed completely, and, as a consequence, the organization of the new or transformed universities reflected no central purpose. Rather, universities became federations coupled by bureaucracy. "Bureaucratic administration," Veysey writes, "was the structural device which made possible the new epoch of institutional empire-building without recourse to specific values. Thus while unity of purpose disintegrated, a uniformity of standardized practices was coming into being."[11]

Market principles invaded universities in several ways. Spokesmen for the American university, for example, were losing a sense of purpose at turn of the century, Veysey has observed. They consequently ran the danger of accepting the standards of their more numerous and influential peers, the leaders of business and industry. The invasion of universities by the market caused more controversy than any other academic trend of the time. In 1902, John Dewey wrote that universities "are ranked by their obvious material prosperity, until the atmosphere of money-getting and money-spending hides from view the interests for the sake of which money alone has such a place."[12] The classic attack on the relations between business and universities came from Thorstein Veblen in *The Higher Learning in America*, a tough, satirical, and penetrating critique that introduced the phrase "captains of erudition" to describe the new, entrepreneurial university leaders who had replaced the clergymen presidents of American colleges before the Civil War.[13]

As Veysey points out, contacts between universities and the marketplace occurred at many levels. Presidents and professors attempted to recruit students by writing articles about the economic utility of collegiate education. At the same time, support for the creation, maintenance, and expansion of universities came from philanthropists, who frequently and often successfully tried to influence the internal life of the institutions they supported. "Of more consequence than donors for the actual conduct of affairs at most universities," claims Veysey, "were boards of trustees," composed largely of businessmen or other non-academic professionals, who often stressed the importance of athletics, businesslike management, and a conservative faculty. Presidents, in turn, often viewed their faculty as employees. "Like shrewd businessmen, university presidents and trustees sought to pay their faculties as little as the 'market price' demanded. . . .most presidents favoured (and practised) a policy of paying professors unequal salaries, so that the 'market price' might obtain on an individual basis." In other words, the labour of faculty had been transformed into a commodity whose price was determined by its value in a novel arena: the academic marketplace.[14]

The transformation of the leading universities signified a new era in the history of capital. In a dramatic and novel way, knowledge – advanced technical and managerial knowledge – had become a resource whose possession was essential to the progress of the vast new corporations and bureaucracies that dominated economic and social life. Science and technology, production and administration, co-ordination and marketing, all required experts and expert knowledge. Until the late nineteenth century, experts and expert knowledge had been produced largely outside of universities. By managing to capture the process through which they were produced and to transfer the actual production of much new knowledge from outside their walls to within them, universities staged one of the great coups in the history of capitalism. Moreover, they met only minimal resistance because the imperial interests of universities and the self-protective instincts of professionals reinforced each other nicely. Together, they made credentials dispensed by universities the hallmark of professional expertise. Universities, thereby, became the gatekeepers of the advanced technical-managerial society.[15]

Until the late nineteenth century, professional education had taken place in a wider variety of settings. Engineers, for instance, frequently were trained in shops; lawyers often began their careers as apprentices in law offices; nurses and social workers, for the most part, received no professional training whatsoever. Although the increasing formalization of university training followed a different pace within each occupation, in all of them great changes occurred between about 1870 and World War I, especially during the 1890s. Enrolment in law schools more than tripled, and in medical and nursing schools it more than doubled. There were about 25 law schools in 1860 and more than 100 in 1900, of which 30 had been founded in the 1890s. The profession that comprised the greatest number of students, however, was education. According to Burke, normal schools enrolled 4 per cent of all students in higher education in 1860, 16 per cent in 1870, and 30 per cent in 1900. A quarter of the graduates of regular colleges became teachers or professors. The increased dependence of colleges and universities on teacher training heightened their efforts to attract women and fueled the rapid rise in female college attendance during the same years. In the 1890s, more than half the undergraduates at the University of Michigan were women and more than 45 per cent of its alumni were teachers.[16]

The expansion of professional education irreversibly blurred the boundaries of universities. Professional schools are dependent on the fields they serve. Because their graduates must be prepared to enter specific occupations and to perform competently, professional training is driven by criteria derived from practice and by the division of labour within specific occupations. For example, the history of curricula within schools of education during the early twentieth century mirrored the history of the educational bureaucracy. As specific jobs proliferated within expanding school systems, schools of education offered courses and degree sequences that paralleled them exactly.[17] University-based professional schools find it difficult to challenge conventional practice without leaving their students at a disadvantage in the job market, and, because they are dependent on the good opinion of the field, they often are reluctant to make sharp criticisms of professionals or their work. This field-dependence undercuts their capacity to lead the development of professions and mutes their potential as critics.

By the late nineteenth century, many universities had already established separate departments of education, and by 1920 separate schools of education had started to appear on campuses across the country. Within these new departments and schools, universities hatched educational research as a new academic field and developed graduate programs for administrators, researchers, and other educational specialists. Through training, textbooks, and consulting, professors of education forged close links with public school systems, and, in this way, strengthened the connections between universities and the state.

During these years universities began to serve the state through many other channels, too. Faculty became increasingly active as expert advisers on governmental policy. Because state and federal governments played such a minimal role in social policy before World War I, university faculty directed their attention to urban problems and city government. The relation between Chicago and its universities provides a vivid case in point. Clearly, one hallmark of the Progressive Era was the attempt to link universities and public service through the application of specialized, expert knowledge to the solution of public problems. Once again, though, circumspection became the price of public trust. Professionals in the service of the state learned to confine themselves to areas in which they possessed recognized technical expertise and to keep their recommendations within the boundaries of acceptable alternatives for public policy. This lesson was one consequence of the great academic freedom cases of the late nineteenth and early twentieth centuries.[18]

Universities, the Marketplace, and the State

The academic freedom cases that rocked Stanford, Wisconsin, Cornell, Pennsylvania, Chicago, and other schools reflected the heightened influence of the marketplace and the state on universities and the transmutation of universities into great bureaucracies led by captains of erudition. Like corporate executives, university presidents in the late nineteenth and early twentieth centuries tried to increase their control over their workers. Within industry, management increased its control of the workplace by reorganizing production in ways that eroded the customary autonomy of skilled workers. Although blocked by constraints that did not exist in industry, university presidents tried to exert their direct authority over faculty in several ways. One was by keeping faculty salaries secret. Another was by demanding that professors not offend trustees or influential sectors of the public. Because of their great dependence on private donors or legislative good will, the early captains of erudition combined their entrepreneurial zeal with political caution.

Within industry, capital exercised its greatest control over labour in the late nineteenth and early twentieth centures by breaking strikes with impunity and blackballing labour leaders. In the same years, it exercised its greatest control over universities by engineering the dismissal of dissident faculty and trying to block their appointment elsewhere. Thus, when some professors (for example, Henry Carter Adams at Cornell, Richard Ely at Wisconsin, Edward W. Bemis at Chicago, John R. Commons at Indiana, and Edward A. Ross at Stanford) refused to curtail their advocacy of free silver, the right of labour to organize, and other causes unpopular in conservative circles, or to restrain their criticism of industries or municipal franchises in which trustees had a direct interest, they were attacked and, often, fired. These sad, sordid, even craven, violations of academic freedom have been chronicled often, and I will not describe their details.[19] The important point here is what these cases illustrate and their consequences. They point to the erosion of the boundaries between the university and the marketplace. As university presidents tried to behave like industrialists who could exact obedience from employees and fire them at will, one of the criteria for dismissal became endangering the financial health of the university by damaging its reputation in influential circles. In these early cases, faculty members fired for openly stating their opinions on public issues received almost no support from colleagues. Nor had they any legal protection. In truth, they were more vulnerable for publicly stating unpopular opinions than for being incompetent.

Faculty mobilized slowly and timidly in response to capital's assault. The conventional landmark in the history of academic freedom is the founding of the American Association of University Professors (AAUP) in 1915. In its early years the AAUP moved cautiously not only because of public hostility but also because of conservatism among faculty. Nonetheless, at its inception, the association adopted a statement supporting academic freedom and tenure. Also in 1915, college presidents organized the American Association of College Presidents (AACP). In its early years, the AACP rejected the AAUP position on academic freedom and tenure and vigorously asserted the right of presidents and trustees to exercise their independent authority in decisions to hire or to dismiss faculty. Although the AACP nearly reversed its stance in 1922, not until 1940 did the two associations agree on a set of principles governing academic freedom and tenure that colleges and universities were willing, albeit gradually and grudgingly, to incorporate into their statutes.[20]

The early AAUP position did not reflect an unlimited commitment to academic freedom. As Mary Furner has shown, during the years of the great academic freedom cases, university faculty had goals beyond protection from arbitrary administrative action. They also were working actively for recognition as professionals with valuable, expert skills. As they manoeuvred to create new disciplines and sell their services to government and industry, faculty developed a defence of academic freedom based on technical expertise and objectivity, and they defended colleagues threatened with dismissal for exercising their professional judgement. Objectivity itself became an ideology deployed in the service of professionalization. Furner makes this point:

> As professionalization proceeded, most academic scientists stopped asking ethical questions. Instead they turned their attention to carefully controlled, empirical investigations of problems that were normally defined by the state of knowledge in their fields rather than by the state of society. Professional social scientists generally accepted the basic structure of corporate capitalism. Abandoning their pretensions to a role as arbiters of public policy, they established a more limited goal:

recognition as experts with extraordinary technical
competence in a highly specialized but restricted
sphere.[21]

Academic mobilization resulted in a compromise.
Administrators could not control faculty in the same way that
corporate presidents could control manufacturing. Veysey points
to the "sense of informal limitations" that constrained the
"exercise of power" at all major institutions. These limits, he
observes, became especially obvious when the "Taylorite
'efficiency' craze began to seek academic targets just after 1910."
Even if faculty were unwilling to support unrestrained academic
freedom, they "guarded certain symbols of self-respect" and
believed that universities were significantly different from
manufacturing concerns. It is important to remember, however,
that academics were ambivalent about the invasion of the
university by the market and the state. Even as they resisted
attempts to circumscribe their academic freedom, they sought
closer ties with government and industry as consultants and
expert advisers, and they solicited outside funds that made
possible the expansion of their research activities and graduate
training programs.[22]

The influence of the state on universities became especially
evident during World War I. For the most part, few professors
protested when their colleagues were fired for opposition to the
war, and many others behaved supinely. Professional historians,
as Carol Gruber has shown, were especially culpable because of
their role as propagandists: they violated the elemental criteria
of their profession by producing patently false and distorted
material attacking America's enemies.[23]

(Relations between universities, the marketplace, and the
state differed in Canada and the United States in at least one
important respect: the relative influence of the private and
public sectors. The private sector in Canada has exerted far less
influence than it has in the United States. For reasons analysed
by Paul Axelrod, private and corporate contributions to Canadian
universities have been much lower, and, even more telling, a far
higher proportion of Canadian university graduates has been
employed in the public sector and a far lower proportion in the
private sector than in the United States.)[24]

By the post-World War I era, many administrators as well
as faculty had become alarmed by the fragmentation of
universities. Rapid expansion, academic and professional
specialization, the proliferation of the elective system, and the
melting boundaries between universities, the marketplace, and

the state had robbed curricula of their coherence. University education appeared to have lost its sense of purpose, and educational programs reflected primarily the demands of disciplines and professions for specialized or technical training. One response in both undergraduate and professional education was the general education movement, which attempted to define a core of knowledge essential to an educated person. The movement's first major achievement was Columbia College's Contemporary Civilization Course, initiated in 1919.[25] It affected graduate and professional training as well; in the field of education one of its major achievements was the introduction of the "foundations of education" as a required subject at Teachers College, Columbia, in the 1920s. The general education movement gathered steam in the 1940s, coasted in the 1950s, and came under attack in the 1960s. Only in the past few years has it reappeared as administrators and faculty once again have voiced alarm over the fragmentation, specialization, and lack of coherence in university programs. This oscillation between a search for coherence and either a purely elective system or pattern of fragmented, specialized programs reflects the tension between marketplace and community in the history of curriculum.

By the start of the World War II, a compromise had been reached within universities between the forces of the marketplace and of the community. Its hallmarks were a core curriculum and an official commitment to academic freedom and tenure. This is the context out of which Clark Kerr's multiversity emerged in the next two decades. Despite the accuracy of his analysis, Kerr's description of the multiversity underestimated the forces that would disrupt campuses not long after his lectures were published. It was, in fairness, difficult to predict the turmoil the Vietnam War would cause or the extent to which the civil rights movement would spread to campuses. Kerr also did not realize the explosive force of the internal contradictions he so actively championed. More concerned with the faculty, he missed the next great challenge to the major tendencies in the history of higher learning, which came, unexpectedly, from the students.

Student revolts on campuses in the 1960s were complex events with several sources: the Vietnam War, the civil rights movement, disenchantment with technology and material progress, and, even, socialization patterns within upper-middle-class families. I want to stress one other source: student radicals attacked the multiversity for neglecting its distinctively educational qualities and for its assimilation to the marketplace and the state. This general criticism underlay many specific complaints: professors who neglected teaching, the presence of secret defence research on campus; restrictions on public advocacy of unpopular causes, and the lack of student participation in university governance. However strident, fuzzy, or disruptive they were, student radicals were the vanguard of the resistance to the multiversity. As faculty assumed their entrepreneurial and bureaucratic roles, it was left to students to take up the task of resistance. Of course, one student demand was "relevance," which, in practice, has proved an ambiguous goal. "Relevance" has had two major meanings. One is the demand for a closer link between university education and jobs. In this sense, students helped accelerate the erosion of the boundaries between universities and the marketplace. The other meaning of "relevance," however, is more consistent with the radical student critique, for it reflects a demand that universities incorporate the great moral and social issues of the day into their curricula.

For many reasons, students could not seriously change the direction of university development or retard the pace of assimilation. The major institutional legacy of their activities was the development of formal participatory structures that included university administrators, faculty, students, and sometimes support staff. These structures have, however, been unable to transform the spirit of academic decision making or to create a sense of community on campuses.

Let me draw on one example from my own experience. In the early 1960s, the Province of Ontario created the Ontario Institute for Studies in Education (OISE) to do research, development, and graduate training in education. The province had been far behind American states in these respects, and, through a sudden infusion of money, it hoped to improve its position rapidly and effectively. OISE was affiliated with the University of Toronto for instructional purposes, and all graduate degrees were awarded by the university. The faculty of OISE grew rapidly from about 20 in its first year, 1965-1966, to more than 40 in its second, and to about 140 a few years later. With nearly unlimited funding for a few years, the province had managed to create a major graduate school of education. OISE's budget included not only money for faculty but internal research and development funds and generous assistance for students. With these resources, the support staff grew as rapidly as the faculty, and the student body, composed mainly of part-time students, mushroomed as well. OISE experienced all the predictable pains of rapid growth, and I will not recite them here. What I want to point to is the question of governance.

OISE was staffed mainly by young faculty deeply affected by the criticism of universities prevalent in the 1960s. They chafed against what appeared to be the authoritarian and bureaucratic patterns of administration in the institute, and they fought for a new form of academic government that would draw on every constituency. The result of their efforts was an experiment: the creation of an Institute Assembly designed to be the precursor of a unicameral form of academic government. The assembly consisted of representatives from every constituency, including the Board of Governors; its powers, however, were only advisory to the administration and the board. Clearly, though, it was a major force. In an effort to permit everyone who wanted to participate in academic government the opportunity to do so, the assembly included four major standing committees. Each of these standing committees, in turn, spun off subcommittees. Each committee and subcommittee were to comprise assembly members plus elected representatives of every institute constituency. A faculty member, chosen by the assembly as its speaker, was to preside over the whole structure and serve as an unofficial ombudsman. I was the first speaker and served for one memorable year.

In a formal sense, we made the assembly work. The assembly took a position on every major decision facing the institute, and neither the Board of Governors nor the administration took any major decision contrary to its wishes. As ombudsman, I mediated some major conflicts and listened to many grievances. Elections were held to fill every committee vacancy. This meant sending ballots to several hundred part-time students for every subcommittee opening. The proportion who voted, not surprisingly, was very small, and the cost of operating the structure — both in money and in time — was great. The issues with which the committees and the assembly dealt were almost entirely budgetary and structural. We discussed almost no issues of educational or substantive research policy. Decisions about what to teach were, by and large, confined to the academic divisions of the institute, and research policy reflected the wishes of individual faculty or was made in the process of awarding internal research funds within the Research Committee. By the end of the first year, enthusiasm for participation in the assembly had begun to wane, and it continued to slide. The faculty now is unionized, and the dream of a unicameral governing body is dead.

The assembly's history contains several lessons. One is the connection between democracy and bureaucracy. Within a large organization, democratic procedures require bureaucratic forms.

Without a widespread sense of commitment and purpose among the participants, form triumphs over substance; practice is governed by routine; and a small number of interested people effectively exert control. Even a new and relatively small academic institution, such as OISE, could not arouse the sustained commitment essential to participatory government in spirit as well as in form. One reason is that, like the multiversity it was in miniature, OISE lacked a core. Faculty had closer ties with their disciplinary colleagues around the continent than with one another. Their first loyalty was to their professional work, defined as research and specialized teaching. Many faculty sought to influence public education directly, which meant muting criticism and building links with the educational bureaucracy. Internal views of what the institute should do were diverse. Few people wanted to take the time to hammer out a coherent statement of purpose or to risk the conflict that a discussion of educational policy entailed. A relatively decentralized system of academic divisions loosely coupled by a bureaucracy remained, in the end, the best assurance of independence. At the same time, students had their own lives to worry about. Most were trying to balance their obligations to jobs, families, and graduate study; few wanted to help run the institution. The support staff probably remained the most interested. To the administration and the Board of Governors, the assembly was a nuisance and sometimes a menace.

I suspect that the history of academic governance in many places travelled a similar trajectory. The legacy of the experience is a collection of structures in which previously excluded groups have a place. In most instances, a relatively small proportion of each constituency probably participates in central, university-wide governance, and the reality is far different from the hopes of the reformers who fought for new governing bodies ten or fifteen years earlier. Nonetheless, central, participatory assemblies remain important. Even if they have little effect on routine operations or on major questions of educational policy (which remain decentralized), they serve as channels through which resistance can be mobilized quickly and effectively in crises or in reaction to events or decisions that outrage the campus. They are, if nothing else, a conscience always brooding over the shoulder of the central administration. This is an honourable and necessary role, though quite different from real communal governance. (Perhaps widespread participation and community can only be sustained within relatively small units where all members are immediately affected by most major decisions. This, of course, is why departmental politics remain so much more lively than central administrative ones. Where central bodies remain the most active, they consist of single constituencies, such as faculty senates or undergraduate assemblies. The reason, again, is the greater commonality of interest among members.)

With its only effective challenge deflected, denatured, or accommodated, the assimilation of the university to the marketplace and the state accelerated. The unionization of faculty on many campuses, which reflects a wage-labour model, is one example. Others are the increased dependence on federal funds and the recent increase in formal ties between universities and the corporate world. Some universities even have based their internal budgetary procedures on a market model. Responsibility-based budgeting, as the model is called, ties the allocation of resources to the enrolment of individual schools and departments and, thereby, fosters competitive, entrepreneurial activity within individual campuses. Some of these developments, of course, reflect the precarious situation of universities caught by inflation, decreased government funding, and a smaller cohort from which to draw students; but they also reflect the lure of government contracts and private sector money. Committed to research, tempted by opportunity, tied more closely to their profession than to their institution, faculty have willingly and eagerly facilitated the erosion of the boundaries of the university and the obliteration of its distinctive features.

The Moral Crisis of the University

Until now, I have deliberately avoided an explicit definition of the key process described here: the assimilation of the university to the marketplace and to the state. Its meaning, which I hope has emerged from my account, has four components. First is the increasing similarity in the principles that underlie the organization and operation of universities and of corporations, especially, the application of the law of supply and demand to internal decisions. Two consequences of the adoption of market principles are the determination of educational and scholarly worth by market value and the transformation of faculty scholarship into a commodity. Second is the increased determination of internal priorities and lines of development by the requirements of corporations and the state. The dictation of research directions by the availability of funds and the structure of educational programs by the division of labour within professions are two results of this aspect of the process. Third, the activities of faculty members increasingly resemble those of entrepreneurs or bureaucrats. Faculty reap their greatest rewards outside the university. Their primary loyalties are to their professional peers around the world and to their clients and sponsors. Fourth, the direction of university development is justified by appeals to the "needs" of the economy, society, technology, or some other great force. A reified imperative drives the history of higher learning and narrowly constricts the availability of alternatives at any point in time. The character of universities becomes inevitable, and their legitimacy rests on their service to the great forces over which they have no control.

What is wrong with this process? After all, Clark Kerr saw in it the triumph of a democratic pluralism and the unprecedented release of energy and creativity in the public service. As Robert Paul Wolff points out in *The Ideal of the University*, however, Kerr "commits exactly the same error which lies at the heart of classical laissez-faire theory," that is, the identification of "effective market demand with true human need." The result is "a covert ideological rationalization for whatever human or social desires happen to be backed by enough money or power to translate them into effective demands." In Kerr's analysis, "national needs" assume the role of the market in classical economic theory. They are above politics and beyond intervention, an inexorable force shaping higher learning. Thus, the responsiveness of the multiversity to "national needs" is "nothing more than its tendency to adjust itself to effective demand in the form of government grants, scholarship programs, corporate or alumni underwriting, and so forth." Although Kerr's analysis invests these demands with moral worth, in truth the university is accepting the priorities only of the government or of some other body for space research, weapons systems, or other goals. Universities, it follows, cannot be genuine critics of the "national purpose" of which they are an instrument, and their independent role in social and political analysis is badly, if not fatally, damaged. The question Wolff poses is this: "at the present time is ... there a greater social need for full-scale integration of the resources and activities of the universities into existing domestic and foreign programs, or for a sustained critique of those programs from an independent position of authority and influence?"[26]

The answer must reflect a position on a difficult question: what distinguishes a university from other social institutions? Wolff offers a compelling definition based on a conception of the ideal university as a "community of learning." The ideal university, he argues, should be "a community of persons united by collective understanding, by common and communal goals, by bonds of reciprocal obligation, and by a flow of sentiment which makes the preservation of the community an object of desire, not merely a matter of prudence or a command of duty."[27] Community implies a form of social obligation governed by principles different from those of the marketplace and state. Laws of supply and demand lose priority; wage-labour is not the template for all human relations; the translation of individuals into commodities is resisted. The difficult task of defining common goals or acceptable activity is neither avoided nor deflected onto bureaucracy.

Nonetheless, modern universities do remain distinct from both the corporate and government worlds, and for all its force, the process of assimilation remains incomplete. The great barriers to the total victory of the marketplace and the state are academic freedom and tenure. Although decisions about tenure often reflect the criteria of the marketplace, tenure is critical for four reasons. First, it restricts the major principle of economic relations in the marketplace: free wage labour. Tenure rejects the prerogative of management to dismiss employees at will; it affirms alternative principles to supply and demand; it rests on an expansive, rather than a restrictive, definition of the reciprocal obligations between workers and employers. Second, it lessens the translation of faculty into commodities whose value is determined solely by their current market price. It prevents the dismissal of academics simply because their work has gone out of fashion. In this way, it protects academics from each other as well as from the marketplace. Without tenure, I have no doubt that, more and more often, competent academics whose work no longer appeared at the forefront of their fields would find themselves without work. Tenure thus restrains the application of pure market value as the sole criterion of continued academic employment. Third, tenure protects academic freedom. Before the introduction of tenure, university administrations succumbed to pressure to fire faculty members with unpopular ideas. There is no doubt that the same process would happen again. Tenure, therefore, is essential if universities are to be effective social critics. Finally, tenure permits internal self-criticism. No institution permits the attacks on its policies and administration that characterize universities. True, even in universities criticism can be muted, but without tenure, there would be almost none.

Despite the existence of tenure — which recent history shows is itself a reversible gain — the forces of community are fragile, and they are losing. The weakness of these forces leaves universities unable to define their purpose; they are increasingly vulnerable because they are unable to mount a credible defence against those intrusions of the marketplace and state that most faculty and administrators even now sense as dangerous or excessive. Universities are less able than ever to define the ways in which they are distinct from other social institutions, how the principles on which they operate differ from those of business and government, and why they should enjoy special privileges. Therefore, the next great crisis of the university may not be demographic, fiscal, or organizational. Instead, it may be moral.

The moral flabbiness of the university weakens every aspect of its life. Take the example of the alleged rape with which I began this essay.[28] Most people who comment on the issues surrounding this incident offer one of three explanations. First, until the 1960s, colleges and universities officially exercised a close watch over the sexual behaviour of their students. After the attack on these restrictions by students in the 1970s, rules were abandoned with stunning speed. Dormitories became co-educational; restrictions on the presence of men and women in one another's rooms disappeared; universities dropped almost all specific rules of conduct; and faculty generally left students alone to do what they chose. Now, it is argued, we are reaping the consequences of neglect.

Second, it sometimes is said that students now suffer from extraordinary stress. Anxious about admission into top professional schools, worried about a tight job market, facing a future where annihilation seems more possible than fulfilment, their behaviour combines an explosive, periodic release of tension with a nihilism deeply disturbing in the young. Of course, and this is the third argument, some would say that there is little especially new in student behaviour. The heavy-drinking students of the 1980s seem more rowdy and noisy than the stoned students of a decade or two ago. Men have always abused and raped women. What has changed is the willingness of women to suffer in silence and the emergence of supportive networks that encourage and help women who are victims to press their case.

Although each of these points has merit, each by itself is partial. We need an explanation not only of student behaviour but of university response. Whatever motivates students, at issue, is a university's capacity for appropriate, effective, and collective response; and the processes underlying the modern history of higher learning have eroded this capacity. Let me illustrate with six questions that emerge from the incident.[29] First, do we treat men differently from women? No assertion angers administrators who handled the case more than the claim that they treated the men involved more fairly than the woman. There can be no doubt of the administration's sincerity on this point. Yet, the process and results best served the interests of the men. The men remained on campus and suffered no interruption in their studies and no disruption of their plans. The sanctions they received were, at worst, an inconvenience. The woman withdrew from the university and suffered greatly. (In the interests of privacy, I will not elaborate on the latter point.) Why did the victim fare so much worse than her alleged assailants? The answer lies in the myriad ways in which the structure of institutions and the nature of legal processes still discriminate by gender. In truth, whatever our intent, there are differences in the way we treat our sons and daughters.

Second, what sort of conduct is acceptable on campus? At the University of Pennsylvania, the brief, general statement about mature and responsible behaviour signals an unwillingness or inability to confront the difficult and divisive ethical issues that an answer requires. One reason the question is so difficult is that the university, like its counterparts, lacks a common centre or any effective sense of community. There are no accepted principles from which a statement on the limits of acceptable behaviour can be written. Some faculty are even reluctant to agree that the university legitimately can proscribe activities that are not clearly illegal. If there are no boundaries between the university and the state, then the state may as well set and enforce all standards of conduct.

Third, what is the responsibility of the faculty for the nature and quality of undergraduate life? The university rewards faculty on market principles, that is, for the quantity and perceived value of their professional productivity. It gives no rewards for attention to undergraduate life. To entrepreneurial and bureaucratic faculty members, undergraduates often are a distraction. Faculty have no incentive to think about the lives of undergraduates outside the classroom; and, even if they felt a fleeting interest or concern, they would have no time to pursue it. Every sort of professional pressure in modern universities pulls energetic, active, ambitious faculty away from a concern with student life. Relations between faculty and students have become increasingly analogous to wage labour: contractual, specific, and delimited.

Fourth, is justice within universities different from justice in a court of law? Do the same rules of evidence, due process, and right to counsel apply within university settings as outside them? Again, without a clear sense of how universities differ from other social institutions, no answer to this question is possible. Yet, it is central to the way in which universities respond to misconduct among students, staff, or faculty.

Fifth, what should be the balance between decentralization and central leadership within universities? The inability of the administration to take clear and decisive control of the case described here reflects structural dilemmas endemic to modern universities as well as the responses of particular individuals. Universities remain remarkably decentralized institutions, for the multiversity is a loosely coupled federation. Critical decisions about educational policy and personnel are made in departments and schools, and every incursion by a central administration is resisted fiercely. Faculty whose own entrepreneurial and bureaucratic activities reduce the boundaries among the university, the marketplace, and the state are quick to invoke the ancient traditions of the university whenever they disagree with an initiative taken by a president, provost, or dean. Yet, they also want an administration that can react effectively to crises, raise money, and mediate equitably among the various interests on the campus. With few, if any, common values or shared purposes to which to appeal, only extraordinary leaders can summon the loyalty and commitment necessary to galvanize faculty sentiment around decisive, controversial, or risky actions. The result is a kind of administrative schizophrenia, which, as in this incident, can cripple the effectiveness of an administration.

Sixth, how do we balance the protection of the institution's reputation with the preservation of its integrity? Or, what are the limits of expediency? Every institution tries to protect itself. Self-preservation is as fundamental to an institution as it is instinctive to a human being. Therefore, institutions (and universities are no exception) prefer to keep embarrassing incidents or facts about themselves private. Allegations of gang-rape on campus do not help raise money or attract students. They do not enhance the image and reputation of the university. The expedient course, therefore, is to deal quietly and privately with the problem. In themselves, privacy and institutional protection are not ignoble criteria. The difficulty is their consequence. For the price of privacy often is moral compromise.

Moral compromise is an especially troublesome course for universities. For all their problems, universities and their faculties remain immensely privileged. They retain a freedom of activity and expression not permitted in any other major social institution. There are two justifications for this privilege. One is that it is an essential condition of teaching and learning. The other is that universities have become the major source of moral and social criticism in modern life. They are the major site of whatever social conscience we have left; without them the civil rights movement, the protest against the Vietnam War, modern feminism, and the anti-nuclear movement would have been immeasurably weaker. If the legitimacy of universities rested only on their service to the marketplace and state, internal freedom would not be an issue. But their legitimacy rests, in fact, on something else: their integrity. Like all privileges, the freedom enjoyed by universities carries correlative responsibilities. In their case it is intellectual honesty and moral courage. Modern universities are the greatest centres of intellectual power in history. Without integrity, they can become little more than supermarkets with raw power for sale. This is the tendency in the modern history of higher learning. It is what I call the moral crisis of the university.

Notes

1. Clark Kerr, *The Uses of the University* (Cambridge, Mass.: Harvard University Press, 1963), pp. v-vi.

2. Paul Axelrod, *Scholars and Dollars: Politics, Economics, and the Universities of Ontario, 1945-1980* (Toronto: University of Toronto Press, 1982); Peter N. Ross, "The Establishment of the Ph.D. at Toronto: A Case of American Influence," in Michael B. Katz and Paul N. Mattingly, eds., *Education and Social Change: Themes from Ontario's Past* (New York: New York University Press, 1975), pp. 193-214.

3. Kerr, *The Uses of the University*, pp. 18, 20.

4. Ibid., pp. 49-50, 90-91.

5. Ibid., pp. 23, 98-99.

6. Ibid., p. 115.

7. Francis Wayland, *Thoughts on the Present Collegiate System in the United States* (1842), in Richard Hofstadter and Wilson Smith, eds., *American Higher Education: A Documentary History*, vol. 1 (Chicago, Ill.: University of Chicago Press, 1961), pp. 356-75.

8. "Francis Lieber on the Purposes and Practices of Universities, 1830," in Hofstadter and Smith, *American Higher Education*, pp. 297-300.

9. Edward Slosson, *Great American Universities* (1910), in Hugh Hawkins, ed., *The Emerging University and Industrial America* (Lexington, Mass.: D.C. Heath, 1970), p. 66.

10. Colin B. Burke, *American Collegiate Populations* (New York: New York University Press, 1982), pp. 214-34.

11. Laurence R. Veysey, *The Emergence of the American University* (Chicago, Ill.: University of Chicago Press, 1965), p. 311.

12. Quoted in ibid., p. 346.

13. Thorstein Veblen, *The Higher Learning in America,* 1st ed. 1918 (New York: Hill and Wang, 1957).

14. Veysey, *Emergence of the American University,* pp. 350-52.

15. On this theme, see David F. Noble, *America by Design: Science, Technology, and the Rise of Corporate Capitalism* (New York: Knopf, 1977).

16. Burke, *American Collegiate Populations,* p. 222.

17. Michael B. Katz, "From Theory to Survey in Graduate Schools of Education," *Journal of Higher Education,* vol. 37, no. 6 (June 1966), pp. 325-34; Arthur G. Powell, *The Uncertain Profession: Harvard and the Search for Educational Authority* (Cambridge, Mass.: Harvard University Press, 1980).

18. Stephen J. Diner, *A City and Its Universities: Public Policy in Chicago, 1892-1919* (Chapel Hill: University of North Carolina Press, 1980). On the academic freedom cases, see Mary Furner, *From Advocacy to Objectivity: A Crisis in the Professionalization of American Social Science* (Lexington: University of Kentucky Press, 1975).

19. Furner, *From Advocacy to Objectivity, passim.*

20. Walter P. Metzger, *Academic Freedom in the Age of the University* (New York: Columbia University Press, 1955), pp. 194-216.

21. Furner, *From Advocacy to Objectivity.* p. 8.

22. Veysey, *Emergence of the American University,* p. 353.

23. Carol S. Gruber, *Mars and Minerva: World War I and the Uses of Higher Learning in America* (Baton Rouge: Louisiana State University Press, 1975).

24. Joel Novek, "University-Industry Interaction: Graduates and Jobs," *Social Sciences in Canada,* vol. 11, no. 3 (Dec. 1983), pp. 8-9.

25. Frederick Rudolph, *The American College and University: A History* (New York: Knopf, 1962), pp. 455-61, 479-85; Daniel

Bell, *The Reforming of General Education: The Columbia College Experience in Its National Setting* (New York: Columbia University Press, 1966).

26. Robert Paul Wolff, *The Ideal of the University* (Boston: Beacon Press, 1969), pp. 36-42.

27. Ibid., p. 127.

28. Regina Austin, Jean Crockett, Michael B. Katz, Robert E.A. Palmer, "Report to the Senate Executive Committee from the Committee to Review the Administrative Actions Pertaining to the ATO Incident," (University of Pennsylvania) *Almanac*, vol. 30, no. 15 (13 Dec. 1983), pp. 3-6.

29. In fairness, it should be pointed out that subsequent to the incident discussed here, the university administration introduced a strong policy on sexual harrassment, initiated a review and reform of internal judicial procedures, and stimulated increased faculty-student contact in various ways, such as making attractive apartments in student residences available to faculty. The administration also tried, with only partial success, to remove the offending fraternity chapter from the campus.

SOCIETY'S EXPECTATIONS: STAYING NEAR THE CUSTOMER

WILLIAM A. COCHRANE

As we approach the twenty-first century and look to the future of our country, it is appropriate that we examine the possible implications for one of the country's most important resources — its universities. Of the many factors that will influence the university's future, none will be more important than the degree of understanding and support provided by Canadian society.

It would seem only reasonable, therefore, to assess society's expectations of its institutions. In the past such expectations have not always been understood by institutions of higher education and, to be fair, have not been clearly communicated. This is true, in part, because society has not, until recently, addressed the issue of what the objectives and goals of a university should be. In turn, the university has generally developed its objectives and programs principally through its own internal activity with only limited exploration or involvement with society.

One of the most important guiding principles of any institution or organization where activities will have a major effect on society should be obtaining, assessing, and responding to the views and expectations of that society.

To this end, one of the most important statements I have heard from business professionals and particularly from senior executives and marketing managers is, "Stay near the customer." This short and simple prerequisite of a successful business should be at the forefront of any activity of universities or institutions of higher education.

Information obtained by staying near the customer would help any organization
— assess the quality of its products and services
— determine the customer's short- and long-term wants and needs
— learn of misinformation and myths and provide an opportunity for correction

29

— decide to discontinue inadequate products or programs and
to reallocate resources
— keep abreast of the competition
— establish a long-term strategic plan
— identify the customers' perception of the institution or
organization.

The last point is extremely important, for so often
perception is reality. Unfortunately, many organizations,
particularly those charged with the responsibility of
management, fail to identify the real perceptions and,
consequently, fail to implement corrective actions or to redirect
the institution.

The principal customers of the university are the general
public, the business or industrial sector, and government. Before
examining their views and their relationships to the university, I
will state some assumptions about Canada's future throughout
the rest of the century and the implications of these for our
universities.

Assumptions and Implications

Throughout the rest of this century, I believe Canada will
experience:

— increased competition, particularly from developing
countries, in manufacturing and natural resource
development, that is, in mining, forestry, petroleum
products, and agriculture
— continued technological development, affecting the kinds of
skills required and the number of personnel employed
— limited economic growth and elevated unemployment
— continued restraint on government expenditures
— increased opportunities for technological development,
industrial transfer, and unique product manufacture
— qualified public support in recognizing the importance of
higher education in determining the country's future
strengths.

The implications for universities of these assumptions include:

— continued financial restraint from government requiring
greater sources of non-governmental revenue
— continued growth in student enrolment as a result of
inadequate job opportunities
— re-examination of educational programs in light of
technological development and decreased "professional"
requirements

— greater emphasis on scientific "innovation," that is, the transfer of scientific discovery into industry for commercial development and industrial growth

— increased awareness, responsiveness, and communication by universities with the various sectors of society

— greater co-operation, integration, and collaboration among academic units of the university and enhanced co-ordination of effort between regional and national academic institutions

— greater unified leadership in economic development, social/political issues, and international relationships.

These implications emphasize one important message for university boards, administrative faculty, and staff: *remain close to the customer.* To expand on this premise, I will now consider the customers of the university and their present perceptions.

Attitudes of the Public toward Higher Education

Opinion surveys over the past five to ten years have assessed public attitudes toward education, including higher education. A U.S. Gallup survey found in 1982 that the overwhelming majority of citizens felt that the education system was very important in affecting the country's future strength and outranked in importance industrial production and the military.

Public attitudes toward education in Ontario were assessed in 1982 as part of an ongoing public opinion survey.[1] Findings revealed that the public:

— wanted current expenditures on public education to be increased, or at least maintained even during the bad economic climate

— saw training as most important and favoured better preparation of high school students by teaching adaptable, basic technical skills

— desired greater business and labour contact with students during high school

— opposed market-related quotas for entrance into post-secondary institutions

— supported a decrease in enrolment to avoid a decline in the quality of education if funds were reduced, but would prefer neither

— favoured enhancing work skills and increasing information through continued learning and self-development, to be carried on principally outside the workplace.

In addition, the survey showed that non-management, salaried professionals and full-time students were the most supportive of educational services; employers, particularly corporate executives, appeared to be more concerned, however, with "financial rationalization" of specific expenditures for educational services. Fifty-two per cent of these interviewed did not favour relating university admissions to job opportunities, but 37 per cent supported such a policy. Responses on this issue varied with income; that is, lower-income respondents were more likely to favour relating admissions to job opportunities.

A 1982 report on the "university purpose" by the senate of the University of Alberta attempted to assess the public's perception and its views for the future.[2] Many of those interviewed had no response to the questions about priorities for the University of Alberta. It was evident that the public was unclear about what universities do and should do; the report suggested that the university community should be sensitive to this observation. The interpretation of the public's response by the university's senate included the following conclusions. First teaching and research functions are of equal importance. Second, the university must do more than provide occupational training, but it must also be sensitive to the public's perception that skills learned at the university will likely enhance opportunities for employment. Finally, universities must provide its graduates with the skills of decision making and effective communication, an aesthetic appreciation, a broad interdisciplinary perspective, and an understanding of ethical problems and social responsibility.

A.S. Hughes examined public attitudes toward post-secondary education in the three Maritime provinces in November 1979 through a telephone survey of 1,163 residents.[3] This report showed that citizens in general were not well informed about many aspects of university activities. Of those interviewed 80 per cent thought that society benefited from publicly supported post-secondary educational institutions, and 8 per cent felt there was no benefit. Lower-income and less-educated groups were among those less confident of societal benefit.

Fewer than a third of those who felt universities benefited society were able to cite an example. Respondents who could identify benefits stated that: more students can go to post-secondary institutions if the schools are publicly supported; the attendees create a better-informed community and population; and acquired competence and greater skills of the work force lead to an improved economy. Those surveyed gave two overall reasons for a college education: it is generally beneficial, and it leads to a more challenging job with greater opportunity for advancement.

Particular university programs were ranked as follows:
— first order of priority: health sciences, agriculture, and forestry
— second order of priority: technical fields, teacher education, law, business administration, and physical sciences
— third order of priority: social sciences, humanities, and fine arts.

The Maritime survey revealed a great deal of public ambivalence about the performance of universities and colleges in that part of Canada. More than 50 per cent of the respondents had no position, and 30 per cent were either very satisfied or not satisfied. Some 54 per cent could not suggest how to improve performance when suggestions were sought, indicating inadequate knowledge and information.

Dr. L. Harris's survey of public opinion toward the University of Prince Edward Island ten years after its inception generally supported the observations of the Maritime survey.[4] One interesting finding was that almost 85 per cent of the respondents agreed that many people outside the university community knew very little about what goes on at a university. My own subjective assessment corresponds closely to these survey results. I believe that a large percentage of the public has a positive attitude toward institutions of higher education and equates university education with better job opportunities and advancement. Yet, most persons are relatively uninformed about what universities do. They have little idea how well the institutions carry out their mandate, and but a few can offer positive suggestions about future directions.

Many persons will be intolerant of universities if they believe that these institutions indulge in benefits and expenditures inconsistent with the economic realities affecting most Canadians. Examples include perceived large wage settlements, job protection through tenure, two- to three-months leave of absence with pay, and sizable capital expenditures for construction projects such as recreational facilities and parking garages at a time of economic difficulty.

Among other matters, the public would like universities to place greater emphasis on the quality of teaching, with perhaps less attention to professors' publishing records, and to be more conscientious about the relationship between the costs and societal benefits of expensive research.

University Response

How might universitites respond to these views in the future?

Universities need to make a greater effort than they have in the past to design better methods of public communication. Although information can be provided to the general media, much more effort should be directed to the opinion makers, university graduates, consumer groups, and elected representatives. Many elected politicians have had little, if any, university experience yet are responsible for allocating resources to universities. Regular invitations to elected representatives to meet, exchange views, and share suggestions would be an appropriate action by university boards and authorities.

Too many universities appear to be isolated and disengaged entities rather than vital elements of daily life. Many seem to be living in a world of many decades ago. To some, this statement by an academic at one of the western universities is appropriate: "The function of the university is not to help with unemployment statistics. We are not a branch of the U.I.C." But for many citizens, the remark is not in keeping with the real world.[5] To maintain the respect and support of the public, all universities must organize ways not only to obtain public views but also to respond to them effectively.

Attitudes of Business and Industry toward Higher Education

Another sector of society that has important and interesting views of our universities is business and industry. During the past twenty years, an unnecessary and harmful schism has developed between business and universities. Many myths and some truths are held by each constituency about the other. I have heard corporate executives express views that reflect a certain disenchantment with our universities. They feel that universities:

— are too insular and are not interested in the needs of business
— are not administered in a financially efficient and businesslike manner
— direct inadequate effort toward ensuring that graduates have basic skills in communications and mathematics
— create a bias against business and teach programs inadequately related to everyday problems
— often conduct costly research that is unrelated to practical problems and that lacks specific objectives, responsible time frames, and adequate evaluation.

It appears that business wants universities:

— to prepare graduates for the realities and shocks of the real
   world following graduation
— to make available dynamic, bright, innovative people with
   problem-solving skills
— to expand their effort in forecasting economic faults and
   demographic shifts
— to increase their responsiveness to issues identified by
   business as important
— to conduct sound basic research and to organize efforts for
   the transfer of discoveries into industrial reality
— to show greater evidence of sound management and
   financial accountability
— to provide assistance in retraining and continuous
   education programs to expand the skills of employees.[6]

Government and Higher Education

Government is the third important participant in the
relationship of universities to the community. Before the Second
World War and for a short time thereafter, universities were
primarily funded through private contributions and student fees.
Universities had closer working relationships with industry and
foundations because they provided tangible support for the
limited resources that existed at our institutions of higher
education. The so-called baby boom of the 1950s resulted in large
numbers of young people presenting themselves for primary and
elementary education. During the late 1950s and early 1960s, it
became apparent that universities would need to respond to the
vast numbers of young people who would seek an advanced
education. The enormous challenges that occurred within a short
time resulted in major strains, imbalances, conflicts, and rapidly
escalating costs and expenditures. In most parts of Canada in the
1950s and early 1960s, one out of every fifteen to twenty
individuals went on to post-secondary institutions — approximately one person out of thirteen of those aged eighteen to
twenty-four.

Governments in Canada, both federal and provincial,
increased financial support to expand existing universities and to
create new institutions across Canada. Education grew from 5.5
per cent of the gross national product (GNP) in 1963 to 9 per cent
in 1970 and was some 8 per cent in 1975. The portion of total
government expenditures (federal, provincial, and municipal) for
education was 16.8 per cent in 1962; it increased to 22 per cent in
1968-1970 and fell to some 16 per cent by the end of the 1970s.

Most universities during this period of rapid expansion were
given significant financial resources by governments to expand

their facilities and staff. Combined with the explosion in numbers of young people seeking higher education was a significant policy change that resulted in a movement toward a more "open door" admissions policy. Funding was enrolment-driven on the basis of provincial grants; this, combined with the general economic prosperity and the priority that had been set by governments, resulted in massive increases in spending on education.

After a period of tremendous expansion with the blessing of governments and the public alike, the growth in educational institutions and their programs suddenly came to a halt. The two principal reasons for this reversal were the change in population growth in Canada and the significant growth in expenditures required to support the educational system from the public purse. By the late 1970s, it was clear that post-secondary educational institutions were in for increased difficulties as financial support from governments diminished.

University enrolments slowed, and enrolment ratio or participation rates became fixed at approximately 20 per cent. It was expected that enrolments would increase until 1982, then decline until 1992, then increase again.

At present it appears that most provincial governments in Canada believe that only a very limited need exists for any significant increase in expenditures for higher education. Although university administration and staff have made many presentations to the public, private citizens do not seem concerned about the serious erosion of university educational programs and facilities. Elected members of the legislatures across Canada appear unconvinced of the universities' plight, and public pressure has been insufficient to effect any attitudinal change on existing fiscal restraint.

There is a perception that universities have generally done well and that the academic staff continue to be a privileged group both in their job protection and their financial reward. The federal government of Canada perhaps did a disservice to the universities in 1977 when the Financial Administration Act removed the restrictions on the 50 per cent federal contributions to post-secondary educational funding and left such funds to be used at the discretion of the provinces. It would seem evident that the federal government should be involved in the development of education policies of national importance in co-operation with the provincial governments.

The public has acknowledged since the post-war years that scientific research should be carried out by Canadian universities, and government support of basic research has steadily developed. Again fiscal restraints, both by provincial and federal governments, have eroded the research strengths within our universities and more particularly decreased the number of personnel receiving skilled training in scientific research. This policy is shortsighted because governments have recently emphasized the importance of research and development (R & D) as a major step in Canada's future economic growth, and they surely must appreciate that high technology is dependent on the availability of skilled personnel and intellectual talent.

Universities have only recently spoken with a clear and collective voice in emphasizing these areas and their importance for the future of the country. As so often happened in university organizations, individual voices and separate views were expressed without considering the benefits of a collective, strong, and singular effort to persuade the public to bring pressure upon their governments to reconsider their existing policies. It is evident, however, that governments are unlikely to provide significantly increased support to universities, because major economic difficulties exist in Canada and present social benefits including social welfare programs will take a higher priority.

University Research and Technology Transfer

The relationship between Canada's economic future and enhanced research and technological development is being increasingly appreciated by those in government, industry, and academic institutions. Economic growth will depend on expanded industrial development, and to a great extent, this development will affect the growth of high technology industries.

Much emphasis has been placed on the need to increase Canadian investment in R & D. Canada expends some 1.0 per cent of its GNP on research and development, with a proposed target of 1 1/2 per cent by 1985. These figures contrast to the 1 1/2 to 5 per cent of GNP now invested in R & D by other industrialized nations.

Although the proposed increase is commendable, one of the major weaknesses in research and development programs is the lack of a "system" or plan for transferring inventions and scientific discoveries from universities to industry. If the government of Canada wishes to increase R & D for the purpose of developing new high technology manufacturing industries, simply providing more money will not accomplish this objective. It is essential that there be a strategy for the transfer of technology from our academic institutions and government research centres, where most of the basic scientific research is carried out, into Canadian industry. Although Canada has able and competent scientists capable of invention, the country has been weak in innovation, that is, the transfer of an invention into scaled-up manufacture and production for commercial marketing.

The innovation process requires a linking of two elements to be productive – the generation of knowledge and the transfer of that knowledge into commercial products and services. For the first, adequate resources must be made available to carry out research. Of major importance is the availability of highly skilled personnel. The progressive decline during the past five to ten years in the number of Canadians with advanced degrees in the physical and natural sciences may have a detrimental effect on the nation's ability to probe the frontiers of science and technology. To ensure the availability of skilled personnel, universities and industry must co-operate in providing adequate programs, resources, and facilities.

The second element, the transfer of knowledge and technology into commercial enterprises to produce products and services, has not been well orchestrated in Canada. Four factors affect the development of new technology and its transfer to industry from universities: attitudes, information, communication, and resources.

Attitudes

Attitudes have been the greatest barrier to the transfer of discoveries into commercial reality. Many myths and erroneous impressions continue to exist in the way industry and universities perceive each other.

The corporate sector holds the view that academic scientists and scholars are not committed to particular goals or time frames, that they have a poor ability to organize and to accomplish certain specific tasks, and that they have little interest in the practical, everyday problems so evident in the commercial world.

Academic scientists believe that business and corporations have little interest in expanding scientific knowledge and are only interested in the practical application and commercial exploitation of scientific discoveries. They also feel that Canadian industry has not contributed to the support of scientific research for the benefit of society in general.

Fortunately, the attitudes of both "solitudes" seem to be changing, albeit gradually. Each is recognizing the mutual benefit of closer contact and co-operation between industry and the university. Frank and open discussion has been almost non-existent, and though there is evidence of recent improvement, it is still necessary to exchange views and ideas and to recognize interdependence to achieve expanded industrial development. The following are three ways to effect improved attitudes through enhanced contact. (1) The appointment of representatives from various business sectors to academic policy and planning committees would increase institution-to-institution contact. This may seem self-evident, but a recent example illustrates insular university thinking. A Canadian university set up a research review committee to look to the future with rather broad objectives. No one, however, had considered the value of adding a member from a high technology company with research experience. The chairman of the committee responded favourably when the oversight was pointed out. (2) The appointment of academic scientists to the boards and advisory committees of Canadian businesses and the promotion of business advisory councils for various faculties and academic units of the university would create opportunities for the exchange of views. (3) The development of a central university office and information centres would also promote and enhance the contact between business and academic staff.

Information

Canadian industry lacks information on the location, expertise, and research interests of academic scientists. Similarly, Canadian scientists are not aware of the location and type of activity in which many small to medium Canadian companies are engaged. Consequently, scientists do not bring discoveries to the attention of Canadian companies, and companies do not contact academic scientists whose expertise may be of considerable assistance to the resolution of specific problems.

One possible solution, as mentioned above, would be the creation of Industrial and Scientific Information Centres in the Maritimes, Quebec, Ontario, the Prairies, and British Columbia. These centres would be a repository of electronically recorded information for businesses and universities in each region; companies and individuals, their interests and activities would be indexed in the system by key words. A business/university advisory committee would oversee the policy and operation of the centre. These centres would be linked nationally so that businesses and university scientists could obtain information beyond their respective regions. Located at each centre would be a very small staff that would include at least one individual with sufficient technical background to be able to visit businesses within the region to offer advice and information and to act as a link with university scientists who could be of assistance to a company.

Communication

Inadequate communication is one of the major impediments to collaboration and co-operation between industry and universities and to the transfer of discoveries to Canadian industry. Enhanced opportunities for co-operation and working relationships are essential for increased communication and understanding.

Canadian business and universities also need to have a closer association to exchange views and concerns through representative generic organizations such as the Association of Universities and Colleges of Canada, regional university organizations, Chambers of Commerce, and the Business Council on National Issues.

Government fellowships and scholarships for industry to engage scientists to work within their industry for limited periods of time would help promote better communication. The secondment of highly skilled staff from universities to industry would be another means of improving relationships between the two sectors. Enhanced co-operative educational programs for both undergraduate and graduate students would also increase communication.

Resources

Both federal and provincial governments have developed grant programs to encourage and support increased R & D in Canadian industry. Grants from the National Research Council under the Program of Industry/Laboratory Projects and under Project Research Applicable in Industry provide limited assistance, but support for costly product development and venture capital from the private sector remains very limited in Canada. The Natural Science and Engineering Research Council has initiated programs to promote greater cooperation and exchange between university institutions and industry. Support for staff exchanges and co-operative research ventures is most valuable and needs to expand.

Industry will need to increase its support for secondment of scientists from universities to industry for defined periods to assist in technology transfer. Opportunities for graduate students to participate in company research efforts must be increased with corresponding financial assistance by industry to back up such programs.

As mentioned earlier, the most valuable resource is skilled personnel. Here universities and industry must join together to convince government and the public to avoid any shortsighted policies that would inhibit the education of badly needed scientific talent.

The Future of Higher Education

What might be the effect of society's expectations on the future direction, activities, and organization of our universities? The effects fall under three headings: students, faculty, and organizations.

Students

There will be less of an "open door" policy and a "right" to attend university and more emphasis on the "right of opportunity" to attend. Higher academic requirements for admission will exist, and greater direct student assistance will be provided by provincial and federal governments. A student with satisfactory academic standing and evidence of motivation will not be precluded from attending university because of economic factors. More "co-operative programs" will exist where more of the students' education will take place in the "marketplace," and greater flexibility will be allowed in completing a degree program.

To address continued high unemployment, "job sharing" will likely grow along with a shorter work week for individuals. As a result, greater numbers of Canadians will seek higher education both to increase their skills and to fill their leisure time. The growth in numbers of part-time students will continue. Industry and labour will both wish greater involvement in program design as they protect their respective interests.

Significant quotas will exist for students wishing to enter such professional programs as medicine, dentistry, nursing, engineering, law, architecture, and teaching, because employment opportunities will be limited. Where services are provided by government, increased expenditures will be controlled by restriction of the providers of these services.

Electronic technology will be exploited to facilitate the self-education of students and will result in more numerous "decentralized" or off-campus programs.

Faculty

Greater emphasis will be placed on developing leaders for a society that needs increased emphasis on social, environmental, and ethical values.

Faculty members will be less organized around the traditional disciplines, such as chemistry, physics, and engineering. They will take part in many multidisciplinary teaching units emphasizing programs to meet the need for broadly educated individuals as opposed to narrow specialists.

There will be rigorous appraisals of performance at regular intervals for faculty with appointments likely for fixed terms of five years and, in some cases, mandatory retraining if employment is to continue. More faculty will also be spending limited periods of secondment to government and business.

Organizations

Universities will develop better means of communicating with the various segments of society and of obtaining information and feedback on the performance of their graduates. Research activity will be linked increasingly to industrial application, with a corresponding increase in joint ventures between industry and university. Government and industry will co-operate in supporting basic curiosity-driven research, with a greater emphasis on the support of individuals rather than projects.

Industry would likely support increased research if universities began to develop specialized or concentrated research thrusts in important scientific areas. One example is the significant support now being given by industry to the University of Waterloo for computer science. Concentrations of effort in selected areas will likely be the pattern for the future, with a corresponding decrease in more general research.

One concern might be expressed at this time. The rapid expansion of new scientific and technical knowledge will require similarly rapid responses by our educational institutions in transmitting information and skills to students. The natural inertia of universities may not allow the redirection and restructuring necessary for accommodating these new developments. A failure to do so could result in other existing institutions of higher education assuming responsibilities that heretofore have been the universities' responsibilities, for example, scientific research and advanced degree educational programs.

The formation of co-operative "consortia" will develop among universities in given regions of the country, and these will enhance teaching and research and will avoid duplication of effort and waste of resources. Greater co-operation between the universities will result in a more sensitive and co-ordinated leadership to address national issues. Although universities have functioned in society as a critic and a resource, they have done so more as isolated sections of a rather poorly organized orchestra emitting a cacophony of sounds whose sweet notes have either not been heard or have been increasingly ignored by many segments of society. A return to an aggressive, constructive, and unified voice will do much to gain general support. Much of Canada's future will depend on the advice and leadership of its intellectual community.

Warren Bryan Martin, scholar in residence of the Carnegie Foundation for the Advancement of Teaching in Washington, D.C., stated:

> The best rationale for the type of university most needed now is not that it is a centre of basic research and sound scholarship, though it is; that it is the place where professional skills are taught and careers launched, though those things happen there, nor that it brings general education, socialization and preparation for citizenship to otherwise benighted students, though it does provide these answers.
>
> The best rationale for the university is that it is the place where the most substantial issues of society — political, economic, social — receive sustained and disciplined attention, where contending theologies and methodologies meet, and where prospects are best for the emergence of appropriate responses to these enduring challenges.

I can support this statement with only one additional comment. Universities will also need to address the issue of ways of implementing these "appropriate responses" and to play a more activist role in the future in implementing these responses than they have in the past.

Notes

1.   D.W. Livingstone, D.J. Hart, and L.D. Maclean, *Public Attitudes Toward Education in Ontario: Fourth O.I.S.E. Survey*, 1982.

2.   The University of Alberta Senate Commission on University Purpose, Apr. 1982.

3.   A.S. Hughes, *Public Attitudes toward Post-Secondary Education in the Maritime Provinces: The A.A.U. Survey Report*, 1979.

4.   L. Harris, *Ten Years Later: The University of Prince Edward Island*, Mar. 1981.

5.   J., Carr, "Universities under Stress, Seek a Role for the Eighties," *The Globe and Mail*, 26 Jan. 1984.

6.   E.S. Jackson, *Working with Universities: What Business Wants*, (Toronto: Institute of Donations and Public Affairs Research, Mar. 1978).

SERVICE OR CAPTIVITY?
BUSINESS-UNIVERSITY RELATIONS IN
THE TWENTIETH CENTURY

PAUL AXELROD

Despite their pristine ideals, honourable intentions, and occasional rebuffs, universities are no virgins when it comes to heeding the corporate siren call. Some may lament the distance that universities keep from their "customers," but from the time North American universities were lured by business and government with land and largess, they literally traded the spiritual for the material world. What the Morill Act in 1862 did for the growth of non-denominational colleges in the United States, in its promotion of "agriculture, the mechanical arts" and the interests of the "industrial classes,"[1] the industrial revolution did for higher education in Canada. According to the *Report of the Royal Commission on the University of Toronto* in 1906, "The two distinct objects of university education are mental culture and practical utility. In recent years the latter has steadily gained upon the former owing to the utilitarian character of the age, the increased expenditures have doubtless been chiefly for the development of this branch of instruction."[2]

Despite the acerbic rebukes by critics of "utilitarianism," like Thorstein Veblen and Robert Hutchins in the United States, and academics W.H. Alexander and Carleton Stanley in Canada, North American universities tightened their bonds with business and government in the early twentieth century. What Hutchins viewed as "the insidious combination of progress, evolution and empiricism in jettisoning the past, in promoting adjustment as an ideal, and in substituting vocationalism for thought as the focus of the university,"[3] was mirrored in Canada by a culture said to have "little use for universities except as purveyors . . . of material comfort."[4] With its insatiable demand for engineers, scientists, and "top-secret" research, the Second World War diminished even further the priority of the humanities on North American campuses. In Canada, only students in the upper half of classes not considered essential to the national interest were allowed to remain in university until graduation during the war.

45

According to one observer, the "laboratory became the first line of defence and the scientist, the indispensable warrior."[5]

After the war, North American universities moved through two distinct phases in their relations with government and business, and by the early 1980s, found themselves on the threshold of a third. As the Canadian experience demonstrated, in prosperous times universities avidly served their corporate sponsors. In the recession of the 1970s, the private sector viewed universities with scepticism and supported them only conditionally. In recent years, corporate interest in higher education has been rekindled, and in the face of limited public funding, North American universities run the risk of becoming the private sector's captive.

If any date can be considered pivotal in raising to unprecedented heights Canadian consciousness over the value of education, especially over the increasing importance of higher education, 1956 would surely qualify. In the previous year, Edward Sheffield, a federal government consultant, released a study to the National Conference of Canadian Universities (NCCU) projecting that, through demographic pressure alone, university enrolment would double to over 120,000 by 1965.[6] The report, which significantly underestimated the actual increase, sparked a period of frenetic activity among educators and businessmen. The NCCU sponsored a special conference in the fall of 1956 entitled "Canada's Crisis in Higher Education," in which the very survival of the country was pinned to the expansion of educational facilities. Papers, speeches, and conference resolutions from some of Canada's most prominent academic figures underlined the crisis. To reach the nation's information nerve centre, the NCCU struck a committee under Claude Bissell, the president of Carleton University, which employed an "effective and simple device" of sending a one-page letter to the editors of all the newspapers in Canada, presenting the statistical case of the Sheffield report and "underlining that in ten years we would have a doubling of our university population."[7] In the same year, a conference of renowned educators, businessmen, and scientists was convened at St. Andrew's, New Brunswick, where similar statements thickened the air and received wide publicity.[8] The conference established a private business-run organization called the Industrial Foundation on Education whose expressed purpose was to promote the cause of and raise money for higher education in Canada.[9] In 1957, the *Final Report of the Royal Commission on Canada's Economic Prospects* drew these threads together, reinforcing the link between Canada's educational development and the country's economic fate. Universities, asserted the commission, "are the source of the most highly skilled workers whose knowledge is essential in all branches of industry. . . . It is incredible that we would allow their services to society . . . to lapse or lag."[10]

Virtually every aspect of education was explored in scores of publications during this period, but for public consumption certain prominent themes stood out. The quietude of the 1950s had been regularly disturbed by lurid accounts of Soviet political ambitions, coldly and at times hysterically documented in the nation's media. Indeed, aside from the public preoccupation with economic growth and material security, the simmering cold war constituted the other major issue that absorbed the attention of North Americans in the post-war period. In 1951 one opinion poll identified the fear of war as the major concern of Canadians (53 per cent). Following the sensational American espionage trial and executions of Julius and Ethel Rosenberg in 1953, 62 per cent of Canadians were prepared to deny Communists freedom of speech; only 26 per cent of the public favoured upholding such a fundamental democratic right. And in 1961, while 42 per cent of Canadians felt that the "free world" could live peacefully with the Russians, fully 48 per cent predicted a new world war.[11]

How did this issue relate to the incessant demands for improved educational facilities? Soviet progress had been generated by a remarkably sophisticated technology, if not equaling, then at least approaching that of the United States. For North Americans, the successful launching of the Sputnik satellite in 1957 underscored these extraordinary developments in a frightening way. Such advances were based on the speedy training of technolgists, engineers, and scientists, financed by the government and educated in universities. One researcher, citing Allen Dulles, the director of the Central Intelligence Agency, reported that the Soviet Union would graduate 1,200,000 students in pure science during the 1950s, while the United States would graduate only 990,000.[12] A statement to the St. Andrew's Conference by James Duncan, a former president of Massey Ferguson, chairman of Ontario Hydro, and a member of the Industrial Foundation on Education, reinforced the perceived link between the economy, the cold war, and higher education:

> In my opinion we are in danger of losing the cold war unless we do something about it and education is very close to the core of our problem. Science and engineering have made such remarkable progress in recent decades that the nation which holds the

lead in these fields holds the initiative in world affairs.

The conference concurred and passed a resolution informing

> the people of Canada that the problem of the universities has become an emergency of grave national concern to the certain disadvantage of our progress as a nation, and can only be solved by energetic and immediate assistance and co-operation of all governments in Canada, of business and industry and of private benefactors.[13]

Without this type of commitment, echoed the Royal Commission on Canada's Economic Propects, Canada, along with other non-communist nations, risked falling victim to Soviet "ecumenical ambitions."[14] On the heels of the Sputnik launching, the Minister of Education in Ontario called a meeting of the province's university presidents, and told them: "It is essential that we do everything we can to reassure those of the public who are anxious about present conditions that everything is being done and will be done to strengthen and to support the services rendered by the Ontario universities."[15]

In demonstrating from an academic perspective that the cold war raised questions about the state of the national culture as much as it did about the condition of technology, Claude Bissell, the new president of the University of Toronto, published an article in *Maclean's* magazine in April 1958, entitled "Universities Must Answer Sputnik with Higher Standards." The NCCU brief to the Royal Commission on Canada's Economic Prospects claimed that the humanities and arts, "from which the soul of man is fed, and through which the heritage of civilized communities is passed to mortal generations," also deserved greater financial support.[16] Senator Donald Cameron, the director of the Banff School of Fine Arts, cited Robert Hutchins on the same theme. "It seems useless to hope that democracy can survive unless all people are educated for freedom. Mass stupidity can now mean mass suicide."[17]

The appeals of the academics were, for the most part, however, as intensely impractical as those of the business community and underscored the utilitarian impulses of the Canadian people. According to the NCCU, "The demand for expert persons, for intelligent persons, with background and perspective, increases with every increase in the population, with every increase in the gross national product, with every requirement for increased investment."[18] No one, in fact, disputed the Ontario government's claim that educational investment was necessary for Canada to become a "modern industrial power."[19]

The task ahead entailed not merely waging ideological war against the nation's potential enemies but securing as well Canada's competitive advantage over the country's economic rivals. The Industrial Foundation on Education (IFE) both marvelled and panicked at the incredible progress Germany and Japan had made since the war. "In 1945 Western Germany lay in ruins and a starving people wandered through the rubble of her devastated cities. Today Germany competes successfully in foreign markets with finished products incorporating the latest technology." The weakness of Canada's educational training facilities was demonstrated by her heavy reliance on skilled immigrants and refugees from other countries. In the first nine months of 1957, disclosed the IFE, Canada brought in nearly 2,150 engineers. For the whole year, this would prove to be some 3,600 "which is over twice as many as graduated from all Canadian universities in 1957."[20] According to the president of Polymer Corporation, "over the next 26 years we will need a minimum of three to four times as many engineers and scientists as are now employed and ten times as many technicians."[21] Indeed, Canada was so far behind her rivals that she spent proportionately one third of funds allotted in the United States to industrial and scientific research and only three fifths of those in the United Kingdom.[22] In a survey that revealed in direct terms the perceived relationship of educational training to corporate performance, the Department of Labour found that:

> The shortage of professional personnel is evident and is not a matter of conjecture. 50 per cent of Canadian employers of professional personnel are experiencing difficulty finding staff. Of the companies surveyed, 47 per cent reported curtailment of production and expansion plans, 33 per cent curtailment of planning and research, 21 per cent overloading of present personnel, 14 per cent liability to offer adequate training, and 11 per cent a shortage of future executives.[23]

On a personal basis, the message cut deeply and effectively, as economists were able to prove in simple and compelling terms that Canadians who were well educated would earn more than those who were not. "Estimates have shown," noted the

Economic Council of Canada," "that better education appears to have raised labour earnings for many by about 30 per cent from 1911-1961."[24] In a 1963 poll, the public revealed how completely it had absorbed such information over the years: 60 per cent of Canadians agreed that a boy should not leave school at age sixteen even if he wanted to, while only 30 per cent said he should be permitted to do so. As if to convince by example, 39 per cent of Canadians in a 1956 poll confessed that leaving school early had been their biggest mistake in life.[25]

Who should pay for the massive expansion of higher education? According to Canadian businessmen, only government could do the job. Contending that students should continue to finance at least part of the education, the editors of the Bank of Montreal *Business Review* admitted that "students can't provide more than a fraction of the increased income that will be required."[26] Similarly, as the president of Falconbridge Nickel of Canada argued, corporations were equally handicapped in their ability to pay.

> The financial problem is entirely beyond the means of philanthropic corporations. It must be remembered that corporations handle the funds of individual investors and have the duty and responsibility of using these funds only for the proper purposes of the businesses and in the best interests of the shareholders. . . . Our educational problem is a national problem.[27]

Lest their corporate brethren were unconvinced by the Gallup Polls, the politicians' speeches, or the academic lobbyists, prominent company spokesmen argued the case of higher education in starkly practical terms, which all businessmen could readily understand and would ignore only at their peril. An editorial in *Trade and Commerce* claimed that "in supporting higher education business is to a certain extent just buttering its own bread. . . . Graduates of engineering and science faculties are being channelled directly into the service of business so that universities are actually saving the businessmen considerable expense that might be encountered in on the job training."[28] "It is out of the universities," emphasized A.A. Cumming, the president of Union Carbide Canada, "that we shall get the professional engineers, geologists, research scientists and others who can lead us forward in the search for technological excellence. They are also the place from which will come the economists, the accountants, the investment people and others for whom a professional economic training is essential."[29]

Despite the small proportion of university income provided by corporate contributions, university officials implored leading businessmen to join university boards of governors. A college comptroller explained why:

> First of all, because they have money themselves or manage it for someone else, they have the required experience. Secondly they might be persuaded to part with some of it once they get a first hand knowledge of the need (for expanded educational facilities). And they know other people of means and can talk them into giving a few thousand or a few hundred thousand, whatever it takes. Thirdly, it's the thing to do — to appoint businessmen. Society expects it. People look up to them, especially government people. If the business community feels there's a need for a university and shows its interest by putting up a good chunk of money, this is a pretty persuasive argument for a provincial grant.[30]

In turn, businessmen, who were swept up in the raging enthusiasm for the expansion of university facilities, were proud to associate themselves with institutions of higher learning. The prestige value of a board appointment was obvious. To be selected by "one's peers," according to one corporate leader, was a badge of honour in the heady days of university development.[31]

While there is little evidence that businessmen profited directly from their associations with universities, they were only too pleased to steer university investments toward companies with which they were connected.[32] The construction industry, in particular, benefited tremendously from the growth of educational facilities. "If the education industry had not increased its investment in construction from 1961-63 by some $211 million, or a gain of nearly 70 per cent above 1961 levels, our $6 billion construction industry would have shown only about half the gain it made during the past two years."[33]

The university was big business, and the corporate executives overseeing the expansion were well aware of the problems and opportunities this presented. They believed they were needed, and this too inspired many of them to join university boards. Although the money they contributed in Canada was not substantial, such aid was precious to the universities because it provided them with a "margin of freedom" to engage in special academic projects, to quicken the pace of expansion, and to enhance the prestige of their own governing boards and campaign committees with prominent business personalities who would gain the attention of government officials holding the purse strings.[34]

Thus, universities were considered essential to the fueling and sustaining of a free enterprise economy. Academics were certainly not unaware of the rampant pragmatism that shaped government policy in higher education, but they were comforted, and in some ways deceived, by the expansion of the "non-utilitarian" areas of university life that accompanied the growth of the professions. After all, did the 1960s not witness the explosion of university general arts programs whose function was cultural, not economic? And did Canadian universities thereby not fulfil the dream of the "Massey" Commission of 1951 of preserving and promoting indigenous culture?[35] In short, was the support extended to general arts not a perfect and powerful indication of society's commitment to the classical educational cause of pursuing truth for its own sake?

The evidence suggests something quite different. Those who viewed the importance of higher education in primarily economic terms included arts programs in their prescriptions. In virtually every major industrial and commercial enterprise, businessmen were firm in their conviction that a student's study of the liberal arts was as vital to the well-being of the economy as was specific professional training. This perception was born of the very complexity of the economy itself, which rendered inadequate narrow, specialized learning, even in the major professions. What employers sought from the universities was the imaginative student who would become the adaptable employee. According to the *Canadian Chartered Accountant*, business training must include not only the tools of the trade, but also such knowledge as "the nature of life in foreign countries, more than one language, and academic work that broadens students' bases of information and makes them generally analytical in their approach to the world in which the businesses... operate" — all talents that would best be provided by a good general arts background.[36] And in the words of the president of Imperial Oil, "Industry has found that it can train an educated man, but it cannot necessarily educate the trained man."[37]

Although they had different concerns, then, the views of businessmen reinforced those of academics on the issue of the liberal arts. The latter could not but be enthralled at the expansion of their own professional opportunities in the humanities and social sciences during the 1960s. While arts professors may not intentionally have been preparing their students for careers in business and science, it is clear that the subjects they taught were viewed as essential by the business community itself. This symbiotic relationship explains a great deal about the depth and nature of support for the expansion of higher education in Canada.

Because the demand for graduates was strong, whatever their academic degrees, all forms of post-secondary education — from engineering to fine arts — were seen as profitable forms of public investment (in a booming economy). If proponents of general education were committed to creating modern-day renaissance men, business did not object so long as these new renaissance men had among their array of talents the capability of working within and contributing to the management of a complex corporation. As business analysts Peter Drucker and John Galbraith observed, knowledge itself was power, and higher education was useful mainly because it had something to sell.[38] None of this is to deny the cultural achievements of the 1960s, which were spurred on in part by university arts courses. The arts thrived, however, on the coattails of a university system designed primarily to serve economic ends.

While support for the expansion of higher education was shaped by broadly based economic demands, the system felt as well pressures to "democratize" access to Canadian universities. Indeed, the "equality of opportunity" argument, heard increasingly in the late 1950s, became almost an article of faith among liberal-minded citizens and politicians in the 1960s. In 1972 both the reports of the Commission on Educational Planning in Alberta and the Commission on Post-Secondary Education in Ontario reiterated this commitment. According to the former, in order for native people and the poor "to be set free, and to be able to function normally in our society, educational opportunities should be made available to them — and to every individual within our province."[39]

Certainly the democratization theme accounts, in part, for the ability of university promoters to elicit the support of those with different interests and competing political persuasions for the central goal of expanding the university system, and it would be foolish to deny its import. In a period when all investment in higher education was viewed as inevitably profitable, however, it was unnecessary for official spokesmen to distinguish between the democratic and the economic benefits of post-secondary education. For the middle and upper classes, universities were the vehicles to professional status. For the less privileged, they held out the promise of upward social mobility. Both of these goals could be rationalized as worthwhile investments in the future of a country starved for highly trained and locally educated professionals. In the context of the overall economic value of higher education to society at large, student aid schemes were themselves considered investments worthy of public support.[40]

Propelled by buoyant economic conditions, favoured by free-spending politicians, and buttressed by widespread public support, higher education during the 1960s became one of Canada's major growth industries. Between 1960 and 1970 full-time enrolment across the country almost tripled to 316,000. In the same period, expenditures by Canadian universities increased 600 per cent to $1.6 billion, and between 1945 and 1970 the number of institutions offering university level training doubled to sixty. All of this was to say nothing of the massive expansion of community college education for the training of students in technical and vocational areas. The spin-off effects of educational investment into other areas of regional economic life, though uncalculated, were unmistakably evident. Popular faith in the economic value of post-secondary education reached unprecedented heights.[41]

Then the balloon burst. Throughout most of the 1970s and into the early 1980s, the country's universities endured a state of permanent underfunding. Despite the consistent growth in enrolments (contrary to public belief), full-time, tenure-stream teaching appointments all but vanished, support staff were laid off, library budgets were ravaged, and plans for new programs were postponed or cancelled.[42] In 1977, the government of British Columbia closed down Notre Dame University, and five years later, the government of Nova Scotia withdrew all funding to the Atlantic School of Education. Throughout the country the fate of other small, "marginal" universities hung in the balance because of inadequate funding.

Like other publicly funded institutions, universities felt the effect of the deepening recession that Canada had been experiencing for more than a decade. Fearful that public spending and higher deficits would only fuel inflation without reducing unemployment significantly, the federal and provincial governments chose instead to restrain wages, particularly in the public sector, and to encourage the expansion of private corporations through direct grants and tax relief. This strategy had not worked by the early 1980s, but the damage to schools, universities, hospitals, social services, and the arts was obvious and profound.[43]

For universities, however, the problems were exacerbated by growing public suspicion about their value as economic instruments. Reports of "surplus" university graduates, especially in the arts, received wide play throughout the 1970s. In 1972 the Manpower and Immigration Department discovered that the 735 companies it surveyed had hired 38 per cent fewer arts graduates than in the previous year, which itself had been 37 per cent below the 1970 figure. A Statistics Canada survey of 1976 university graduates found that two years after graduation, 8.2 per cent were unemployed and only 42 per cent of those with jobs believed that their university training was directly relevant to the positions they held. For Ph.D. holders in the arts, the problem of underemployment (that is, the occupation of positions for which they were over-qualified) was especially severe.[44]

These conditions, combined with the wide belief that universities had been bathed in luxury for far too long, led a number of economists, including those working for the Economic Council of Canada, to reverse their positions on the value of investing heavily in higher education. Claiming to have "refined" their earlier models measuring the "rate-of-return" on educational spending, economists produced conclusions consistent with the growing demand for restraint in the public funding of higher education.[45] Politicians used these studies to rationalize their imposition of higher tuition fees. Students, they now argued, benefited more from higher education than society did as a whole. Therefore, they should pay a larger share of the cost. No one put the argument more crudely than the Ontario Minister of University Affairs who introduced his restraint program in 1971 with the demand that universities should produce "more scholar per dollar."[46]

Revolted by student unrest, worried about the "productivity" of the universities, and convinced that professors "spend too little time teaching. . . and too much time researching books and articles for a fee," Canadian businessmen added their own voices to this obsessive concern with efficiency and profitability in the workings of the country's universities. Annual surveys of approximately three hundred major companies between 1971 and 1978 revealed that the proportion of the corporate donation dollar going to higher education fell from 37 to 25 per cent.[47] Once extolled as the most vital of public investments in a growing economy, post-secondary education had become, in the eyes of many, a major part of the economic problem.

This was not to suggest that the universities of Canada were in imminent danger of being closed down—en masse. Despite the uneven demand for graduates, certain areas of higher educational training still served the private sector well. The demand for engineers, business graduates, and computer scientists remained relatively strong throughout the 1970s and early 1980s, though in the face of enduring recession, the future of even these fields was uncertain. Students responded to their perceptions of the market by enrolling increasingly in the "pragmatic" disciplines at the expense of arts and general education.[48]

The stated priorities of the federal and provincial governments reflected this selective interest in the activities of Canadian universities. In the fall of 1981, Ottawa promised to reduce dramatically its support of higher education through the Established Programs Financing arrangement and to redirect its funds toward university programs and research designed to serve the country's economic needs.[49] In every region, provincial governments took initial steps to control the growth of academic programs, to avoid "duplication" of facilities, and to encourage universities to "rationalize" their development in accordance with economic demand. Perhaps the most extreme example of this approach was in British Columbia where an Academic Council, created in 1978, was assigned unprecedented authority over colleges and universities.

> It provides for articulation committees to recommend on the equivalency of courses given at one institution or university as compared to courses given at another institution or university. In cases of dispute, the Academic Council is to have power to make a ruling on the matter, apparently in this respect being able to override university decisions on admissions. This power, if exercised, might well conflict with provisions of the Universities Act, and it certainly flies in the face of widely accepted and indeed minimal notions of the academic responsibilities of the university.[50]

Recession, rationalization, and restraint—these were the watchwords that shaped higher education in the 1970s and early 1980s. Against such odious and debilitating pressures, the goals of widening accessibility, fostering social criticism, enhancing cultural development, and preserving institutional autonomy struggled to assert their priority in the framing of post-secondary educational policy.

Thus, in good times and bad, universities were judged primarily on their ability to contribute to economic growth. Aware that government funding is unlikely to be as bountiful as in the 1960s, universities have turned increasingly to the private sector for their economic salvation. Owing to the recent revolutions in biotechnology and microelectronics, some corporations are actively purchasing university resources to satisfy their insatiable appetites for research and development. Many, like the Canadian Corporate Higher Education Forum, favour this trend.[51] Enthusiastically, they point to the growing number of contract research and joint venture projects involving corporations and Canadian universities. Won't such arrangements make universities more self-sufficient by getting the government bogeyman off their backs? Won't they compel universities to become more sensitive to community needs? Won't intellectual life be revitalized and enhanced?

There are grounds for scepticism. Some influential businessmen, with money to spend, have a very narrow view of the value of higher education. According to Donald Chisolm, chairman of Bell-Northern Research Ltd., a subsidiary of Northern Telecom Ltd., Canada's largest private investor in industrial development, "I find about 85 per cent of university research isn't worth reading. . . . Most university work is curiosity-oriented and unfortunately pure (that is, pure theoretical as opposed to applied) and not particularly relevant."[52] Sydney Jackson, president of Manufacturers Life Insurance Company concluded: "Business . . . tends to regard universities as citadels populated by the woolly-minded and inward looking, somewhat removed from the cut and thrust of the real world."[53]

If the university's financial fate depends upon tapping the resources of the private sector, and if the attitudes of the private sector are reflected in the above comments, then can we envision the university of the future? Donald Chisolm, cited above, thinks he already has, and for him it works. His model is Stanford University in California because "it's an industrial park, not a science park." Arrangements by which private corporations provide universities with capital or operating grants in exchange for both considerable influence over the direction of research and exclusive licences on patentable discoveries made in laboratories are even more common in prestigious universities in the United States than in Canada. Among a number of such contracts at Stanford is one with the Centre for Integrated Systems, an agency representing seventeen microelectronics firms. For a $12 million grant, the centre's own scientists are allowed to be on site full time, "thereby providing them with virtually unprecedented access to graduate students and academic research in progress."[54]

A larger deal involves the Hoechst Pharmaceutical Company of Germany, which signed a $70 million contract with Massachusetts General Hospital, an affiliate of Harvard, to create a Department of Molecular Biology. In addition to its privileged access to research, the company was permitted to appoint its scientists working at Mass General to the faculty of Harvard.[55] The Massachusetts Institute of Technology received $100 million from the Whitehead Institute of Biological Science, whose employees, according to *Business Week*, were to be granted professorships.[56]

Some critics have raised questions about the effect of such "profitable" contracts on the nature and terms of university research. Economist and engineer Seymour Melman contends that when large agencies dangle huge amounts of money before financially hungry universities, such grants have a "magnetic" effect.[57] Young professors and graduate students will structure their research according to what they perceive is required by profit-oriented organizations. Pure research that takes too long to produce results, or research projects that stand outside of or even conflict with those of the sponsor, could well be ignored. Stanford immunologist Leon Wofsy makes the following observations:

> For a young scientist ten years ago, who was at the beginning of his career — if he was good — the kind of question in planning his career was, first, do I have a problem that's really interesting; and, can I make an outstanding contribution from an intellectual and scientific point of view that will win respect for me in the academic community? And if you could answer those questions positively, the chances are that the grant support would be forthcoming. At the present time, the young scientist at an equivalent stage of his career has to pose the questions in a very different way. He has to say — if I choose a question and it's interesting, but doesn't lead necessarily to something exploitable or productive with some commercial potential, can I get support?[58]

University administrators undoubtedly view such contracts as a case of the university serving "community" needs. This is too easy a defence. The community is not one undifferentiated mass. It consists of competing and sometimes irreconcilable elements. A university heavily dependent on funding from the private sector will inevitably minister to those segments of the community that can afford to purchase its services at the expense of those too poor to pay. Are universities willing to take responsibility for being partners in projects that cause workers to lose their jobs or environments to be contaminated? Community service, under these conditions, turns the university into the corporation's client.

Consider, in addition, the possible effect of sponsored research on academic and institutional credibility. A pesticide company might provide a university scientist with funds to investigate the safeness of the company's product. If the research concludes that the product is indeed safe, he may not be believed because of the source of his funds. If he issues his results under the university's name, it too could be brought into question. All of this could happen even if the scientist's conclusions were correct and his integrity intact. If his advice were ignored, decisions damaging to the community might be made. Perhaps, in everyone's interest, this sort of applied research could go on in an industrial park outside the university. The price paid for the corporate grant may well be too high.

Can a university be worthy of the name without a commitment to the principle of open dissemination of information and research? Companies that are able to strike favourable "early warning" research and licensing agreements with universities may succeed in stalling for a considerable time the sharing of basic research within the academic community. According to Derek Bok, president of Harvard, "Because the financial stakes are high, investigators may not merely withhold ideas from publication; they become closemouthed and refrain from the free, informal discussions with colleagues that are essential to the process of discovery."[59] Academics who willingly or accidentally divulge such information could (along with their universities) be subject to law suits. (The Massachusetts Hospital-Hoechst contract compels the hospital to submit to the company drafts of all manuscripts at least thirty days before they are submitted for publication.)[60] Furthermore, do universities wish to encourage their own academics to hide and horde their research in the hope of selling it to the highest commercial bidder? Excessive academic entrepreneurship is yet another consequence of the new relationship being forged between universities and the private sector. Despite his general support of closer ties between business and universities, Derek Bok offers the following warning:

> It is one thing to consult for a few hundred dollars a day or to write a textbook in the hope of receiving a few thousand dollars a year. It is quite another matter to think of becoming a millionaire by exploiting a commercially attractive discovery. With stakes of this size, the nature and direction of academic research could be transmuted into something quite unlike the disinterested search for knowledge that has long been thought to animate university professors. In short, the newfound concern with technology transfer is disturbing not only because it could alter the practice of science in the university but also because it threatens the central values and ideals of academic research.[61]

In spite of everyone's good intentions, academic entrepreneurship can indeed sully the working environment of a university. At McGill University in Montreal two professors of microbiology (one the head of a department) took leaves of absence in late 1983 amid a swirl of controversy about their research activities. Engaged in the development of a process that could facilitate the cleanup of toxic and radioactive waste, the two professors conducted their research in space provided by the university, and they chartered three companies (in Holland, in the United States, and in Canada) to market their product.

Concern emerged at the university on several fronts: the alleged use of university facilities and federal research money for private commercial purposes; a dispute over the patent rights to the product — which led to the launching of a $500,000 lawsuit by a former research associate of the scientists; and the successful imposition of an injunction brought by the scientists against the McGill student newspaper, preventing it from publishing information about the invention.[62]

Problems such as these apply mostly to the areas of biotechnology and microelectronics, which in recent years have received the lion's share of corporate support. What about those academic disciplines that make no claim to contributing directly to corporate profitability and the gross national product? What about the arts? However prevailing the utilitarian ethic in the 1950s and 1960s, at least the arts survived and flourished on the strength of the investment theory celebrating the value of "human capital." University presidents can still be heard hailing the arts as the core of the university, but public funding restraints on the one hand, and the research priorities of the private sector on the other, belie this rhetoric. The life of arts faculties, according to Canadian economist Eric Kierans, has been "drained out into the management schools, the engineering schools, the medical schools and the law schools."[63] Are the humanities and social sciences, more decisively than ever, becoming high technology's mere handmaidens?

Let the last word go to Dalton Camp, a well-known Canadian journalist and commentator, who spoke to a conference in 1983 on business and the universities.

> I have long believed the research undertaken by the universities should be free, independent and determinately nonutilitarian. I have also believed all a university should expect from the business community is money. And all that the business community should expect from the university is to be asked for it.... The choice is clear: starve the humanities or put them on short ration, in order to feed the sciences. This choice would ultimately assign the humanities to another jurisdiction, something for later life perhaps, or to some station in purgatory between the nonessential and the obsolescent.... Thus the universities will be producing in greater numbers than they do now, the inarticulate, the functionally illiterate, the ethically sterile, the politically passive, and the morally inert.... We will be packaging people who took no English but who mastered in jargon. The literature of our language will become something to be buried among other academic toxic wastes — philosophy and history.[64]

Welcome to the brave new university of the twenty-first century.

Notes

1. Lawrence R. Veysey, *The Emergence of the American University* (Chicago, Ill.: University of Chicago Press and Phoenix Books, 1970), pp. 15, 82; Richard Hofstadter and Wilson Smith, eds., *American Higher Education: A Documentary History*, vol. 2 (Chicago, Ill.: University of Chicago Press, 1961), p. 568; Derek Bok, *Beyond the Ivory Tower: Social Responsibilities of the Modern University* (Cambridge, Mass.: Harvard University Press, 1982), p. 62.

2. *Report of the Royal Commission on the University of Toronto* (Toronto: L.K. Cameron, 1906), p. liv.

3. Frederick Rudolph, *The American College and University: A History* (New York: Alfred Knopf, 1965), pp. 479-80; Robert Hutchins, *The Higher Learning in America* (New Haven, Conn.: Yale University Press, 1936).

4. W.H. Alexander, 1939, cited by Michiel Horn, *Globe and Mail*, 22 Jan. 1983; Carleton Stanley, "School and College," paper delivered to the National Conference of Canadian Universities, 1934, *President's Office Papers*, Dalhousie University Archives.

5. Charles E. Burke, "Science, Technology and Research in the Canadian Democracy," pamphlet in McMaster University Archives, 1948; Wartime Bureau of Technical Personnel, *Annual Report* (Ottawa: Department of Labour, 31 Mar. 1944).

6. "Canadian University and College Enrollment Projected to 1965," NCCU *Proceedings*, 1955, pp. 34-36.

7. C.T. Bissell, ed., *Canada's Crisis in Higher Education* (Toronto: University of Toronto Press, 1957); and Bissell, *Halfway Up Parnassus: A Personal Account of the University of Toronto, 1932-1971* (Toronto: University of Toronto Press, 1974), p. 44.

8. Stanley Deeks (an organizer of the conference and an employee of the Industrial Foundation on Education), private scrapbook of newspaper clippings, and *Interview*, 12 May 1976.

9. Industrial Foundation on Education, *The Case for Corporate Giving to Higher Education,* 1957. See also Paul Axelrod, *Scholars and Dollars: Politics, Economics, and the Universities of Ontario, 1945-1980* (Toronto: University of Toronto Press, 1982), chap. 2.

10. *Final Report of the Royal Commission on Canada's Economic Prospects* (Ottawa, 1957), p. 452.

11. *Public Opinion News Service,* 6 Jan. 1951; 16 May 1953.

12. Wilson Woodside, *The University Question* (Toronto: Ryerson, 1958), p. 30.

13. Cited in Industrial Foundation on Education, *The Case for Corporate Giving to Higher Education,* pp. 4-5.

14. *Final Report,* p. 19.

15. "Colloquium held in the Senate Chamber of the University of Toronto, 17 January, 1958 with the Principals and Presidents of Ontario Universities and the Heads of Mathematics Departments," RG-2 P3, Archives of Ontario.

16. *Submission of Canadian Universities to the Royal Commission on Canada's Economic Prospects,* presented by representatives of NCCU, 6 Mar. 1956, p. 5.

17. "Education: The Key to Survival," *Cost and Management,* July 1961.

18. *Submission of Canadian Universities,* p. 5.

19. *Submission of Ontario to the Royal Commission on Canada's Economic Prospects,* 1956, p. 57.

20. *The Case for Corporate Giving,* pp. 3, 10.

21. J.D. Barrington, cited in *Financial Post,* 15 Sept. 1956.

22. *The Case for Corporate Giving,* p. 18.

23. Cited in H.J. Somers, "Private and Corporate Support of Canadian Universities," in Bissell, ed., *Canada's Crisis in Higher Education,* p. 20.

24. G. Bertram, *The Contribution of Education to Economic Growth*, a study prepared for the Economic Council of Canada (Ottawa, 1965), pp. 61-62; see also Economic Council of Canada, *Second Annual Review* (Ottawa, 1965), p. 87.

25. *Public Opinion News Service*, 7 Apr. 1965; 29 June 1963.

26. Bank of Montreal, "Canada's Expanding Universities," *Business Review*, 27 Nov. 1961.

27. H.J. Fraser, "The University and Business," in *Canadian Universities Today* (Toronto: University of Toronto Press, 1961), papers presented to the Royal Society of Canada, 1960.

28. "What Does Business Owe to Education?" *Trade and Commerce*, Aug. 1960.

29. A.A. Cumming, "The Business Community's Responsibility to Higher Education," at Kenneth R. Wilson Memorial Luncheon of the Business Newspapers Association of Canada, 18 June 1964, reprinted in *Monetary Times*, Sept. 1964.

30. Cited in G. McCaffrey, "Canada's Newest Universities Need Executives to Start," *Executive*, Nov. 1962.

31. Interview with David Mansur, former member of the York University Board of Governors, 21 Aug. 1981. See Paul Axelrod, "Businessmen and the Building of Canadian Universities: A Case Study," *Canadian Historical Review*, vol. 63, no. 2 (1982).

32. Minutes of meeting of York University Board of Governors, Feb. 1969, detail short-term and long-term investments of the university in companies with which board members were associated.

33. R. Edsall, "Education: The Boom That Never Goes Bust," *Canadian Business*, Oct. 1963.

34. H. Byleveld, "Business Aid to Universities: A Margin of Freedom," *Canadian Business*, Jan. 1967.

35. *Report of the Royal Commission on National Development in the Arts, Letters and Sciences* (Ottawa, 1951), pp. 132-37.

36. "Education and Training Power," *Canadian Chartered Accountant,* Oct. 1963.

37. *Imperial Oil Review,* Sept. 1959. For a fuller discussion of this issue, see Paul Axelrod, *Scholars and Dollars,* pp. 105-10.

38. See John Galbraith, *The New Industrial State* (Boston: Houghton Mifflin, 1967), pp. 377-80.

39. Report of the Commission on Educational Planning, *A Future of Choices — A Choice of Futures* (Edmonton: Queen's Printer, 1972), p. 60; Commission on Post-Secondary Education in Ontario, *The Learning Society* (Toronto: Ministry of Government Services, 1972), p. 147.

40. Speech to Legislative Assembly of Ontario, by Premier Leslie Frost, 10 Feb. 1958, p. 70, introducing new student assistance program; House of Commons, *Debates,* 14 July 1964, p. 4442, speech by Minister of Finance Walter Gordon.

41. See, for example, J.R. Nininger with F.W.P. Jones, *A Survey of Changing Employment Patterns at Lakehead Cities of Port Arthur and Fort William* (Ontario Economic Council, 1964), which relates economic growth to educational development. See also J.A. Cleworth et al., *The Economic Impact of McMaster University on the City of Hamilton and Surrounding Localities* (McMaster University, Office of Institutional Research, 1973).

42. See, for example, Ontario Council on University Affairs, *System on the Brink: A Financial Analysis of the Ontario University System* (1979); The Maritime Provinces Higher Education Commission, *Second Annual Report,* 1975-76 (Fredericton, 1976); "Cuts, Cuts, Cuts, Restraint, Restraint...," *University Affairs,* November 1982; Peter Leslie, *Canadian Universities: 1980 and Beyond* (Ottawa: Association of Universities and Colleges of Canada, 1980), pp. 65-129.

43. For a lucid discussion of the economic crisis of the 1970s, see Cy Gonick, *Inflation or Depression* (Toronto: Lorimer, 1975). See also previous footnote.

44. *Financial Post*, 23 Sept. 1972; W. Clark, Z. Zsigmond, *Job Market Reality for Post-Secondary Graduates: Employment Outcome by 1978, Two Years after Graduation* (Ottawa, 1981).

45. David Dodge, *Returns to Investment in University Training: The Case of Canadian Accountants, Engineers and Scientists* (Kingston: Queen's University, 1972); David Sewell, "Educational Planning Models and the Relationship Between Education and Occupation," in S. Ostry, ed., *Canadian Higher Education in the Seventies* (Ottawa, 1971); Economic Council of Canada, *Design for Decision Making Eighth Annual Review* (Ottawa, 1971), pp. 210, 212. See also Ivar Berg, *Education and Jobs: The Great Training Robbery* (Penguin, 1970).

46. *Toronto Telegram*, 8 Mar. 1971; "Statement on Operating Support of Provincially Assisted Universities for 1971/72 and 1972/73," by Ontario Minister of University Affairs, Apr. 1971.

47. *Corporate Giving in Canada, 1971-1978*, Institute of Donations and Public Affairs Research (Montreal, 30 Mar. 1978).

48. Statistics Canada, *From the Sixties to the Eighties: A Statistical Portrait of Canadian Higher Education* (Ottawa, 1978), p. 35.

49. Government of Canada, *Fiscal Arrangements in the Eighties: Proposals of the Government of Canada* (Ottawa, 1981); *Financial Post*, 21 Nov. 1981.

50. Leslie, *Canadian Universities*, p. 76.

51. The Corporate-Higher Education Forum was formed in May 1983 with membership from the academic and business worlds. See its publication, *Partnership for Growth: Corporate-University Cooperation in Canada* (Montreal, 1984). See also Ronald Anderson, "Corporate, Academic

Links are Becoming More Intimate," *Globe and Mail*, 4 May 1984, p. B2.

52. "Business as the Broker between Science, Society," Conference Report: Business and the Universities, *Financial Post*, 14 May 1983.

53. Sydney Jackson, "Working with Universities: What Business Wants," address to a seminar, "On Universities," sponsored by the Institute of Donations and Public Affairs Research, 30 Mar. 1978.

54. For detailed information on these projects, see three articles by Barbara J. Cullitin in *Science*: "The Academic Industrial Complex," 28 May 1982; "The Hoechst Department at Mass General," 11 June 1982; "Monsanto to Give Washington U $23.5 Million," 18 June 1982.

55. Cullitin, "The Hoechst Department at Mass General."

56. "Business and Universities: A New Partnership," *Business Week*, 20 Dec. 1982, p. 61. See also "More Firms Marrying Up with Labs in Universities," *Financial Post*, 1 Oct. 1983.

57. Canadian Broadcasting Corporation, *Ideas Series*, "The Academic Industrial Complex" (Transcript, 1982), Interview, p. 3.

58. Ibid., p. 15.

59. Bok, *Beyond the Ivory Tower*, p. 150. See also Rob M. Rosenzweig and Barbara Turlington, *The Research Universities and Patrons* (Berkeley: University of California Press, 1982).

60. Cullitin, "The Hoechst Department at Mass General."

61. Bok, *Beyond the Ivory Tower*, p. 142.

62. See articles by David Wimhurst in the Montreal *Gazette*, 29 Oct., 15 Nov., 17 Nov., 18 Nov., 22 Dec. 1983.

63. Cited in John Spears, "Firms, Academia Groping for New Ties," *Toronto Star*, 22 July 1984.

64. Dalton Camp, "Liberal Arts in Danger of Dying Lonely Death," Conference Report: Business and the Universities, *Financial Post,* 14 May 1983.

SCIENCE AND THE PUBLIC TRUST:
THE NEED FOR REFORM

ALBERT H. MEYERHOFF

In the coming years, few issues in the "post-industrial" United States will be more important than the direction of new technology. Present-day decisions in various fields will determine how our abundant, but nevertheless fixed or diminishing, resources are to be allocated. In agriculture, choices are being made between ever-increasing reliance on toxic chemicals and alternative means of pest control; in energy, between nuclear power or coal and the "soft" energy path; in medicine, between new wonder drugs and preventive medicine; in industry, between automation and job creation through more labour-intensive means of production. Such decisions usually are not this dramatic but instead, more subtle, reflecting diverse factors, including the predisposition of individual scientists, the views of peers, the marketplace, the needs of the society – and the availability of adequate financial support.

In short, science is no longer "pure" or neutral, if it ever was. To the contrary, as Anna Harrison, past president of the Association for the Advancement of American Science, noted in a thoughtful and important article:

> Every technological innovation, regardless of how great its positive impact on society, also has a negative impact...the benefits and the negative impacts may be experienced by different subsets of society and in different time frames...the allocation of public moneys to the support of basic research is an act of faith.[1]

Given the effect of technology on the public at large, the need for continuing trust in key decision makers thus becomes paramount. Fortunately, scientists remain at or near the top of public opinion polls in terms of credibility. Yet, not so paradoxically, public concern over rapidly developing new technology – characterized by some as "science anxiety" – is also

69

a real and growing phenomenon. This is understandable in a world where medicines like DES (diethylstilbestrol) become poisons, sugar substitutes cause cancer, nuclear power plants threaten to melt down, and genetically engineered new life forms evoke memories of the Andromeda Strain.

It is against this framework that what has been characterized as the "commercialization" of American university research and development must be evaluated. Faced with rising operating costs and the prospect of cuts in government funding, universities around the country have been in an unprecedented race to increase their ties to private industry. This has been true of private as well as public universities. A parallel development has been growth of the "faculty entrepreneur," especially in the exploding field of biotechnology. Private firms are springing up adjacent to universities, established and staffed by university scientists who are doing for-profit work often overlapping their university work.

Serious questions exist about these trends. Universities not only influence choices made about the direction of new technology, they also serve as our "brain trust." Every day, university scientists and other specialists are brought forward as experts to influence public policy decisions on such wide-ranging subjects as health care, fiscal policy, toxic chemicals, offshore oil exploration, and the effect of nuclear war. To what degree does "assimilation" by the corporate sector of university scientists, either subtly or not so subtly, influence such advice and such opinions? How serious is "the prospect of significant contamination of the university's basic research enterprise by the introduction of strong commercial motivations and conflicts of interests on the part of faculty members with respect to their obligations to the corporations in which they have consultancies or equity"?[2]

These are important questions. They have not yet been fully answered, within the university community or elsewhere.

Financial Disclosure at the University of California

Although corporate-university ties may serve important purposes in creating a new financial base for research and in improving the transfer of technology, it is a relationship filled with risk. A case in point involves the University of California (UC). Over its strenuous opposition and following lengthy hearings before that state's Fair Political Practices Commission, University of California faculty were recently required to disclose equity interests, sources of income, and other forms of financial involvement with corporate or other private sponsors of their research. This disclosure requirement resulted from the filing of an administrative complaint under that state's Political Reform Act of 1974, adopted through initiative by the people of California, at least partially in response to the Watergate scandal.

The Political Reform Act required disclosure of such financial interests by all government employees and prohibited individuals from participating in decisions where there might be a conflict of interest, but the Fair Political Practices Commission had previously granted a wholesale exemption from application of the act to university research. The citizens' petition, filed in August 1981, challenged this exemption and urged that the commission adopt regulations making the state's conflict of interest laws fully applicable to the University of California faculty. After public testimony raised the issues of academic freedom, university autonomy, and the misuse of tax moneys by university faculty, in March 1982, the Fair Political Practices Commission adopted by a four-to-one vote final regulations requiring full disclosure by university scientists of most financial interests held in business entities sponsoring their research through gifts, grants, or contracts. Rules also were approved requiring the establishment of specially empanelled university committees to review decisions on research where potential conflicts were present. Left unanswered at that time were what guidelines or regulations would apply once a serious conflict was discovered. Although flawed in several respects, the regulations imposed were by far the most stringent financial disclosure requirements for university faculty anywhere in the United States.

The original petition filed with the Fair Political Practices Commission identified less than a dozen actual "cases" of potential conflicts of interest at the University of California, in part because without disclosure, hard information was difficult to come by. One of those cases, illustrative of many of the problems that may result from closer ties between private firms and universities, was that of a biotechnology firm known as "Calgene." This firm was co-founded by UC professor Raymond Valentine, who was also its vice president. A prominent scientist, Valentine's research identifying *nif* genes could allow certain plants to produce their own nitrogen from air. This work was potentially of significant commercial value. According to the petition filed with the California Fair Political Practices Commission, shortly after providing a $2.3 million grant to UC to support Professor Valentine's research, the Allied Corporation also purchased a 20 per cent interest in Calgene at a cost of nearly $2 million. The Allied contract was to fund five co-investigators for five years, one of whom was Valentine. For the University of California, the grant was a large one, roughly equal to the average annual receipt of all other gifts and grants made in support of agricultural research. Reaction occurred quickly to the Calgene situation, both within and outside the university. One letter, signed by numerous members of the UC Bacteriology Department, indicated their view that "involvement of experiment station members in Calgene constitutes a clear conflict of interest." Also disturbing were reports from graduate students that they were unsure whether their research was intended to benefit the university or Calgene.

One memorandum from a distinguished member of the UC faculty, Dr. Daniel Epstein, to Dean Charles Hess touched the heart of the matter. In it he stated:

> Charlie, one aspect that I believe to be exceedingly important was not included in the discussion of this matter by the College Faculty on Tuesday, November 24.
>
> Occasional consulting and other relatively minor extramural activities are often beneficial all around, but long-term commitments involving substantial financial interest are something entirely different, and particularly so if the extramural entity is a business run for profit. The damage such involvement may cause – is already causing on our campus – is this: the vital ingredient of academe, free and mutually stimulating exchange of information and ideas, is stifled.
>
> In the past, it was the most natural thing in the world for colleagues to swap ideas on the spur of the moment, to share the latest findings hot off the scintillation counter or the electrophoresis cell, to show each other early drafts of papers, and in other ways to act as "companions in zealous research."
>
> No more. Any U.C.D. scientist with a promising new slant for the improvement of nitrogen fixation or the enhancement of salt tolerance of crops or accelerated *in vitro* culture of plant tissue will think twice before talking about it to anyone who is connected with either of the two Davis crop genetic private enterprises – or even with colleagues who in

turn might speak to any such person. I know that this type of inhibition is already at work on this campus.

In addition, graduate students of faculty members connected with these businesses are in danger of being directed in ways more tailored to the requirements of those enterprises than the students' educational and professional advancement.

It should be made clear to University people associating themselves with businesses of this kind that in so doing they may cut themselves off from the essential spontaneous, free flow of information and ideas that is the very lifeblood of the academic enterprise, and that the integrity of their direction of graduate students may no longer be unquestioned.

No matter what formal policies are promulgated, conscientious University scientists will take what measures they individually can to protect their own, the University's, and the public's right to their ideas and findings, and to safeguard the rights of graduate students. As a result we have this new guardedness, caution and suspicion.

I therefore have my doubts about any very "positive" approach to this development. I feel that in any statement on this problem by the University the inevitable damage to the academic enterprise that I have discussed here should be clearly spelled out. In effect, what this intimate connection of some of our faculty with corporate business is doing amounts to no less than an insidious but nonetheless real abridgement of the academic freedom of all members of our college and their graduate students. That, I believe, is the main issue that must be confronted.

Faced with increasing criticism, Professor Valentine was finally instructed by UC either to sever his relationship with Calgene or to relinquish his position on the Allied-funded project. He chose the latter. Among other potential conflicts of interest identified in the original Fair Political Practices Commission petition was the now well-publicized involvement of Professor Herbert Boyer with Genentech. Other university faculty members had stated publicly that they believed Genentech, now a multi-million-dollar private concern, was actually started in a University of California laboratory. Faced with the Valentine and Boyer cases and several other examples, the Fair Political Practices Commission finally reached its decision and required disclosure by faculty of financial interests in research sponsors. Over the objections of the petitioners, the commission refused, however, to require disclosure of financial interests in companies that may directly benefit from other government-funded research so long as such entities did not actually serve as a sponsor.

In 1982, the first annual summary of University of California disclosure statements was filed with the commission pursuant to these new regulations. Some 340 "positive" cases were identified where university scientists had some financial interest in business entities also sponsoring their research. Some of these potential conflicts were relatively minor; others were serious and involved consulting income, stocks, stock options, board directorships, and equity valued in the tens and even hundreds of thousands of dollars. A few examples are useful:

- A scientist of the University of California, Los Angeles (UCLA) proposed a research project with Cetus Corporation, in which he had an investment of between $10,000 and $100,000, as well as income of $1,000 to $10,000. Although the director of the university's Molecular Biology Institute stated that "the contract calls for work ... at the border of basic research and technology," the project was approved. Cetus received an exclusive, worldwide, royalty-bearing licence to any patentable discoveries.

- Another UCLA scientist working on a project with Genetics Institute was paid $20,000 as a consultant to the project's sponsor. He also owned $30,000 in stock in the concern, with options to acquire additional shares worth $375,000. The contract provided Genetics Institute with royalty-bearing licences.

- A third University of California scientist was involved in a project with Global Geochemistry, of which he was president and 100 per cent owner. He also held an investment of between $10,000 and $100,000 and received more than $10,000 in outside income from Global. Global's contract with the university was eventually not renewed.

- Another UC scientist proposed a research contract with Serex International from which he had been promised consulting income of $10,000 per year and a 5,000-share stock option as a "signing bonus." Serex was to receive exclusive patent rights.[3]

Controversy over the proper application of conflict of interest laws at the University of California continues unabated. In a recent uproar, it was learned that in the 1982 report, UCLA failed to identify some 29 positive cases of potential conflicts and, further, had withheld from the commission documentation concerning the 33 cases that were reported. The commission issued a strongly critical statement, and, following significant media attention, UCLA eventually reluctantly complied with commission directives, documenting a total of 62 cases *in toto*.[4] In only a handful of the 340 positive cases identified by the commission in its 1983 report has any serious action been taken by UC to remedy the apparent conflicts of interest presented.

In 1984 the university proposed revised "guidelines" to be used by its specially empanelled committees once a potential conflict of interest is discovered. These guidelines were the subject of a commission hearing held in April 1984. They are vague, ambiguous, and certainly on their face do not prevent research from going forward where apparent conflicts of interest exist, such as in the examples listed above. The guidelines instead merely require committees to "consider to the extent possible the nature and extent of the financial interests in the relationship of the principal investigator to its sponsoring entity" and to "give special consideration" where a researcher has "a significant ownership in the sponsor, . . . the opportunity to receive financial benefit from the sponsor (*e.g.* bonuses, stock options) . . . [or] a long-term consulting relationship." Confusing conflicts of interest with scholarship, the guidelines also put a high premium on merits of the research as opposed to the potential for personal gain by the publicly employed university scientist.

Indeed, the guidelines conclude that "in many, if not all of the projects under review, it may not be possible" to take into account potential financial effects of research on a sponsoring entity or on the researcher. This is alleged to be the case because research "typically leads to unexpected results," and "it is difficult, if not impossible, to predict the applications of research."[5] In an era of technological assessment, applied research, and very specific goals indicated by sponsors for agreed-to patent rights of significant financial value, this statement is entirely disingenuous. Nonetheless, at its April 1984 hearing, the commission signed off on these guidelines, and in an act of questionable legality, continued to delegate authority over ensuring compliance with California conflict of interest laws to the University of California itself.

Problems with Leverage:
Agricultural Research at Land Grant Colleges

It must be emphasized that these issues are not merely questions of individual university scientists possibly making a profit from decisions involving the allocation of public funds. On the contrary, in some ways, such abuses are the *least* important concerns flowing from closer ties between universities and the business community. Of much greater significance are the social, economic, political, and environmental consequences that may result from encouraging increased private funding for American universities. This is due to the very real threat that university research may become even more tailored than it is already toward commercial considerations and profit while giving short shrift to improving the quality of life – and learning – in the United States.

One example involves the ties between large-scale agriculture and the fifty land grant universities in the United States. Literally billions of public dollars are expended each year at land grant universities for both basic and, increasingly, applied research. Development of such new technology plays a major role in establishing the direction of American agriculture for decades to come. For many years, the focus of allocating the overwhelming bulk of these resources has been to promote a system of large-scale, production agriculture, with an ever-increasing reliance on a combination of chemical pesticides, fertilizers, growth regulators, water projects, and machinery. Resulting increases in agricultural productivity have been dramatic, although during the last decade they have begun to level off. For crops where surpluses have become a problem, efforts to curtail production focused on acreage while technological development directed toward large-scale agriculture continued, largely unquestioned.

Rising costs of productive inputs, especially petroleum, have meant, however, that continuing to develop technologies based upon short-term needs may prove to be disastrous from a public policy perspective. Research targeted to foster intensive use of energy and capital also has contributed most to farm specialization, concentration, and environmental degradation. Because much of the good land is now in production, and because serious problems are resulting from the diminution of prime farmland due to development pressures, we have lost the flexibility to shift to more land-extensive agricultural practices.

Spurred by the promise of higher yields and at least in part because of the historically close ties between the personnel of land grant colleges and representatives of production agriculture, universities have been woefully slow in taking into account the environmental and social hazards flowing from industrialized agriculture. Minimal resources have been allocated to alternative practices less likely to do permanent harm to the rural social system or to deplete fixed natural resources. Instead, long-term problems are frequently shunted aside to deal with this year's or next year's immediate crisis.[6] Yet, the range of such long-term effects is truly staggering. They include, for example, jeopardizing food production by too closely tying agricultural productivity to potentially unavailable petroleum and petroleum-based products; permanently damaging the soil through overuse, abuse, and saturation by chemical-based fertilizers; depleting and contaminating both irrigation and drinking water; irreversibly changing the quality and nutritional value of crops; seriously threatening human health from exposure to toxic substances; and contributing to the deterioration of the quality of rural life by swallowing up small family farms, displacing farm labour, and bankrupting dependent small businesses.[7]

Consider the case of large-scale agricultural mechnization. Although it is certainly possible to debate the pros and cons of using tax funds to automate harvesting in agriculture, it cannot be seriously denied that the development of such new technology will come with serious social costs. When the harvesting of cotton was mechanized in the late 1940s, 250,000 jobs were eliminated in the first three years. Between 1945 and 1965, more than 4 million people were displaced, the majority being blacks from the rural South. The costs, first in terms of human suffering and then in social welfare, were staggering. Some attribute the overpopulation and urban blight found in many northern and eastern cities to the mass migration following cotton mechanization.[8]

The University of California is now in the process of using large sums of public funds to mechanize at least thirty-four different crops. One study completed for the United States Department of Labor indicates that such mechanization will eliminate at least 128,000 jobs in California alone over the next ten years.[9]

How were decisions made to use public funds for this purpose? A lawsuit brought by a group of California farmworkers and small family farmers sheds some light on this fundamental question. According to the plaintiffs, these research decisions were heavily influenced by the availability of private funds for research. One survey conducted anonymously by UC Professor Isao Fujimoto found that the large majority of department chairs and researchers identified outside funding as the principal determinant of what research gets done. One researcher put it this way: "You have to gear your research to the funding sources. . . .There is big money available from production ag with which you can dig your own grave. . . . I had to go where the money was . . . which was the chemical companies."

Earmarked grants and gifts for research on agricultural mechanization research are, of course, commonplace at UC from such agribusiness giants as Sunkist, Eli Lilly, Chevron, and Union Carbide. Further, members of the UC board of directors and the vice president in charge of the university's agricultural budget have served as past directors of Del Monte Corporation, the world's largest fruit and vegetable processor, which uses university-developed harvesters in its tomato fields. These same officials owned stock in Del Monte, and the university itself is the fifth largest stockholder in the company, with 155,000 shares. University scientists frequently serve as consultants to large-scale agricultural interests and, further, receive 50 per cent of all net patent royalties resulting from commercial use of their inventions. (One of the developers of a plant thinning machine has already received royalties in excess of $235,000, and the three inventors of a tomato harvestor have received more than $340,000.)

In 1963, the tomato harvester developed at UC was put into commercial production. By 1970, the industry was completely mechanized. The number of harvest-time jobs dropped from more than 50,000 in 1964 to fewer than 18,000 in 1970. The number of tomato farmers plummeted from more than 4,000 in 1963 to only 593 in 1973. The average tomato plot grew from 32 acres to 363 acres. During this period, the price of processed tomatoes increased by 111 per cent; other fruits and vegetables rose substantially less.[10]

These projects, and others like them, continue while the university publicly denies responsibility for or competence even to assess the potential far-reaching social, economic, and environmental costs that will necessarily be incurred. Yet, as former U.S. secretary of agriculture Bob Bergland noted in a 1980 speech:

> I find it difficult if not impossible to justify the use of federal funds to finance research leading to the development of machines or other technologies that may increase production and processing efficiency but at the same time damage the soil, pollute the environment, displace willing workers, and reduce or eliminate competition.

I do not believe a federally financed research effort ought to benefit a small number of individuals, corporations or narrow interest groups to such an extent and in such a way as to make it possible, in time, for the beneficiaries to gain control of the farm to market structure, monopolize the sources of finance at every step, and increase their profits by selling what may well be an inferior product at a price that is insulated from competition.[11]

Tampering with the Brain Trust: The Charles Hine Case

As noted above, the availability of private funds to universities not only significantly influences the direction of research but also has a second deleterious effect: it potentially compromises the objectivity of the very university faculty that serve as the society's "brain trust" on numerous important public policy matters. Such influence can, of course, be subtle; it can result not only from the potential of increasing personal income as a "faculty entrepreneur" but from the availability of substantial grant money for university research as well.

Consider the case of Dr. Charles Hine, a researcher and toxicologist at the University of California in San Francisco, and his role in regulating the pesticide dibromochloropropane, or DBCP. This highly toxic chemical was finally banned by the Environmental Protection Agency in the late 1970s after being linked to male sterility, birth defects, and cancer. First called to national attention after chemical workers exposed to DBCP were found to have become sterile, the pesticide was later found both in the food chain as well as in the drinking water of up to 1 million Californians.

Early toxicological tests on DBCP were performed by Dr. Charles Hine twenty years previously, in the late 1950s. Press reports in the *Los Angeles Times* and elsewhere indicate that Dr. Hine had served as a consultant for one of DBCP's registrants, Shell Chemical Company, for thirty years. Research by Dr. Hine showing that the chemical caused testicular atrophy in rats at levels as low as five parts per million was reported to Shell in 1958 but not to appropriate government officials until three years later. Dr. Hine indicated that the study was treated as confidential because work on it was partially funded by Shell, which from the late 1950s through the late 1970s, had donated almost $400,000 to the school for medical research on the toxicity of pesticides and related chemical products.[12]

At the time of the DBCP report, Dr. Hine worked for both the medical school and for Shell as a consultant. Despite the laboratory findings of testicular atrophy and sterility, press accounts indicated that no research was done to confirm a safe or no-effect level, and DBCP became a widely sold and commonly used pesticide. Since then, ninety-five men who worked with or near DBCP in chemical companies have been found to have low or no sperm counts. Dr. Hine has since been sued for $20 million by twenty of the now-sterile workers and also was subpoenaed by the California Department of Industrial Relations to testify about his research on DBCP and his relationship with Shell Oil Company.

Hine also has worked as a consultant for Dow Chemical, for the Clorox Corporation, for Du Pont, and for a law firm that represents tobacco companies. He became the medical director of the American Smelting and Refining Company (ASARCO) and also runs Hine, Inc., a successful private toxicology lab in San Francisco. Dr. Hine has testified as an expert witness before legislative committees, has done consultant work for the California Department of Health, and has served as a medical examiner for the California Workers Compensation Appeals Board. This is in addition to his duties as a salaried clinical professor at the UC Medical School. Thus, Dr. Hine in some ways typifies the dual relationship between some university professors and industry.

Moreover, according to another press account, Dr. Hine has sometimes served as an expert witness without making public his other outside activities. In August 1977, just before California voted on a smoking-in-public restriction, Hine wrote a lengthy letter to the *San Francisco Examiner* indicating that the claim that non-smokers may be harmed by tobacco smoke "contradicts medical facts. A non-smoker cannot contract cancer or other diseases from secondhand smoke." At the end of the article, Hine was described as a UC professor and consultant for the California Department of Health; his consulting for a law firm representing tobacco companies was not mentioned. Likewise, in November 1975, Hine submitted testimony to the State Air Resources Board. The board was attempting to set a safe standard for airborne levels of lead in the workplace. Overexposure to lead can result in a wide variety of serious acute and chronic health effects. Hine urged that the ambient lead standards proposed were too low and identified himself at hearings as a private citizen and a professor at the University of California. No reference was made to the fact that he was also medical director of ASARCO, the major lead producer in the United States.[13]

The extent to which Dr. Hine's actions regarding DBCP, or his various testimonies as an expert witness, were influenced by his ties to industry is, of course, difficult to assess. The appearance of conflict of interest is certainly present here and, when publicized, undermines the general public's faith in academia, in science, in our brain trust. At a minimum, these interests should be disclosed during any testimony or offering of expert opinion on government policy or regulatory action so that the decision makers involved can use their own judgement about objectivity. Dr. Hine's case is not unique, but it joins several issues that still remain unaddressed by universities throughout the country.

The Response of Academia

To date, the response of the university community to the public policy issues raised by increasing availability of private funds has been slow and singularly unimpressive. In late March 1982, a conference was convened at the secluded California retreat of Pajaro Dunes. ·Its purpose was to establish ground rules governing the relationship between universities and private corporations performing commercial research on campus. Participants included the presidents of Harvard, the Massachusetts Institute of Technology, Stanford, the University of California, and the California Institute of Technology. Also invited were the chief executives of eleven "high tech" corporations involved in biotechnology, including Du Pont, Eli Lilly, and Genentech. Finally, a handful of faculty members were selected, chosen principally for their previous involvement in the commercial application of biotechnology. Participation by other segments of the public was neither solicited or allowed, and the conference was closed to members of the press. Yet at issue was the question of how to make decisions about the disposition of literally hundreds of millions of public research dollars from federal and state coffers.

Concerned about the narrow makeup of the conferees and the closed door meeting procedures, a group of university faculty members from throughout the country, as well as the leadership of several national environmental and consumer organizations and of organized labour, wrote to these five university presidents urging that a follow-up conference be convened, seeking alternative viewpoints. That conference has never occurred.

Perhaps more important than the comparatively narrow makeup of the Pajaro Dunes conference was the paucity of its results. The final document produced by the conferees consisted only of vague generalities and platitudes. It failed to address most of the vital issues surrounding conflicts of interest by university faculty or to consider the propriety of providing exclusive patents to business entities contributing to university research projects. The Pajaro Dunes report has subsequently been roundly criticized:

> What the five university presidents produced last weekend doesn't really get to the problems. It is largely a statement of unexceptionable general principles, combined with hortatory language on the need to preserve "basic academic values" and so forth. It winds up, disappointingly, as "an agenda of issues" not of "attempted" answers. Perhaps this was inevitable, considering the narrowness of the group. But the effort shouldn't stop here. Universities, and science as a whole, would benefit from an attempt to hammer out rules to guide the development of new relationships with business that won't endanger academic science.[14]

Conclusions

All of this is reminiscent of what President Eisenhower warned against in his farewell address:

> The prospect of domination of the nation's scholars by federal employment, project allocations and the power of money, is ever present — and is gravely to be regarded. Yet, in holding scientific research and discovery in respect, as we should, we must also be alert to the equal and opposite danger that public policy could itself become the captive of a scientific-technological elite.
>
> It is the task of statesmanship to mold, to balance and to integrate these and other forces, new and old, within the principles of our democratic system, ever aiming toward the supreme goals of our free society.

In sum, if the relationship between universities and the business sector becomes too blurred, the public trust that university scientists now command in such high measure will eventually erode. True academic freedom will be threatened as will the honest interchange of new ideas or of the latest research findings. Graduate students and faculty members alike will risk having their efforts more tailored to commercial needs than to scholarship or to the best interests of society as a whole. In short, it is time for universities to stop debating and, instead, to develop consistent policies, addressing whether:

— exclusive patent licences should be provided to corporate or private sponsors of research where public funds and resources are expended

— "faculty entrepreneurs" should be permitted to engage in business ventures that parallel their university functions and make use of "intellectual property" created at public expense

— private funds should be provided to university scientists "earmarked" for specific research, thereby potentially leveraging greater amounts of public money for commercial purposes

— scientists should be disqualified from participating in research where they have a direct financial interest in its private sponsor

— public disclosure should be required by university scientists of financial interests in business firms or other sources of income that foreseeably may benefit from publicly financed research and development efforts.

Society has a right to know that decisions on research are being made in the public interest. It is, after all, *our* university. If the university community continues to fail to clean up its own house then, sadly, the task will fall to state and federal governments to provide the bulk of funding for university research in the United States.

Notes

1.   Anna Harrison, "Reflections on Current Issues in Science and Technology," *Science*, vol. 215 (1982), p. 1061.

2.   Testimony of Stanford president Donald Kennedy, U.S. Congress House of Representatives, Committee on Science and Technology, Subcommittee on Oversight and Investigation, 16-17 June 1982.

3.   *Staff Report to the Fair Political Practices Commission*, 1 Sept. 1983, pp. 10-14, 20-22.

4.   Ibid., pp. 1-3.

5.   *Proposed Guidelines for Disclosure and Review of Principal Investigator's Financial Interest in Private Sponsors of Research*, revised Mar. 1984, on file with California Fair Political Practices Commission.

6.   See United States Congress, Office of Technology Assessment, *An Assessment of the United States Agricultural Research System* (Washington, D.C.: U.S. Government Printing Office, 1982).

7.   See United States Department of Agriculture, *A Time to Choose: Summary Report of the Structure of Agriculture* (Washington, D.C.: U.S. Government Printing Office, Jan. 1982).

8.   Gutman, "Black History Seduced and Abandoned," *The Nation*, 22 Sept. 1979.

9.   See California Institute for Rural Studies, *Labor's Dwindling Harvest* (Davis, Calif., 1977); Friedland, Barton, and Thomas, *Manufacturing Green Gold* (New York: Cambridge University Press, 1981).

10. Friedland and Barton, *Stalking the Wily Tomato* (Davis: University of California, 1974).

11. Remarks delivered by U.S. Secretary of Agriculture Bob Bergland before USDA's Science and Education Administration, Reston, Virginia, 31 Jan. 1980.

12. *Los Angeles Times*, section II, p. 1, 18 Oct. 1977.

13. Linn, "The Man in the Middle of the DBCP Scare," *New West*, 17 Dec. 1979, p. 141.

14. *Washington Post*, 5 Apr. 1982.

BALANCING PURE AND APPLIED
RESEARCH

HANS KORNBERG

It has been estimated that in the United Kingdom, most – possibly two thirds – of the nation's basic research is carried out in the universities;[1] they also carry out a significant amount of applied research. Although the division of scientific inquiry into "basic" and "applied" is an arbitrary one and, indeed, has engaged many people in the philosophical niceties of attempting to categorize different types of work as "fundamental," "strategic," and "applied," I propose here to adopt the definition of the Frascati Manual,[2] which is now commonly used by official bodies throughout Europe. In this, *basic research* is defined as "experimental or theoretical work undertaken primarily to acquire new knowledge of the underlying foundation of phenomena and observable facts, without any particular application or use in view." *Applied research* is also "original investigation undertaken in order to acquire new knowledge. It is, however, directed primarily towards a specific practical aim or objective." Since, in the jargon of the trade, research and experimental development are often lumped together under the abbreviation "R & D," it may be helpful to complete the definition by adding that "*experimental development* is systemic work, drawing on existing knowledge gained from research and/or practical experience that is directed to producing new materials, products or devices, to installing new processes, systems or services, or to improving substantially those already produced or installed." I shall not consider this type of activity in this paper.

However one may actually choose to define what is done in the scientific laboratory, it is clear that, in advancing knowledge in this manner, universities play an important role in the fulfilment of national aims, not least in the supply of scientifically educated people on whom the generation of wealth through technology will ultimately depend. Although this role has always been implicit in the universities' involvement in science, both the proportion and the total amount of effort devoted to basic and applied research have risen dramatically since the end of World War II to unprecedented levels in the late 1960s. Now, however, there are unmistakable and ominous signs that the capacity of the universities to engage in basic research is under increasing threat and that, by the next century, this capacity may well have decreased to levels that should cause concern. For a scientist, particularly one who (like myself) engages in an empirical discipline (which, to quote the admirable definition of the *Shorter Oxford Dictionary*, "is based on, or guided by, the results of observation and experiment only"), this change in capacity is probably the most important aspect of the future of the university. We scientists who are also academic teachers know that teaching and research must go hand-in-hand, and that we teach largely what we deduce from our own experiments. If we do not experiment, our teaching will become stale. We cannot base our teaching solely on the research of other scientists in other countries; although knowledge is a common good, it is rapidly transferred only between those who are actively engaged in its creation. Hence, research — and, for me, this means *basic* research — is not a luxury (or, as someone has unkindly put it, "a form of occupational therapy for academics"), but an absolute necessity.

It is for reasons such as these that I propose to examine the changes that have occurred and are occurring in university research, and their implications. My data are drawn preponderantly from sources in the United Kingdom, since those are the only data readily available to me. I believe, however, that the record of the past that they provide, and the trends that may be discerned from them, are not confined to the United Kingdom and will find their counterpart in Canada and in the United States.

The Rise of Scientific Research in Universities

Two main forces were brought to bear on official thinking toward the end of World War II to cause a major expansion in the number of universities in the United Kingdom and the effort devoted nationally to primarily basic research. In October 1943, two distinguished physicists wrote to the Royal Society of London to call attention to the needs of research in fundamental science after the war. They pointed out "that it was no longer possible to leave the development of fundamental physics in this country entirely to the local initiative of the various universities but that some central guidance on major matters of policy was not only desirable but essential, if the case for increased resources is to be adequately put to the relevant Government authorities." Consequently, the Council of the Royal Society set up committees to consider post-war needs in several sciences and published a report[3] that urged the government – through the University Grants Committee (UGC), which in the United Kingdom acts as the medium through which universities and the government communicate on financial and other matters – to include adequate provision for research in their financial allocations to individual universities. Looking at Table 1, one cannot help but be astounded at the modesty of these sums. On the assumption that the purchasing power of the pound is now 5 per cent of that of 1939, the estimate for scientific research is of the order of $40 million. In fact, a recent offical report[4] shows that the expenditure on university research that is funded by the U.K. government's Department of Education and Science alone amounts to more than forty times this estimate – roughly $1800 million – and this is by no means all of the sums that are expended in universities for basic and applied research.

TABLE 1: Total "Ordinary" Expenditure by Subjects

Subject	Average for Pre-1939 Year ($m)	Estimated for Normal Post-war Year ($m)
Physics	4.12	12.0
Chemistry	6.00	16.0
Geology	1.08	3.0
Biology and biochemistry	3.44	9.0
Total	14.64	40.0

Note: Data are adapted from *Report on the Needs of Research in Fundamental Science after the War* (London: The Royal Society, 1945), by assuming that one pound in the original table equals $40 at current prices.

In addition to the pressure exerted by leading scientists through the Royal Society, an even more powerful drive toward the expansion of universities was provided by the realization that far too few able boys and girls had the opportunity to experience higher education. Moreover, as the war neared its end, it became clear that the number of student places then available was quite insufficient to meet the growing needs of the community for scientifically trained people. The student population, in the fourteen universities and eight university colleges that then existed in the United Kingdom, was only about 50,000, of whom only about one in four read science. A Committee on Scientific Manpower was therefore set up and reported in 1946; it recommended that the national interest demanded the doubling of the output of graduates in science and technology. The report, which did not differentiate between the two categories of scientists and technologists, hoped that this expansion would be achieved in ten years. It was, in fact, achieved in five. The total number of full-time students in pure science and technology increased from 13,000 in 1938-1939 to 27,000 in 1952-1953. The number of students in pure science increased by 121 per cent, and the number in technology by 89 per cent. During the same period, the number of students in the humanities increased by 56 per cent.

A further and major impetus to the growth of student numbers, particularly in science and technology, was provided ten years later by the so-called Robbins Report.[5] This quantified some of the thinking that had been expressed qualitatively since World War II. It demonstrated, for example, that there was an increasing tendency for pupils in schools to stay on to what in Canada would be high school. Second, there was a "bulge" in the birth rate after the war, and these individuals would be of an age to enter universities in the late 1960s: the population of eighteen-year-olds was predicted to rise from 533,000 in 1959 to 812,000 in 1965. Third, the report pointed out a considerable imbalance between social classes in the chances of obtaining a university place and recommended that urgent action be taken to rectify this. Whereas about a third of the children born in 1940 to parents who were skilled professionals, such as doctors and lawyers, went on to university, only 1 per cent of children born to semi-skilled or unskilled workers did so. Fourth, it was felt that Britain lagged behind other advanced nations in the proportion of eighteen-year-olds who went into higher education: in 1958-1959 only 4.5 per cent of eighteen-year-olds did so in the United Kingdom, compared with 7 per cent in France, 10 per cent in Sweden, 5 per cent in the Soviet Union, and 20 per cent in the United States. (It should be remembered, however, that 2.4 per cent of this age group in Britain ultimately obtained degrees in science or technology; this compared well with the 2 per cent that did so in France, Germany, and Sweden.) Moreover, the proportion of students who went into technology was felt to be too low. In 1959, first degrees in technology as a proportion of first degrees in science and technology were only 36 per cent compared with 65 per cent in Canada, 48 per cent in France, 68 per cent in Germany, and 49 per cent in the United States. Some rebalancing was needed.

As a result of this thinking, the number of universities was increased from fewer than thirty to more than fifty during the next decade. This was done by upgrading a number of colleges of advanced technology to university status and also by building a number of new universities from scratch. The upshot of this activity was that by 1967-1968, the total number of students had risen to 200,000, and by 1980-1981, to 300,000. Moreover, whereas only 25 per cent read science (pure and applied) in 1939, this proportion is now roughly 40 per cent. Similarly, the number of full-time academic staff in all subjects rose from roughly 10,000 in 1956-1957 to more than 40,000 in 1981-1982. This expansion in university numbers was accompanied by an increase in financial support for research, largely from government sources, that more or less kept pace and, until the end of the 1960s, enabled almost any member of an academic staff who wished to advance learning through research to obtain a research grant for that purpose.

The Loss of Faith in Scientific Research

This massive expansion in university education, and in the resources devoted to scientific research that were associated with that expansion, was followed after the 1960s by an equally rapid disenchantment with science that, to some extent, is still with us today. Many factors contributed to this disenchantment. One was the realization that advances in scientific knowledge often bring with them disadvantages: the legitimate and widespread concern over environmental pollution by industrial practices or products is one symptom of this unease. Even medicine is not exempt: advances in hygiene, therapeutics, and surgery have brought great benefits to mankind, but have also ensured that more people survive to have children of their own and that the balance between the number living and the number dying has created an alarming rate of population growth. Populations all over the world are aging, with consequent economic strains, not only because their birth rates decline but also because people no longer die from those diseases that carried off their forebears in youth and middle age. That one man's profit is another man's loss has, of course, long since been realized: as J.D. Bernal pointed out in 1939,[6] the commercial synthesis of aniline dyes in ninteenth-century Britain brought starvation to the million Hindu agricultural labourers whose indigo was no longer needed.

The great triumphs of technology that marked the end of the 1960s were also tainted both by their provenance and by their apparent disregard of social priorities. The enormous expenditure of public funds on the space programs of the United States and the Soviet Union would surely not have occurred had rockets and satellites been devoid of military potential. Although the achievement of placing men on the moon and bringing them back to earth safely was rightly admired as a technological triumph, the applause was tempered by a sense of foreboding. Moreover, it was asked, if money was available to the staggering extent necessary to sustain adventures in space, were there not matters demanding more urgent attention on which that money could be spent more usefully and more humanely? Sentiments such as these gave rise, in the United States and to a lesser extent in Britain, to "a widespread unease (amounting among some of the young to despair) because moral skills applied to social institutions have not kept pace with scientific skills applied to technolgoical needs."[7] It was this mood that, in the 1960s, persuaded many youngsters either to study what was perhaps misleadingly called "social sciences" (which were, in their effects, often anti-social, and were certainly not science), or even to opt out altogether from further study.

Another factor that contributed to the reduced faith in science was the growing awareness that the premises on which some of the more euphoric predictions of the 1960s were based were wrong. Among the considerations, for example, that led to the Robbins Report was the belief in a connection between higher education and economic growth. Since the end of World War II, Britain had experienced a growth of the gross domestic product (GDP) of only 2.5 per cent per year compared with 4.6 per cent attained by France and 7.6 per cent by Germany; indeed, Britain's was the lowest in Europe. Similarly, the growth rate in productivity in the United Kingdom was only 2.4 per cent per year, which was the second lowest in Europe.[8] An expansion of scientific education seemed to be necessary to achieve increased growth rates. Such a prescription was also supported by an interesting study in which the growth rate of the GDP and the numbers of university students per thousand primary students were compared.[9] These two indices were 7 and 48 per cent for Japan, 11 and 41 per cent for Germany, 5 and 17 per cent for Sweden, 5 and 35 per cent for Italy, and 5 and 28 per cent for France, but were only 2 and 20 per cent for England and Wales.

The belief that increased investment in scientific research could provide a cure for the country's economic ills was accompanied by another belief (which has not been abandoned even now in some quarters): that the speed of attaining that cure was proportional to the amount of money invested in scientific training and research. These beliefs were based on the simplest model of the innovation process, in which research leads directly to development (its application) and hence to the desired end-product, which is often equated with economic growth. In this sequence, each successive step is the logical outcome of its predecessor: to feed in research at one end would be to ensure economic growth at the other.

The available evidence suggests, however, that this is far from being true. An amusing demonstration of the falsity of this model was provided by B.R. Williams,[10] who compared the proportionate expenditures on research and development of a number of countries from 1950 to 1959 with an index of rising prosperity in those countries — the average compound growth of output per person employed — from 1955 to 1964 (see Figure 1). The difference of five years in the time scales was estimated to be the period required for any research to result in economic benefit. Although this five-year time lag is probably in error, there should nonetheless be a correlation between the two sets of figures: on the simple model, high research expenditure should be associated with high rates of economic growth. Not only was there no such correlation, however, but one is led to the ludicrous conclusion that the highest rates of growth were associated with the lowest research expenditure. In other words, research impedes economic growth! (A similarly misleading conclusion can be derived from a quite different field of endeavour.[11] In studies of eighteen developed countries, A.L. Cochrane and his colleagues found that higher infant death rates are correlated with a higher number of pediatricians per birth and, indeed, the more doctors there are per person, the higher is the death rate in general. It is but a short step from noticing such an interesting correlation to advocating a reduction in the number of medical students, as a measure of obvious benefit to public health.)

Since there was no clear economic benefit that could be attributed to the greatly increased national investment in (largely basic) research, the attitude steadily gained ground in official circles that, in the United Kingdom at any rate, we must be doing predominantly the wrong kind of research. I shall consider this point in the penultimate section of this paper.

Figure 1

Expenditure on R & D and Output per Person

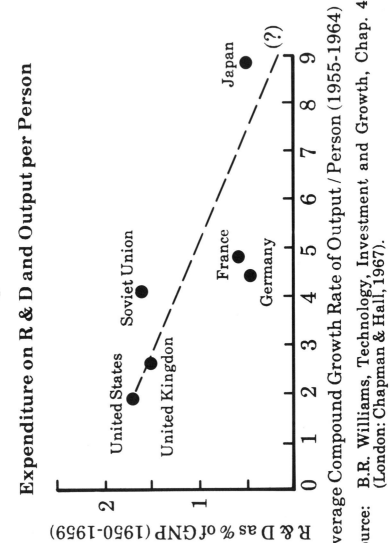

Source: B.R. Williams, Technology, Investment and Growth, Chap. 4 (London: Chapman & Hall, 1967).

The Dual Support System

The nature of the financial provisions for university research in Britain, and the pressures that are being increasingly applied to alter these financial provisions, cannot be fully understood without some discussion of the *dual support system*. This term is used to emphasize the fact that there are two main channels through which money enters the universities. By far the most important channel flows from that sector of government that is labelled "Department of Education and Science" (DES), but this channel itself has two branches. On the one hand, the science budget of the department provides funds for the basic research carried out under the aegis of the five research councils. Of these, four deal with science; they are the Agricultural and Food Research Council (AFRC), the Medical Research Council (MRC), the Natural Environment Research Council (NERC), and the Science and Engineering Research Council (SERC). A further portion of the science budget also supports scientific research sponsored by the British Museum (Natural History) and the Royal Society.

The stated purpose of the department's science budget is "to develop the natural (and social) sciences, including engineering, to maintain a fundamental capacity for research and scholarship and to support relevant higher education at the postgraduate level."[12] The research councils achieve these objectives by making grants to research workers in universities as well as elsewhere, and by directly operating their own research establishments. These establishments may themselves be associated with universities as research units or research groups (which differ in the length of time for which support is assured); or they may be central facilities that any one university would find too expensive to maintain and that are therefore provided for the use of universities; or they may be separate institutes that have only tenuous links with universities.

The second and major branch that channels funds from the department to universities is that which falls under the auspices of the UGC. Funds that flow into universities via this route do so in the form of block grants that cover both research and teaching, it having been officially accepted for the past fifty years that these two activities go hand-in-hand. Even as far back as their report of 1936, the UGC disagreed with Cardinal Newman's assertion that "to discover and to teach are distinct functions" and endorsed the quotation from the inaugural lecture of the principal of Owen's College, Manchester (now the University of Manchester), that "he who learns from one occupied in learning drinks of a running stream. He who learns from one who has learnt all he has to teach drinks the green mantle of a stagnant pool."

In the science fields, the intention of the UGC's support of research is that it shall provide the basic research capability that university departments need to have if speculative ideas are to be generated and to be developed to the stage where they may attract further support from external sponsors, which may include the research councils. Since the research activities of universities and their general expenditure cannot be clearly separate, and the UGC's objectives in funding research cannot be clearly distinguished from the wider objective of funding all aspects of the university system, the actual sums derived from the UGC for university research can only be guessed at. The UGC has, however, estimated that the contribution to university research from the funds it allocated in the year 1978-1979 was nearly $600 million; for comparison, the research councils have estimated that they supported university research in that year to the tune of $390 million.

These two sources of government support, the research councils and the UGC, are not the only legs of the dual support system. In addition, significant funds are derived from a proportion of the fees paid by students, from industry, from charitable bodies, from government departments other than the DES, and from private benefactors. The great benefit of having a system that is so flexible is that, from the UGC provision alone, an academic teacher should in theory be assured of his or her own salary, of the overheads of his laboratory, and, more often than not, of the salary of at least some technical assistants who can provide continuity to the work of the department and who, often, possess tenure equivalent to that enjoyed by the teacher. This level of basic support is assumed to be sufficient for academic staff at least to taxi along the runway: if they wish to become airborne in their research, they will of course need to seek support from external funding agencies. Even without such further support, it is intended that they can at least keep in touch with the frontiers of their subject and can thereby enrich their teaching. The availability of assured basic support should not only help newcomers to academic staff to become established and to develop their research to a point where it will attract further support but, most important, should provide a buffer that to some extent protects the research worker from the pendulum swings, from penury to affluence and often back again, that characterize dependence wholly on external sources. That was the theory, and that was how it worked up to the late 1960s. The system has been progressively eroded since then by a decrease in total funding, particularly by repeated cut-backs in the UGC contribution on which chiefly rests the dual support system, and also by deliberately favouring support of applied research.

Threats to Basic Research: Erosion of the Dual Support System

The government minister who in the United Kingdom has the ultimate responsibility for allocating sums of money both to the UGC and to the research councils is advised in this latter function by an Advisory Board for the Research Councils (ABRC). A working party of the ABRC reported in July 1983 on the support given by the research councils for in-house and university research and stated "unreservedly that the dual support system is currently under severe strain and is not working properly."[13]

Chief among the reasons for this conclusion, as far as universities are concerned, are the financial economies that have been imposed in recent years by the government through repeated cutbacks of UGC funds. Many reasons have been advanced for these cutbacks. One important consideration has been precisely that which, a quarter of a century earlier, inspired the Robbins Report — the expected abundance of eighteen-year-olds in the population. As shown in Figure 2, the number of these young men and women is projected to fall steeply from the present 2.75 million to only about 1.9 million in 1996 and thereafter to rise again (of course, no projection beyond the years 2002 is possible). It was no doubt in the minds of those who calculated financial allocations to univerities that a fall in the eighteen-year cohort by more than 31 per cent over the next twelve years should be anticipated by an appropriate reduction in financial provisions. What may not have been sufficiently realized, however, is that the fall in the total number of eighteen-year-olds does not necessarily mean a concomitant reduction in the number of university entrants. There is evidence that the birth rate among professional classes from whom the student population largely comes has been remarkably constant and will not exhibit the fluctuations shown in Figure 2.

Still, population projections cannot be the sole reason for the erosion of UGC funds. As shown in Figure 3, the total student load rose steadily by 24 per cent between 1971-1972 and 1978-1979 from about 251,000 to 310,000. Concomitantly, the expenditure on academic salaries rose from $533 million to $645 million (at constant prices); this presumably reflected the rise by 13 per cent in the number of academic staff, from 29,400 to 33,300. (It will be noted that this percentage increase in the

Figure 2

Population of Eighteen-Year-Olds in the United Kingdom, 1970-2002

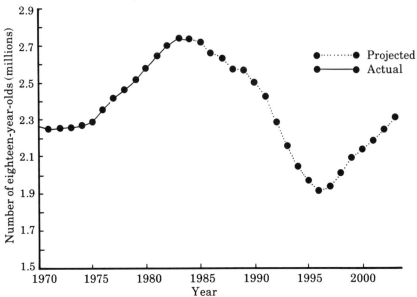

Note: The numbers plotted for any one year are the sum of the actual or projected populations for that year and for the two preceding years. Thus, 1980 = 1978 + 1979 + 1980.

Source: United Kingdon, *Report of a Joint Working Party on the Support of University Scientific Research* (London: H.M.S.O., 1982).

Figure 3

**Academic Salary Costs, Departmental Expenditures, and Number
of Students in U.K. Universities, 1971-1972 to 1978-1979**

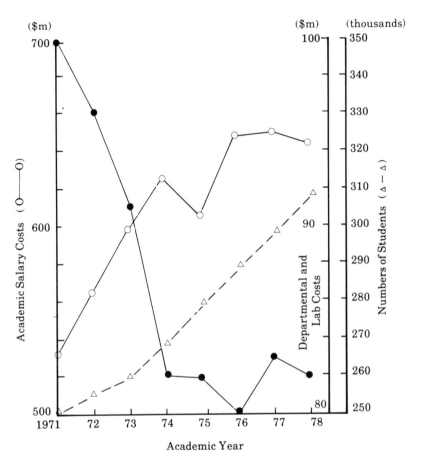

Source   United Kindom, *Report of a Joint Working Party.*

number of staff is only half that of students; this increase in teaching load inevitably also encroaches on time devoted to research.) In contrast, and despite these sizable increases, departmental and laboratory expenditure decreased by 19 per cent, from $100 million in 1971-1972 to slightly more than $81 million in 1975-1976. Expressed as a reduction in this type of expenditure per member of academic staff, the change is 28 per cent, from $3,420 to $2,470. This percentage has decreased still further since; there is no good reason to hope that that decrease has yet been arrested.[14] The effects of these reductions are disproportionately severe, not only in curtailing the purchase and maintenance of small items of equipment, and in operating costs, but also in inhibiting travel and attendance at conferences. Indeed, funds for these latter purposes have been virtually eliminated from British universities.

Of all the pressures on university scientific research, the cutback in the UGC grants for equipment has had the most severe effects. This is because there exists a Catch-22 element in the inter-relation of the two branches that channel government money into the dual support system. The research grants offered by the research councils are deficiency grants; they are expected only to top up resources that cannot be supplied from the UGC sector. Consequently, such research grants are given only to laboratories that are "well-found"; they are certainly not intended to supply basic equipment that should be supplied from university sources for the research proposed. One is more and more driven, therefore, into the ridiculous situation that the UGC funds are insufficient to supply this basic equipment, yet without it one cannot hope for any alternative source of funds.

The intensity of this pressure may be illustrated by data published in 1982.[15] It is generally accepted that the equipment grants in 1973-1974 were adequate, and that year is now used as the inventory base for subsequent estimates. The first major cutback in government expenditure caused the equipment grant in 1974-1975 to be cut to about half the value of the previous year at constant prices — $65 million compared with $139 million. The difficulties this caused were rather tardily recognized by the government, and additional funds were made available in both 1979 and 1980. The shortfall and, more seriously, the large accumulated deficit over the years has, however, posed immense problems for science departments. The increasing sophistication of the equipment used even for subjects that were once regarded as relatively inexpensive has meant that replacement of obsolete apparatus costs far more than did the original equipment, yet the funds available for purchase of such equipment have decreased alarmingly. If this situation is allowed to continue much longer, and there is no sign to the contrary, it is not too fanciful to predict that, in the United Kingdom at any rate, first class basic research in science will become confined to just a few favoured departments in a few universities.

Threats to Basic Research:
The Increasing Importance of Being Applied

Since the mid-1960s, the progressive decreases in the allocation of government funds for basic research have been accompanied by the undeniable realization that if the nation is to benefit from the scientific research being done in universities, the knowledge gained has to be translated into activities that generate wealth: in the immediate context, this means industrial processes and industrial products. This is not a new demand to university science. Advances in basic research in, for example, physiology, biochemistry, pharmacology, botany, and other biological sciences have in general quickly found their applications in medicine and agriculture; similarly, the research work of chemists in universities has traditionally been linked closely with the chemical industry. It is equally undeniable that, for a variety of reasons, many discoveries made in British laboratories have been exploited commercially largely outside Britain. Again, to cite examples from biology, one has only to think of penicillin in the 1940s and of interferon and monoclonal antibodies now. As a government minister succinctly put it at a public meeting in March 1984, Britain has gained sixty-three Nobel Prizes whereas Japan has won only three, yet, largely as a result of developments in high technology industries, the rate of growth of GNP is far greater in Japan than in Britain. Clearly, means have to be found for technology transfer from the university laboratory bench to the production line.

These considerations have over the years led to steady pressures being exerted on the research funding systems to encourage university scientists to form links with industry. Inevitably, the hope is that scientists will work to a greater extent on problems that will lead to new processes and products in the near rather than the distant future and that are, therefore, directed primarily toward specific aims and objectives. In other words, it is hoped that university scientists will increasingly engage in applied research.

These pressures have been exerted through the research councils in a number of ways. Of greatest importance both in the range of activities and in the amount of money it disburses is the Science and Engineering Research Council. When this research council was established in the late 1960s, it was called the Science Research Council (SRC); it acquired the "and Engineering" relatively recently. (Similarly, in 1984 the Agricultural Research Council became the Agricultural and Food Research Council.) These changes in terminology reflect changes in emphasis. In the definitive statement issued by the government in 1972 on the manner in which government R & D should be conducted, the role of the then SRC was clearly defined: "Its primary purpose is to sustain standards of education and research in the Universities."[16] The SERC, however, supports links between industry and universities in ways that have nothing directly to do with that primary purpose. It runs, for example, a Teaching Company Scheme that pays for high calibre graduates to work in an industrial company to solve problems in manufacturing, under the joint supervision of the firm and the university concerned; an Integrated Graduate Development Scheme that enables new graduate recruits to the manufacturing industry to receive intensive induction training organized jointly by their employer and a university; Collaborative Training Awards that support short-term training projects of twelve- to fifteen-months duration, which are principally related to industrial production problems in smaller companies; and, together with the Royal Society, an Industrial Fellowship Scheme that supports members of academic staff for secondment to an appropriate industry for up to two years to help the particular company undertake a research project related to its own research program. All these schemes, valuable as they are, have only marginal relevance to sustaining "standards of education and research in universities." Similarly, the introduction of the "F" into the title of the Agricultural Research Council indicates that a greater proportion of the resources available through that council will now be used to underpin the food processing industry in the United Kingdom.

Pressures of this kind are also being applied through awards to graduate students. For many years now, the SERC has offered Cooperative Awards in Science and Engineering (CASE) that support post-graduate training through research jointly supervised by a member of an academic staff and by a partner from an industrial laboratory. These awards are fundamentally different from the post-graduate studentships in pure science. Whereas the latter are allocated to university departments for distribution to those students who, in the opinion of those departments, are best fitted to continue their education by working for a Ph.D., the CASE have first to be approved by virtue of the topic to be studied, and only then is a suitable student sought to fill them. The student is also expected to spend several periods of work in the industrial partner's laboratory as part of the training.

It is fervently to be hoped that all these schemes will achieve the desired end. So far, industry spends only about $70-80 million per year in universities, which is less than 8 per cent of the moneys currently being spent on scientific research in universities. It is obviously necessary to increase this proportion and to lessen the universities' overwhelming dependence on government funds. One is perhaps less than enthusiastic in commending schemes to foster closer research links between universities and industry when one realizes that these measures have been accompanied by only a small increase in support for research from industry but have constituted a major diversion of funds from the basic research component of the dual support system.[17] They, therefore, exacerbate a trend that has already led to severe impairment of precisely those areas of scientific inquiry that, over the years, have been recognized by Nobel Prizes and other evidence of international esteem. I believe that, if this trend is not speedily checked, it will also defeat the very purpose for which the redeployment of funds is being made.

Many attempts have been made to trace the path from basic research to the successful development of some product or process, with the aim of shortening the delays between these events and in the hope of predicting future success from today's endeavour. A particularly careful and detailed analysis of the history of five innovations was prepared by the Illinois Institute of Technology Research, for the U.S. National Science Foundation, sixteen years ago and published under the title *TRACES — Technology in Retrospect and Critical Events in Science*.[18] The subjects chosen were (1) magnet ferrites, a class of material widely used in computer memories and telecommunications, (2) the video tape recorder, (3) the oral contraceptive pill, (4) the electron microscope, and (5) matrix isolation, a then-new technique for the study of mechanisms of chemical reactions. The key papers in the scientific and technical literature that contributed to these developments were traced and classified, on the basis of their technical content and of the motives that impelled that research, into "non-mission" (basic) research, "mission-oriented" (applied) research, and research associated with development and application. A remarkably uniform picture emerges from consideration of these five very different subjects. In each case, about 70 per cent of the key papers reported research that was clearly basic, and only 20 per cent were applied. In each case, nearly half of this work had been done thirty years or more before the product was achieved. In each case, about nine years elapsed between the achievement of a clear concept of the device or process and its successful development. (This achievement of the concept is defined in the report as "conception," which is a term less than felicitous when applied to the contraceptive pill.) Since in each case about 90 per cent of all the relevant basic research had already been completed a year before the point of conception, it is evident that this research was performed without any knowledge of the final process or product to which it contributed.

This important conclusion emerges also from current industrial applications of biology, particularly the exploitation of genetically engineered cells that form the substances of what is now called "biotechnology." A key component of this technology is the ability to recognize particular sequences of the genetic message, encoded in DNA, to excise them, and either to splice them into other pieces of DNA or to copy and modify them before they are incorporated into a suitable vector. All these activities emerge directly from basic research in molecular biology that was carried out without any intention of applying it to industrial ends and that was largely carried out within the last dozen years. Indeed, the successful outcome of these exciting researches was not, and could not have been, predicted at the time. Nor, I suspect, would it have been possible to achieve these successes earlier if a "crash program" had been instituted before the time was ripe: the rate-limiting step was the acquisition of new insights into molecular mechanisms, generated by scientists who were free to follow their bent without coercion and did so solely in the conviction that the problems they were studying were exciting and ripe for solution. Any increase in the "mission-orientation" of university research will be counter-productive in the long run if it stifles this type of free inquiry on which unpredicted, and as yet unpredictable, advances in the future will undoubtedly rest.

Basic and Applied Research in Universities of the Next Century

Fortunately, the omens are that a major increase in applied research will not necessarily mean the death of basic research, provided that the universities remain alive to the needs for maintaining their basic research capability. Two universities in the United Kingdom have already gone far down a path that I suspect many other British universities will have to follow as they move into the next century. One, the Cranfield Institute of Technology, is unique in that it is largely a graduate, science-

and technology-based institute, of university status, that does not receive funds from the UGC; it is perhaps analogous to the Massachusetts Institute of Technology in the United States. The Cranfield Institute has perforce had to rely on its own initiatives to generate an income that, for the more traditional British universities, came almost automatically. It appears that the efforts to exploit research in science and technology have forged many links with industry that have enabled the institute not only to avoid becoming a contract organization, but to expand its basic research activities. "I think the force at work here," the vice-chancellor wrote to me when I was preparing this paper, "is that knowledge of the applied problems itself stimulates more basic enquiry. We intend therefore to expand even further our applied research policy as a means of bringing in its wake an increasing amount of pure research."

A second university that has also been forced increasingly to generate funds by forming links with industry is the University of Salford. Here the primary driving force was necessity: in the academic year 1983-1984, the UGC grant to Salford was cut by more than 40 per cent. In forging such new relationships, the university realized at the outset that major changes in management structure, within the university and ancillary to it, would have to occur. The traditional academic management structure of universities is based on academic disciplines, such as chemistry or biological sciences or history, that are primarily concerned with the acquisition of knowledge and the passing on of that knowledge to future generations; this "passing on" includes the freedom to publish without outside censorship other than the peer review provided by the editors of learned journals. The requirements of industry are quite different. In general, the solution to an applied problem is wanted by an industrial concern in a form that will be immediately useful, is supplied to specification, and is supplied to time; it may also require a moratorium on publication. The type of internal research committees that have been suggested as a means of permitting universities to monitor and to allocate the scarce resources available to them from all sources are not capable of meeting such demands.[19] Recognizing this, the University of Salford set up an Industrial Centre that is an independent incorporated company, whose profits go to the university. This organization is legally and managerially independent of the university, has to trade at a profit, and has full-time employees, including a general manager and part-time directors who also hold appointments in the university. It has also set up another body, with the acronym CAMPUS, that helps to establish, and then manages, those relationships between the university and industry that go beyond the simple "contract research" operations that, in general, do not contain any basic research component. CAMPUS also sponsors the limited tenure appointment of senior people who will work part-time in industry and part-time in the university. These kinds of activities may provide a link between the academic and the industrial environment that is not only effective in its immediate aims but is also strong enough to ensure that industrialists are made aware of the basic research questions raised by industrial problems, of the advantages of undertaking basic research within the university, and of the long-term benefits that may accrue to them by sponsoring such research.

Knowing how little of the present situation could have been foreseen twenty years ago, when it seemed that the cornucopia of government support for science would shower riches upon the universities in increasing measure and forever, I am reluctant to prophesy how research in universities will fare in the twenty-first century. I think that the trends, discouraging as they may seem from the vantage point of the past, still leave room for hope. No one would deny the necessity for universities, particularly in the United Kingdom, to apply their research in greater measure to the benefit of the society that ultimately pays for that research. To enable this to be done without destroying the universities as centres of intellectual excellence and of innovation requires that those who commission research — whether it be government or industry — continue to be reminded also of the vital necessity that basic research continues to flourish. By the same token, those who administer, teach in, and perform research in universities will have to recognize that they must modify many of the procedures traditional to British universities and must anticipate them in good time. Although such changes will undoubtedly make British universities twenty years hence rather different from what they are today, this need not impair their vigour: indeed, they will serve to make universities in the United Kingdom much more akin to those in North America.

Notes

1. United Kingdom, *Report of a Joint Working Party on the Support of University Scientific Research* (London: H.M.S.O., 1982), Cmnd. 8567.

2. *The Measurement of Scientific and Technical Activities* (Paris: Organization for Economic Cooperation and Development, 1980).

3. Royal Society, *Report on the Needs of Research in Fundamental Science after the War* (London, 1945).

4. United Kingdom, *Annual Review of Government Funded R & D, 1983* (London: H.M.S.O., 1984).

5. United Kingdom, *Higher Education* (Robbins Report) (London: H.M.S.O., 1963), Cmnd. 2154.

6. J.D. Bernal, *The Social Function of Science* (London: Routledge & Kegan Paul, 1939).

7. E. Ashby, "Science and Anti-Science," *Proceedings of the Royal Society* B, 178, 29 (1972).

8. M.M. Postan, *An Economic History of Western Europe 1945-1964* (London, 1967).

9. M.C. Kaser, in *The Economics of Education*, ed. E.A.G. Robinson and J. Vaizey (London, 1966).

10. B.R. Williams, chap. 4 in *Technology, Investment and Growth* (London: Chapman & Hall, 1967).

11. A.L. Cochrane et al., *Journal of Epidemiology and Community Health* 32, 200 (1978).

12. United Kingdom, *Annual Review*.

13. Advisory Board for the Research Councils, *The Support Given by Research Councils for In-House and University Research* (London: H.M.S.O., 1983).

14. Ibid.

15. United Kingdom, *Report of a Joint Working Party.*

16. United Kingdom, *Framework for Government Research and Development* (London: H.M.S.O., 1972), Cmnd. 5046.

17. Unitd Kingdom, *Improving Research Links between Higher Education and Industry* (London: H.M.S.O, 1983).

18. Illinois Institute of Technology Research, *TRACES — Technology in Retrospect and Critical Events in Science* (Washington, D.C.: National Science Foundation, 1968).

19. United Kingdom, *Report of a Joint Working Party.*

PART II

MACHINES AND MINDS

THE CYBERNETIC DREAM
OF THE TWENTY-FIRST CENTURY

MORRIS BERMAN

> *In the future the community of the learned will have to propose this new and humane technology which is natural philosophy and positive magic . . . . However, if the sense of the individual [that is, of particular entities] is the only good, how will science succeed in recomposing the universal laws through which . . . the good magic will become functional?*
> - William of Baskerville, fourteenth century, in Umberto Eco, *The Name of the Rose*

> *The main point is that the world of life is to a great extent created and maintained through the expression of emotional energy. It is this energy through which magic operates . . . . The control and manipulation of emotional energy is the secret of all magic . . . .*
> - Father Sylvan, in Jacob Needleman, *Lost Christianity*

It was in the mid- to late 1960s that an idea with a long but obscure ancestry finally came to fruition, one that many, myself included, found very difficult to grasp. This idea was that science possessed no epistemological superiority over any other mode of thought, that it had no monopoly on the truth, and that in the last analysis, it was a mythology — that is, it functioned as a type of religion for Western industrial societies. The general public identified this argument most closely with Theodore Roszak, who asserted that science was not some sort of absolute, transcultural truth, but rather a cultural construct, that is, a "construct in which a given society in a given historical situation has invested its sense of meaningfulness and value."[1]

Why was this argument so difficult to grasp, let alone accept? Largely, because all of us were brought up within the philosophical boundaries Roszak had chosen to call into question. These boundaries have their origins in the Scientific Revolution of the seventeenth century, and are generally summed up by historians of science as the "mechanical philosophy." Briefly, this philosophy holds that spirits of any kind are delusions, that consciousness is epiphenomenal (that is, arises from a material base), and that matter and motion are the only real entities. The favourite image of the universe was that of a clock, wound up by the Almighty to tick forever. Nature was thus seen as mechanical, and all explanations of its behaviour had to be material ones. For the most part, this is still what the dominant culture believes, as can be seen by consulting virtually any modern textbook in the natural or social sciences, or, for that matter, the daily newspaper.

Roszak's idea, had a long tradition behind it, a tradition, interestingly enough, that was heavily academic. Edmund Husserl, Martin Heidegger, and Ludwig Wittgenstein had broached the subject in various forms. The Frankfurt School for Social Research, notably Max Horkeimer and T.W. Adorno, had wrestled with these problems in books such as *Eclipse of Reason* and *Dialectic of Enlightenment.* The so-called externalist school of the history of science, following the mode of analysis of Karl Mannheim, pointed out that both the content and the method of modern science were "situation-bound," highly localized in time and space. In other words, modern science was put together over a period of roughly 150 years, and principally in four countries – Italy, England, Holland, and France. If one studies the social, economic, and religious history of those nations between 1550 and 1700, one begins to understand why scientific conceptions of reality took root at that time and in those places. The logical conclusion was that this mode of perception was and is a cultural construct, a mythology, a complex and elaborate world view that permeates Western industrial societies and provides them with meaning.[2]

During the 1960s, however, the real critic of the scientific world view was not Theodore Roszak but Herbert Marcuse, whose book *One-Dimensional Man* constituted a major attack on the claim of science to be value-free. At a time when it was still fashionable to argue that science and technology could be used for good or evil, Marcuse argued that science possessed no real neutrality but was, from its inception, haunted by a particular bias, which he termed the "logic of domination." His attack, paradoxically enough, was based on an examination of the one feature that modern science regards as a *guarantee* of its neutrality, namely, its purely formal or abstract character. In a word, the science of Galileo is about relata, not about contents. The law of free fall, $s = kt$, is descriptive rather than normative. Where Aristotle saw a falling body as going "home," moving toward the center of the earth, and thereby living out its teleological destiny, Galileo saw only an abstract relationship between distance and time.

Modern science is thus based on the abolition of the notion of *telos*, or inherent purpose, and it does this by positing a purely formal reality, one that can be bent to any situation. It is precisely here, said Marcuse, that it reveals its bias, for the ability to be bent to any situation implies a purely instrumentalist character. $S = kt$ has a latent but powerful message, for it projects a world of pure form and essentially says that only this is real. In Galileo's time, it was still possible to maintain a notion of two realities. Hence the father of modern science, as he has been called, supposedly argued before the Inquisition that "physics tells how the heavens go; it does not tell how to go to heaven." It proved to be a feeble dichotomy, however, and one difficult, as the centuries passed, to maintain. The two realities ultimately collapsed into one, hence the title of Marcuse's book. Having left value behind, this single dimension of reality could then claim to be value-free. Marcuse argued, however, that this very neutrality constituted the bias of the whole methodology. There could be nothing neutral about a methodology, said Marcuse, that swallowed up the entire *Lebenswelt*, that created, for literally everyone in the culture, a single mode of seeing and interpreting the world. "When technics becomes the universal form of material production," he wrote, "it circumscribes an entire culture; it projects a historical totality – a 'world.'" Amorality, in short, was a species of morality; "value-free" really meant "scientific values."[3]

The combined result of this thinking, or at least, conspicuously concomitant with it, was the eruption on an unprecedented scale in Europe and North America of cults of various sorts. The feeling was, quite simply, that science had gone astray; if it were a mythology, there were reasons to believe it had outlived its time, and other realities were equally valid or perhaps even superior to it. By the mid-1970s, interest in the occult – astrology, alchemy, sorcery, numerology, witchcraft, Scientology – was extremely widespread. Not since the heyday of the Renaissance had the non-rational enjoyed such a vogue. The growing disenchantment with science partly explains this development, but one still has to ask, why magic? What was there about the occult tradition that was so attractive to a large counterculture jaded with science? There are undoubtedly many answers to this, but I suspect that one of the most important of these is that magic has strengths in precisely those areas where, according to Marcuse, science is weak. The occult sciences are anything but formal and abstract. They are sensuous and concrete, and magic rituals typically engage all of the senses, including taste and smell. Magic is embodied in a way that science is not; it emerges from the whole person, not just from the intellect. Although magic certainly has a manipulative, or exoteric, aspect, its historical context down to the early modern period was a sacred one. That sacred (or ecological) context meant that magic was not value-free or instrumentalist, and there was always a severe injunction against using it in a purely manipulative way. Goethe's *Faust* is, in fact, a modern version of this ancient injunction: the attempt to divorce fact from value has a price, that being nothing less than the loss of the soul. As Marcuse recognized, that divorce is the essential drama of the modern era.[4]

Finally, magic was attractive because it provided an epistemological shock. Many of those who got interested in magical practice, myself included, had a real surprise in store: it works. Reality is flexible enough that perception can influence it; in fact, that is why *science* works, and why it can rightly be called the magic of the modern era. As it turns out, the occult subculture was not the only circle that was interested in alternative realities. Soviet and American intelligence organizations had been investigating the paranormal — extrasensory perception, psychometry, psychokinesis, etc. — since the 1950s or 1960s and discovering what magical practitioners have known for centuries: mental attitudes can make a difference for physical effects.[5]

As noted, all of this suggested to many people that Western consciousness may be in the midst of a mythological shift, or that a new scientific revolution might be in progress. This perception, however, was definitely not confined to investigators of occult phenomena. A large "new paradigm" literature began to develop, arguing for a convergence of modern physics and archaic spiritual tradition, for example, or seeing in ecology or systems theory a new mode of constructing the world.[6]

As for myself, I played with magic long enough to satisfy my intellectual curiosity, but I have to confess that I never managed to acquire any great magical powers. Furthermore, my interest was in a post-Cartesian philosophy, not a pre-Cartesian one, and this pretty much put me in the "new paradigm" camp. When I stumbled across the work of the cultural anthropologist Gregory Bateson, I found what I was looking for: a scientist who talked like an alchemist. Precise, empirical, experimental, Bateson's categories of thought nevertheless had a living, sensuous quality to them. As I began to wade through the opaque prose of his book

Steps to an Ecology of Mind, to puzzle over essays like "The Cybernetics of 'Self'" and "Form, Substance and Difference," it began to dawn on me that this man had somehow managed to bring fact and value back together in a way that was rationally credible. Although he often used a cybernetic or systems theory terminology, the pages of the book oozed life, because the theory emerged not from abstractions but from concrete solutions. Patiently, over the decades of his life, Bateson lived and studied among the Iatmul of New Guinea and the Balinese, alcoholics and schizophrenics, and dolphins; it was from such contexts that his most famous concepts, such as schismogenesis, circuitry, and the double-bind, had emerged. Bateson was the living embodiment of his own theoretical analysis; the philosophy was incarnated in the practice. This was a "process" reality, formally identical to the magical tradition, yet radically different in content. There was a clear resonance with Taoism, with quantum mechanics, with the work of Carl Jung and Wilhelm Reich; and it spoke directly to questions of ecology and man's relationship to the environment. The Gregory Bateson of *Steps,* I concluded, could well be the most brilliant, and most desperately needed, thinker of the twentieth century. I would still, to a great extent, defend that view.[7]

Unfortunately, in his later work Bateson was not able to hold together the synthesis of the sensuous and the scientific — what Umberto Eco calls "natural philosophy and positive magic." The first hint that something was amiss occurred to me in 1979 when Bateson published *Mind and Nature: A Necessary Unity.*[8] The holistic epistemology of *Steps* was still there, but despite the subtitle of the book, mind and nature were tending to float away from each other. In Bateson's revision of Darwin, for example, evolution was presented almost entirely as a mental process. Real dinosaurs and butterflies seemed to be absent from the picture. By mid-1980, just before Bateson's death, this tendency was taken to its logical conclusion. His last talk, "Men Are Grass: Metaphor and the World of Mental Process," solves the mind-body problem by doing away with the body altogether. The cybernetic philosophy presented there is, when you come down to it, essentially Neoplatonic or Augustinian. The flesh withers, the soul is immortal — a convenient philosophy, of course, if you know you are about to die, but a retreat from reality into a world of pure abstractions nonetheless. By turning into pure form, Batesonian holism succumbed to the very problem that haunted the mechanical philosophy.[9]

Those who seriously reject mechanistic science today largely fall into the two categories I have identified: occult practitioners and what we might call cybernetic or holistic thinkers. I will not comment further on the first category, principally because I do not believe it has any real future: it is very unlikely that we could revert to an earlier era and world view, and I am not convinced it would be a good idea in any event. I will focus my attention, therefore, on the second category, where I have begun to have some serious doubts. Whereas Bateson managed, at least for a time, to hold mind and matter together, the holistic or cybernetic thinking of the 1980s is simplifying the problem by dispensing with matter before the game even begins. As a result, an epistemological consensus is emerging in philosophical circles, which, in one form or another, claims to refute and replace the mechanism and materialism of the past three hundred years but which, in most of its forms, falls prey to the same philosophical problems that plague modern science as they were identified by Herbert Marcuse. It is purely abstract and formal, capable of being bent to any reality. Although it often appears to be value-free, it in fact projects a *Lebenswelt*, a total vision of reality that circumscribes an entire world.

Nor is this occurring only in philosophical circles. The new mythology is appearing in three realms of society, which overlap, interpenetrate, and reinforce one another, and which are often very difficult to distinguish. The first, as noted, is that of abstract philosophy, which includes a rather eclectic mélange of writers and scientists, figures as diverse as Ken Wilber, Marilyn Ferguson, David Bohm, Douglas Hofstadter, and Rupert Sheldrake.[10] The second is that of the professional disciplines, including history, biology, education, ecology, and psychology, to name but a few. The third is the daily life of the ordinary citizen, which is increasingly filled with video games and home computers. The three realms are not identical, and in sociological terms, there is no way I can prove they are even related. Yet it seems to me that it would be naive to believe that this new mythology had somehow emerged within our culture at three different points and that these three manifestations were nevertheless not part of the same social process. I take it as a given that they *are* structurally related, even though I cannot establish any concrete causal connections. Taken as a whole, they propagate the mythology of a new "process" reality, a type of abstract "mentation" or consciousness that, despite a fanfare of propaganda about being a new liberating epistemology, is in fact just as disembodied and value-free as its mechanistic predecessor. These problems, which I see operating in all three domains, are the focus of my critique. Before returing to abstract philosophy, or "new paradigm" literature, toward the end of this paper, I shall concentrate on the more concrete manifestations of the new cybernetic consciousness.

In many ways, daily life is the most significant, the more so for being the least sophisticated. The Italian historian Carlo Ginzburg has argued that the way to discover what a culture is about is not to study the ideas of its leading intellectuals, but rather to examine what fills the heads of its ordinary citizens.[11] Unfortunately, we are at an impasse here, for it would seem to be too early to discern this. As far as I am aware, no one has made exact studies of the effect of video games or home computers on the individual, so I have to rely on general impressions. The image I have — everyone has seen it — is of a group of teenagers crowded around a Pac-Man machine in a drugstore or games arcade. The thing that interests me most here is the eyes of the players. They are glazed. The phrase that recently entered the English language, "video addict," is quite apropos, because the machine instantly takes the player out of this world. He becomes, in effect, unconscious; his eyes take on an absorbed, drugged quality that reflects the all-encompassing power of the screen. As with any drug, the video screen effectively enables the addict to leave his body and thus the cares of the world. I recently discovered that an organization called Vidanon has emerged, dedicated to getting people unhooked from this addiction.[12]

In this way Pac-Man, and frequently the home computer as well, is really the modern fulfilment of the Gnostic vision. For whether the screen presents a computer program or asteroids to be blown out of the sky, it enables the user to escape, at least momentarily, from boredom, anxiety, and other emotional difficulties, all of which are felt in the body. This is not to say that the intended use of home computers is identical to that of video games, but as things work out in practice, both encourage disembodied activity and both help to diffuse a similar mode of perception throughout the culture. In this way our culture is starting, without much questioning or critical evaluation, to acquire a kind of "computer consciousness." Strictly speaking, home computers fall into the category of professional activity; but it is very doubtful that all or even most of the 27 million units sold between 1978 and 1983 are being used in this way.[13] Exact mode of use, however, is not the point. The real issue here is that both video games and home computers create a similar view of the world for millions of people. Both present the viewer with a screen and a set of images to be operated upon. Both convey the notion that reality is a function of programming, and children as well as adults pick up a certain vocabulary from their use. The general result, I suspect, is a vast subculture that lives entirely in its head, that sees reality as essentially neutral, value-free, and, especially, disembodied, a form of pure mental process.

An example of what I am talking about was provided by a friend named Susan who teaches high school in northern Florida. Many of her students have home computers. When Susan assigns a paper, her students immediately run home and feed all the key words into their machines, which are hooked up to data banks and library resources, and proceed to string this information together. One of Susan's students, Frank, stayed after class one day to show her his mass of computer printouts on the latest topic she had assigned. "Frank," she finally said, "stop a moment. I think it's great that you've gathered all these facts about the subject, but put them aside just for a second. Look at me and tell me in your own words: what do you *feel* about this issue?" Frank stared at her for a moment and finally replied, "I don't know what you mean." Susan told me that if she could afford it, she would retire to Key West and spend the rest of her life scuba diving. In fact, she may not have long to wait. Increasingly, the direction of secondary school education is to do away with teachers entirely. In one survey conducted by the Sperry Univac Corporation, 50 per cent of the high school students polled said they would prefer to be taught by a machine and gave as their reason that they wished to be left alone.[14]

I feel very uneasy with developments of this sort; they show how people get completely caught up in a world view without any notion that such a thing is happening to them. I fear we will see much more of this in years to come. Recently, the University of Victoria concluded an agreement with IBM Canada whereby the two institutions will work together to develop applications for computer software to be used by students from kindergarten up. Computers are also being designed for the purpose of rocking a baby's cradle and singing it lullabies. "It is already technically possible," says Seymour Papert, professor of mathematics and education at the Massachusetts Institute of Technology, "to make a machine that can interact with a child from the beginning of its life." Papert's research team discovered that infants can become addicted to computers, and he comments that the interference of parent-infant bonding by such machines is a turning point in the history of child rearing. By cutting these early ties, he says, "we could easily turn up a generation of psychotic children, of psychotic adults."[15] Susan's student, Frank, may seem like an aberration today, but a decade from now he may be fairly typical. Three decades from now, there may be no problem, for there may be no one around who does not possess a cybernetic consciousness. The "psychotic" label is a matter of social definition. In a predominantly psychotic world, psychotic becomes healthy, and healthy, psychotic. We must stop and think about developments of this sort before daily life is completely transformed.

The second domain I referred to is that of the professional disciplines. I have no opposition to cybernetic technology as technology; its utilitarian aspect is not the focus of my critique. Computer technology clearly makes possible many desirable things, such as scanning the retina in eye operations or arranging airline flights and schedules. For such purposes it is a valuable tool. What I am worried about is how it acts on the emotional, social, and perceptual aspects of human existence. I question what the widespread adoption of computer technology is doing to our modes of perception and to our relationship to ourselves, to one another, and to the environment. Within professional research, the effect is becoming more noticeable every day.

In the field of professional history writing, and in virtually all of the social sciences, computer studies have become the *sine qua non* for obtaining a grant, and in some cases, professional respect. Robert Fogel and Stanley Engerman's classic work of a decade ago, *Time on the Cross*, is a case in point. Computerized data enabled the two historians to argue that the system of slavery in the American South was really part of the cash economy and thus that, in material terms, American slaves were not really an oppressed population. Several scholars subsequently challenged the way the authors used and interpreted their statistics and were able to throw the argument into serious doubt. Yet the major issue it seems to me — and some reviewers did point this out — is that there is something seriously amiss with the methodology being used, beyond the question of faulty statistical analysis. What this methodology can never capture is the experience of slavery as it was actually lived; and this can only be recaptured, if at all, through testimonial evidence. There will always be the problem of how representative any testimony is, but at least this sort of evidence is not blind to the subjective experience of daily life. As one black reviewer remarked, "there are differences between being a slave and being free, even if those distinctions cannot be analyzed by high-speed computers."[16] Yet for the most part, historians and social scientists have tended, in the ensuing decade, to *follow* the path blazed by Fogel and Engerman, rather than to realize that it is ultimately a dead end. As they move ever farther into this rarefied atmosphere of quantitative analysis, the vital subjective dimension of human life recedes from view. Attitudes, perceptions, ideologies, emotions, modes of cognition, frequently even class affiliation — none of these things is amenable to computer analysis, and as a result, they increasingly tend to get dropped from the research agenda and thus from the historical picture in general.

A good deal of historical research is now being designed with the computer in mind. The tool is thus becoming the master, rather than the servant, and in doing so it creates a very skewed version of what the historical record actually contains. Unfortunately, it is in the omitted areas I mentioned that we tend to find the real life of human beings, the locus of meaning, and the value system of a culture. As the Chilean biologist Francisco Varela once remarked, the hard sciences deal with the soft questions and the soft sciences with the hard ones.[17] The more the humanities, history, and the social and behavioural sciences succumb to the glamour and professional pull of computer analysis, the more precise they will be and, I suspect, the less they will have to say.

The popular belief about these fields is that we are learning more because we increasingly have more information available. In fact, the range of thought is actually being narrowed, because all of the information is of the same kind. In Orwell's *1984*, the goal of the state was to create a system of thought that embraced all the rest. This is what is effectively happening, albeit not through any deliberate conspiracy. The technology itself discourages any kind of thinking that jumps the rails, that is central to truly creative work; and this narrowing tendency is rapidly being incorporated into institutional procedures. Some universities in the United States are now considering the feasibility of putting the card catalogues of their libraries on computer tapes, which will do the searching for you. One university library has apparently closed its stacks to students and faculty alike, and all search and request work is done by computer terminals. The outcome should be obvious. Many scholars will tell you that their best finds have come through pure chance: they went to the stacks to locate some particular item and accidentally stumbled across a book that proved to be a revelation, that altered the entire direction of their work. The new system would make such serendipity completely impossible.

History and the social sciences are not the only disciplines that are being cyberneticized. Among other fields, ecology, biology, and clinical psychology are now being heavily influenced by a systems theory approach. The dominant trend in American ecology since the Second World War has been increasingly reductionist and managerial. The cybernetic approach is to abstract data from the organic context in the form of "bits" of information. These are then manipulated according to a set of differential equations to generate a "trajectory" for the ecosystem and plan its "rational" management. The word "ecosystem" itself comes from systems theory, having been developed to replace the older, more organic phrase, "biotic community." The cybernetic approach to resource management is perhaps exemplified by the Club of Rome, which sees the planet not as a web of life, with regional peculiarities, but as an abstract globe whose resources can and should be moved around according to ecosystem trends formulated by simulated cybernetic models. The result is the destruction of the holistic vision, or organic unity, that lies at the heart of the man-nature relationship, just as the science and technology of the modern era managed to do. This is no less a disenchantment of the world than the one referred to by Max Weber, no less a logic of domination than the one discussed by Herbert Marcuse. Waving a holistic banner here in the name of ecology is truly meaningless.[18]

Cybernetics has also made great headway in biology, and recent textbooks, as well as numerous research papers, are starting to describe living organisms as "systems of information." In his book *Algeny*, Jeremy Rifkin notes that "survival of the fittest" is being replaced by "survival of the best informed." Life itself is now described as "self-programmed activity." Rifkin warns that if a New Age is indeed dawning, it is the Age of Biotechnology, in which "cybernetics is the organizing framework . . . the computer is the organizing mechanism, and living tissue is the organizing material." What is disturbing about this, as with ecology, is that holistic thinking originally held out the promise of abolishing the fact-value distinction attacked by Marcuse and of restoring the sense of nature as being alive and sacred. Instead, just the opposite is happening. The one professional field most clearly directed to the study of life is becoming totally disembodied in its theoretical approach – a continuation of the mechanistic paradigms. "Life as information flow," writes Rifkin, "represents the final desacralization of nature."[19]

My third and last example of cybernetics come to the professions is that of clinical psychology. A genre of self-help books has appeared, designed to get the reader to induce changes in his life by thinking of himself as a cybernetic system. By and large, these books are translations of Norman Vincent Peale or Dale Carnegie into cybernetic terminology. In *Psycho-Cybernetics*, Maxwell Maltz describes the human unconscious as a "goal-striving 'servo-mechanism' " and tells his readers that they can achieve their goals by getting this mechanism to oscillate between positive and negative feedback signals. Eugene Nichols, in *The Science of Mental Cybernetics,* provides his readers with twenty-three "mental-action cards," sketches of IBM punch cards with slogans on them. Expressions like "input," "feedback," and "mental data processing" fill literally every page.[20] Although I regard all of this as somewhat amusing, and even somewhat sad, it cannot be dismissed as aberrant or even a misapplication of the cybernetic idea. It is only an *application* of the theory, not a *mis*application, for the concept of self-corrective feedback is central to all varieties of cybernetic thinking; and there is no convincing reason, from a theoretical point of view, why it should not be extended to human interaction. It is also not aberrant, because it is precisely through this sort of popular usage that a world view most effectively spreads. The same thing happened in the early modern period in Europe when clock metaphors began to appear, such as "running like clockwork" or "I'm all wound up."[21]

In a similar fashion, we now have a jargon for therapy that urges the patient to "erase old tapes" and "reprogram his consciousness" so that negative events no longer "push his buttons." Within the past few years, a whole new therapy, called neuro-linguistic programming (NLP), has arisen, which is based explicitly on a cybernetic model. It would be difficult to find a better example of disembodied consciousness, the fact-value split, desacralization of nature, and the projection of pure form than NLP. It is truly a New Age gem. The bible of the movement is significantly titled *The Structure of Magic,* by Richard Bandler and John Grinder. The authors wrote the book after observing three of the great therapists at work — Virginia Satir, Fritz Perls, and Milton Erickson — and by generating a cybernetic model of how they treated their patients. Each of these three was or is an intuitive genius, akin to Zen masters, and their talent is legendary. Bandler and Grinder broke down all of their therapeutic interactions into "bits" of information and then reassembled them into a generalized cybernetic pattern. Hence, the "structure of magic" has supposedly been distilled and scientized.[22]

The thesis here, and the authors are clear about this, is that the scientized version of the original therapy is transferable; anyone with half a brain can copy and apply it successfully. "Our purpose in this book," they write, "is to present to you an explicit Meta-model, that is, a Meta-model which is learnable." They emphasize that the model is purely formal and content-neutral and claim that this makes it universally available and universally applicable. What the authors fail to grasp is that the structure of magic is not the same thing as magic itself. Fritz Perls was able to heal people not because he was following some cybernetic formula, but because of his physical presence, his personal power. Like Erickson and Satir, Perls was a wizard. He had a genius for grasping what his patient's drama was, tricking him into a psychological dead-end around the issue, and catalyzing an emotional breakthrough. The crux of his talent was ineffable, and it was hardly a matter of technique.[23] This is what makes the whole approach of NLP so bizarre. What we have here, once again, is mechanism in updated clothing; we are not better off for having invented a "process" model of therapy.

The third realm affected by the new mythology is the philosophical. The epistemological issues are very complex; and one cannot, as Marilyn Ferguson wishes to do, lump all "process reality" thinking together. There are varieties of holism and real differences between them. Still, with very few exceptions, such as Gregory Bateson's earlier work, all of this theoretical analysis is subject to the same criticims Marcuse made of mechanistic science. Classical science and much contemporary holistic thinking, which includes cybernetic thinking, turn out to be not all that different. Both appear to be value-free, at first glance, and yet can be shown to project a *Lebenswelt*. Both generate a purely formal, abstract reality that can be bent to any situation. Both are disembodied. Cybernetic thinking, and more generally holistic thinking, does not automatically take one out of the world of Newton and Descartes, as so many holistic theoreticians claim. The cybernetic mechanism may be a more sophisticated model of reality than the clockwork model of the seventeenth century; but it is still, in the last analysis, a mechanism. Two types of holism thus have to be distinguished here. The first is a sensuous, situational, living approach to process, as the early Bateson exemplified. The other, an abstract form, is a type of "process mechanism" present in the work of many philosophical spokesmen of the New Age; it is, in a now more psychologically appealing garb, the last phase of classical science, not the beginning of a new paradigm at all. Cybernetics and general systems theory turn out to be the last outpost of the mechanical world view — a continuation of the scientific project of the seventeenth century rather than the birth of a truly new way of thinking.

As noted earlier, many examples of "holism gone astray" are available. To combat the mechanical philosophy of the past three hundred years, we now have "implicate orders," "morphogenetic fields," and "holographic paradigms," among other things. All of these notions are ingenious, and some of them may even be "true," if the word can be said to mean anything in this context; but for the most part, they are disembodied, value-free, and content-neutral. David Bohm's concept of the "implicate order" is purely formal; it deals with boundary relations, in which reality is viewed as a process that Bohm calls "enfolding" and "unfolding," or "holomovement." Similarly, Rupert Sheldrake's notion of formative causation by means of "morphogenetic fields" – a brilliant hypothesis if there ever was one – is also purely formal, as the name itself implies. It is not grounded in any concrete or sensuous reality, and it is certainly capable of being bent to any situation. It has been used thus far only in a positive sense, to explain, for example, the growth of the anti-nuclear movement in politics, successful evolutionary adaptation in biology, or the process of learning in general. Yet the same theory can be used to explain contagion, the rise of Facism, the spread of nuclear weapons, or addiction. *La Peste*, by Camus, is a perfect description of a morphogenetic field. As with classical mechanism, the theory is not able to discriminate by content. The whole world dissolves in form. Here, as with Bohm's work and that of so many other "process" thinkers, human beings somehow disappear from the picture. The whole thing becomes cosmic, a vast mental process divorced from specific physical situations. Alfred Korzybski's famous dictum, "the map is not the territory," is not without relevance here.[24]

One of the most prominent thinkers in this category – and his work is explicitly cybernetic – is Douglas Hofstadter, whose book *Godel, Escher, Bach* appeared in 1979. Hofstadter's work illustrates the general point I am making here extremely well. The book is not easy reading, for most of the text deals with the nature of mathematical paradox of the sort formulated by Zeno of Elea in the fifth century B.C. Despite its density, the book has been lionized, selling hundreds of thousands of copies and winning Hofstadter the Pulitzer Prize and a spot as a regular columnist for *Scientific American*. As I plowed my way through it, I began to have an uncomfortable feeling: the book had no real content. It was all about puzzles and tautologies, designed to show that everything in our world, including the subjective concept of "I", was essentially symbolic patterned activity. Reality somehow disappeared from its pages. Everything was programming; the whole world had turned into artificial intelligence. I began to sense in Hofstadter a kind of computer jockey who got so fascinated by cybernetic operations that he decided they could and should be extended to the entire world.

There is a scene in the film *War Games* (1983) in which the young whiz kid, who has accidentally tripped into the Pentagon terminal and is busy simulating nuclear war on his home computer while the Joint Chiefs of Staff are actually preparing to bomb Russia, asks his machine: "Is this a game, or is it real?" His computer replies: "What's the difference?" As John Searle pointed out in a review of Hofstadter's second book, *The Mind's I* (co-authored with Daniel Dennett), this simple point has been lost on Hofstadter. You can, says Searle, get a computer to print out the words "I am thirsty"; but no one in his right mind would attempt to pour a glass of water into the machine as a result. Plainly put, Hofstadter's brand of holism is completely out of touch with reality.[25]

I heard Hofstadter speak in 1981 at an East Coast university where I was then teaching. The turnout was so great that the overflow had to be siphoned off into a room with closed-circuit television. Hofstadter spoke for ninety minutes, and it was vintage stuff: what Achilles said to the tortoise and other Zenonian brain-twisters. Like *Godel, Escher, Bach*, the talk was rich in form and devoid of content. I was, that year, teaching a course on the historical relations between holistic and mechanistic thought, and so some of the students in that class came up to me after the talk and wanted to know what I thought. "Well," I said, "I'd be curious to know what Dr. Hofstadter thinks dreams are." To my surprise, one of my students took off, elbowed his way through the enormous crowd that surrounded Hofstadter, and came back within ten minutes. "I asked him," he said, panting for breath. "He told me that dreams were confused brain programs." I will not repeat my reaction to this bit of cybernetic wisdom, but suggest only that one contemplate this: more than eighty years after Freud's *The Interpretation of Dreams*, nearly seventy years after Jung's *Psychology of the Unconscious*, and millennia after the Greeks, the Egyptians, the Essenes, and aboriginal peoples from all over the planet recognized the value of dream symbolism for human life, a leading spokesman of the cybernetic age is telling his audience that dreams are "confused brain programs." I wonder if the language of the body is also, for Hofstadter, a type of confused programming, and whether he finds animal and plant life disorganized and in need of cybernetic management. One has to ponder what it means in the history of a civilization when a thinker of this sort can come to be regarded as a man of penetrating insight, a mind truly to be reckoned with.

I am not categorically opposed to holistic thinking. Far from it. I wrote a whole book arguing that mechanism had no philosophical future, and I still believe that. My point is that the real issue, ultimately, is not mechanism versus holism, but whether any philosophical system contains an intrinsic ethic – and not a value-free one – and whether it is a truly embodied approach to the world. On these grounds, mechanism would seem to be disqualified, as Marcuse so effectively argued. The holistic case is not so simple, however; there is holism and there is holism. In *The Reenchantment of the World*, I argued that the magical tradition is reviving in a way that is scientifically credible. It is precisely this impulse that underlies the research of David Bohm and Rupert Sheldrake, and from that point of view, their work is definitely worthy of our attention and respect. Such thinkers are quite literally the modern equivalents of Descartes and Newton; they recognize that the old paradigm is crumbling, and they are out to construct a new one. What I am concerned about is that the magic will somehow get left behind in the process. By "magic" here I do not mean sticking pins in dolls; I mean the affective, concrete, and sensual experience of life. The paradigm I have in mind would be grounded in the real behaviour of man in the environment. It would incorporate the sort of information that arises from our dream life, our bodies, and our relationship to plants, animals, and natural cycles. Moreover, I am absolutely convinced that this paradigm would usher in a profoundly creative and liberated period in the history of the West. Unfortunately, most holistic thinking today, and certainly that of the cybernetic variety, is moving in a very different direction. In the name of enlightenment, we are getting reification; we are drifting into a hall of mirrors. What is being lost, in all three of the areas I discussed, is any sense of unmediated reality,[26] as is celebrated in Japanese haiku or which comes to us through dreams, through body awareness, or through any extended experience with nature. Instead, we are now moving toward a world of pure metaphor, "programming," "patterned activity," what one writer has called "mysticism without a soul."[27] "Mysticism without flesh" might be more accurate.

Yet I do not believe this tendency is inevitable. In the philosophical and professional domains, at least, we might conceivably be able to exercise some epistemological restraint. Cybernetic thinking does not have to be disembodied and formulistic. In his book *The Gift*, Lewis Hyde cites the example of a gift-giving ceremony among the Maori of New Zealand that reveals a cybernetic structure, but Hyde is well aware that the power of this structure is derived from its actual embodiment in a concrete situation: a history, a tradition, a gestalt that is felt to be alive by those who participate in it.[28] Paul Ryan, the American video artist and author of the book *Cybernetics of the Sacred*,[29] once put it to me this way: God is Relationship. By "relationship" he did not mean a set of abstract relata, but a practice, a praxis, a living and embodied reality. There *are* no "circuits," there *are* no "feedback loops"; all that is fantasy. To think such things exist apart from real situations is a Neoplatonic dream; it is to fall into what Alfred North Whitehead called the "fallacy of misplaced concreteness." The French philosopher Maurice Merleau-Ponty recognized this tendency as early as 1960 and wrote the following in his essay "Eye and Mind":

> Thinking "operationally" has become a sort of absolute artificialism, such as we see in the ideology of cybernetics, where human creations are derived from a natural information process, itself conceived on the model of human machines. If this kind of thinking were to extend its reign to man and history; if, *pretending to ignore what we know of them through our own situations*, it were to set out to construct man and history on the basis of a few abstract indices . . . then, since man really becomes the *manipulandum* he takes himself to be, we enter into a cultural regimen where there is neither truth nor falsity concerning man and history, into a sleep, or a nightmare, from which there is no awakening.
>
> Scientific thinking . . . must return to . . . the soil of the sensible and opened world such as it is in our life and for our body — not that possible body which we may legitimately think of as an information machine *but that actual body I call mine*, this sentinel standing quietly at the command of my words and of my acts.[30] (Emphasis added.)

We are at a crossroads now, and it is a crucial one, for this is the heart of the mythological shift I have been discussing. In our eagerness to reject the mechanistic science of the past three hundred years, we need to be wary of what we are replacing it with. The thing to ask of any new philosophical statement, any extension of computer hardware into schools, universities, or therapists' offices, and of any new toys such as Pac-Man or Apple II, is only this: does it take me into the things I fear most, and wish to avoid, or does it make it easy for me to hide, to run away from them? Does it enable me to shut out the environment, ignore politics, remain unaware of my dream life, my sexuality, and my relations with other people, or does it shove these into my face and teach me how to live with them and through them? If the answer to the latter is yes, then I suggest that we are on the right track. If the answer to the former is yes, then it is my guess, as Merleau-Ponty says, that we are sinking into a sleep from which, in the name of enlightenment itself, there will be no easy awakening.

Notes

1.   Theodore Roszak, *The Making of a Counter Culture*
        (Garden City, N.Y.: Doubleday, 1969), p. 215.

2.   Edmund Husserl, *The Crisis of European Sciences and
        Transcendental Phenomenology*, trans. David Carr
        (Evanston, Ill: Northwestern University Press, 1970);
        Martin Heidegger, *The Question Concerning Technology,
        and Other Essays*, trans. William Lovitt (New York:
        Garland, 1977); and Karl Mannheim, *Ideology and Utopia*,
        trans. Louis Wirth and Edward Shils (New York:
        Harcourt, Brace and World, reprint of 1936 edition). It
        should be noted that Heidegger made strict distinctions
        between the categories of Being, technology, and scientific
        truth, and it might be argued that Roszak and others
        tended to confuse them. It was one of Heidegger's
        students, however, Herbert Marcuse (see below), who was
        able to show that although these categories might be
        philosophically distinguishable, they were not really
        separable; and that in actual practice, they easily got
        scrambled. Thus Marcuse argued, for example, that
        scientific truth as it developed in the seventeenth century
        actually had a technological *a priori*, or hidden
        technological agenda; and that by the twentieth century,
        this had largely come to define Being in Western
        industrial societies.
            The later notebooks of Wittgenstein reveal his
        perplexity with the "grammar of theology" versus the logic
        of science, and the inability to establish the
        epistemological superiority of the latter. For a general
        overview of the Frankfurt School see Martin Jay, *The
        Dialectical Imagination* (Boston: Little, Brown, 1973). As
        for the "externalist" school in the history of science, there
        is a large literature in this genre, but the classic studies
        probably remain those of Robert Merton and Edgar Zilsel,
        done in the 1930s and 1940s. See also the essays in Hugh
        F. Kearney, ed., *Origins of the Scientific Revolution*
        (London: Longmans, Green, 1964).

3.   Herbert Marcuse, *One-Dimensional Man* (Boston: Beacon
        Press, 1966), esp. chap. 6.

4.   For a more extended discussion of this, see chap. 3 of my
        The Reenchantment of the World (Ithaca, N.Y.: Cornell

University Press, 1981). Descriptions of magical practice can be found in various works by the early twentieth-century British occultist Dion Fortune (Violet Firth). A more recent text is David Conway, *Ritual Magic* (New York: E.P. Dutton, 1972).

5.   On Soviet and American research into the paranormal, see Michael Rossman, *New Age Blues* (New York: E.P. Dutton, 1979), pp. 167-260, and Ronald M. McRae, *Mind Wars: The True Story of Government Research into the Military Potential of Psychic Weapons* (New York: St Martin's Press, 1984).

6.   See, for example, Firtijof Capra, *The Tao of Physics* (Boulder, Colo.: Shambhala, 1975); Gary Zukav, *The Dancing Wu Li Masters* (New York: William Morrow, 1979); or Itzhak Bentov, *Stalking the Wild Pendulum* (New York: E.P. Dutton, 1977).

7.   Gregory Bateson, *Steps to an Ecology of Mind* (New York: Ballantine, 1972).

8.   Gregory Bateson, *Mind and Nature: A Necessary Unity* (New York: E.P. Dutton, 1979).

9.   Gregory Bateson, "Men Are Grass: Metaphor and the World of Mental Process," 9 June 1980, published by the Lindisfarne Press. I have tended, in this paper, to blur the distinction between the concepts "value-free" and "disembodied." (Marcuse, it seems to me, does this as well.) Strictly speaking, they are not the same thing Bateson's later work was certainly disembodied, but it was never value-free. His concept of "circuitry," for example, or of "Mind" (capital "M"), both of which he took from cybernetic theory, essentially added up to what in certain Eastern religious traditions is called "karma," a kind of non-linear law of cause and effect. On this reasoning, the universe is not value-free, but rather is suffused with a pattern that is self-defining or reflexive. Meaning is thus built into the system. In actual practice, however, a disembodied system can easily take on a purely formal character and fall into the "value-free" camp; and I discuss the susceptibility of Bateson's work, and of holistic/cybernetic thinking in general, to this tendency in chapter 9 of *The Reenchantment of the World*. Another

way to see this distinction is to examine the difference between the magical tradition and Aristotelianism. Formally, a *telos* is definitely present in the Aristotelian world view, and meaning — for example, the concept of natural place and motion — is embedded in the universe. Natural place and motion are, furthermore, very much a part of the occult tradition and fall into the category of "sympathy," the theory that "like knows like," a notion present in Orphic and Greek shamanic traditions and in the writings of some of the pre-Socratic. Aristotle, in fact, may in some way represent the intellectualizing of this tradition, following the pattern of Plato's "inversion" of occult sources (on this see E.R. Dodds, *The Greeks and the Irrational* [Berkeley: University of California Press, 1951 –]). The problem is that once the living tradition gets disembodied, the system is still technically endowed with meaning or value, but only in an abstract sense. In actual practice, the purely formal aspect comes to the fore, and Marcuse wrestles with this in *One-Dimensional Man* (pp. 137-39, 147), saying that it is a precursor or anticipation of seventeenth-century science.

This same tension lies at the heart of the problem with Bateson's legacy. To put it succinctly, the early Bateson was an alchemist, the later Bateson an Aristotelian. All of his work, as I have noted, was "value-laden," but the disembodied character of the later work turned it into a kind of cybernetic catechism, and thus, in practice, it would seem to be as instrumentalist as the mechanism of the seventeenth century.

10. Marilyn Ferguson, *The Aquarian Conspiracy* (Los Angeles: J.P. Tarcher, 1980); David Bohm, *Wholeness and the Implicate Order* (London: Routledge & Kegan Paul, 1980); Douglas Hofstadter, *Godel, Escher, Bach* (New York: Basic Books, 1979); Rupert Sheldrake, *A New Science of Life* (Los Angeles: J.P. Tarcher, 1981). Ken Wilber is the author of several works, recently published, including *The Spectrum of Consciousness*, *Up From Eden*, and *The Atman Project*. Wilber is, however, critical of certain aspects of "new paradigm" thought; see Ken Wilber, ed., *The Holographic Paradigm* (Boulder, Colo. Shambhala, 1982), pp. 157-86, 249-94.

11. Ginzburg develops this theme very effectively in *The Cheese and the Worms* (Baltimore, Md.: Johns Hopkins

University Press, 1980), and more recently in *The Night Battles* (Baltimore, Md.: Johns Hopkins University Press, 1983); both books translated by John and Anne Tedeschi.

12. "Addicted to video games? It's Vidanon to the rescue," *Victoria Times-Colonist* (British Columbia), 8 Oct. 1983; from an article in the *Los Angeles Times*.

13. This figure was given by Edward Lias of Sperry Univac Corporation at a conference entitled "Future Mind," University of South Florida, Tampa, 14-16 Apr. 1983.

14. Ibid.

15. "Computer Harm to Children," *San Francisco Chronicle*, 26 Dec. 1983.

16. Robert W. Fogel and Stanley L. Engerman, *Time on the Cross*, 2 vols. (Boston: Little, Brown, 1974); review quoted is by N.I. Huggins, writing in *Commonweal*, vol. 100 (23 Aug. 1974), p. 459. For an update of the debate, see "Historian Calls for 'New Moral Indictment' of Slavery," *The Chronicle of Higher Education*, vol. 27 (11 Jan. 1984), pp. 7, 12.

17. At a conference entitled "Andere Wirlichkeiten" (Other Realities), Alpbach, Austria, 7-11 Sept. 1983. For a holistic paradigm which I believe differs from the models being criticized in this essay, see Humberto Maturana and Francisco Varela, *Autopoiesis and Cognition* (Dordrecht, Holland: D. Reidel, 1980). At the Alpbach conference, Varela frequently emphasized the importance of a holism that did not leave human beings out of the picture.

18. "Cybernetic ecology" is discussed by Carolyn Merchant in *The Death of Nature* (New York: Harper & Row, 1980), pp. 103, 238- 39, 252, 291. For the Club of Rome report, see Donella H. Meadows et al., eds., *Limits to Growth*, 2d ed. (New York: Universe Books, 1974).

19. Jeremy Rifkin, *Algeny* (New York: Viking Press, 1983), esp. pp. 191, 213, 221, 228. For a good example of a biology textbook in the cybernetic genre, see Lila Gatlin, *Information Theory and the Living System* (New York: Columbia University Press, 1972).

20. Maxwell Maltz, *Psycho-Cybernetics* (New York: Pocket Books, 1969); R. Eugene Nichols, *The Science of Mental Cybernetics* (New York: Warner Books, 1971).

21. For some interesting examples of this see the *Oxford English Dictionary* under the entry for "clock." Miners began to describe the direction of veins of ore as "lying at 9 (or whatever) o'clock"; W. Fenner, in *Christ's Alarm* (1650), says you must wind up your conscience every day "as a man does his clock."

22. On this and the following, see Richard Bandler and John Grinder, *The Structure of Magic, Part I* (Palo Alto, Calif.: Science and Behavior Books, 1975), esp. pp. 18-19, 158. For an example of *body* therapy reduced to cybernetic terms, see Yochanon Rywerwant, *The Feldenkrais Method: Teaching by Handling* (New York: Harper & Row, 1983). I am grateful to Mr. Brian Lynn for pointing these works out to me and for the helpful discussions we had on current trends in New Age "therapy."

23. "True magic works," writes Father Sylvan, "through the phenomenon of resonance. One must know the exact words to say and one must say them in exactly the right place and the right time . . . " (Jacob Needleman, *Lost Christianity* [New York: Bantam Books, 1982], p. 87).

24. On Sheldrake and Bohm see note 10 and also Renee Weber, "The Enfolding-Unfolding Universe: A Conversation with David Bohm, " in Ken Wilber, ed., *The Holographic Paradigm*, pp. 44-104. For an example of morphogenetic fields applied to the political (anti- nuclear) sphere, see Ken Keyes, Jr., *The Hundredth Monkey* (Coos Bay, Oreg.: Vision Books, 1982). Korzybski's statement was first given in *Science and Sanity*, published in 1933, and is repeated in the works of many other writers, including Gregory Bateson.

    I raised the issue of the ethical neutrality of the implicate order with Professor Bohm, and he subsequently wrote to say that in its simplest formulation, the implicate order was indeed value- free. He has successfully dealt with that issue, at least, in a forthcoming paper, "Soma-Significance: A New Notion of the Relationship between the Physical and the Mental," and I am grateful to him for sending me a copy of the manuscript version of his essay. The paper essentially argues that the implicate order, and in fact, the entire universe, has meaning (or value) embedded in it, in an intrinsic fashion, and that an improper ethic introduces destructive elements that destabilize the system as a whole. Although there are some very important, and novel, insights in this essay, it seems to me on the whole to be very similar to the ethics and epistemology developed by Gregory Bateson: a cybernetic, self-referential world in which violations of the homeostatic order (the network of Minds and Sub-Minds) can be regarded as evil or insane. This certainly takes it out of the value-free category; yet the whole approach is reminiscent of Bateson's later work. That is, despite frequent references to "soma" in Professor Bohm's discussion, the mode of analysis has a purely cerebral or disembodied quality to it; or at least, that is how I read it. See the earlier discussion of Bateson (above) and note 9.

25. Douglas R. Hofstadter and Daniel C. Dennett, *The Mind's I* (New York: Basic Books, 1981); John R. Searle, "The Myth of the Computer," *New York Review of Books*, vol. 29 (29 Apr. 1982), pp. 3-6.

26. Strictly speaking, this is not true of such games as Pac-Man. Addictions do provide unmediated experience because of their absorbing intensity. The problem, of course, is that the world in which the addict is absorbed is unreal, and thus the pattern is one that might be termed "pseudo-holistic." Bateson discusses this in his essay "The Cybernetics of 'Self': A Theory of Alcoholism" (reprinted in *Steps to an Ecology of Mind*).

27. Father Sylvan, in Needleman, *Lost Christianity*, p. 140. Cf. Murray Bookchin's comments on the whole issue in "Sociobiology or Social Ecology, Part II," *Harbinger*, vol. 1, no. 2 (Fall 1983), pp. 28-38.
    Not all criticism of artificial intelligence, I am happy to report, comes from traditional "humanistic" quarters. Joseph Weizenbaum, one of the pioneers of artificial intelligence, has had some serious reservations about the field and its alienating tendencies. He has discussed this in a review of a book entitled *The Fifth Generation*, by Edward Feigenbaum and Pamela McCorduck, which argues that artificial intelligence is indispensable to all

spheres of life. In this review (*New York Review of Books*, vol. 30, no. 16 [27 Oct. 1983], pp. 58-62), Professor Weizenbaum writes: "The knowledge that appears to be least well understood by Edward Feigenbaum and Pamela McCorduck is that of the differences between information, knowledge, and wisdom, between calculating, reasoning, and thinking, and finally of the differences between a society centered on human beings and one centered on machines."

28. Lewis Hyde, *The Gift* (New York: Vintage Books, 1979), pp. 17-19.

29. Paul Ryan, *Cybernetics of the Sacred* (Garden City, N.Y.: Doubleday Anchor, 1974).

30. Maurice Merleau-Ponty, "Eye and Mind," trans. Carleton Dallery, in James M. Edie, ed., *The Primacy of Perception* (Evanston, Ill.: Northwestern University Press, 1964), pp. 160-61.

COMPUTERS AND EDUCATION
IN THE TWENTY-FIRST CENTURY

PATRICK SUPPES

Historical Perspectives

To put into historical perspective the great educational innovations of the past, we can identify five major technological innovations comparable to the current computer revolution: written records, libraries, printing, mass schooling, and testing.

Written Records

The first major educational innovation was the introduction of written records in ancient times for teaching. We do not know exactly when the use of written records for instructional purposes began, but we do have, as early as Plato's *Dialogues* written in the fifth century B.C., sophisticated objections to the use of written records.

Today no one would doubt the value of written material in education, but there were strong and cogent objections to this earliest innovation in education. The objections were these: a written record is impersonal; it is very uniform; it does not adapt to the individual student; it does not establish rapport with the student. Socrates and the Sophists, the tutors of students in ancient Athens, objected to introducing written records and destroying the essential personal relation between student and tutor.

It has become a familiar story in our own time that a technological innovation has side effects that are not always uniformly beneficial. It is important to recognize that this is not a new aspect of innovation but has been with us from the beginning.

Libraries

The second innovation was the founding of libraries in the ancient world, the most important example being the famous Alexandrian Library established around 300 B.C. Because of certain democratic traditions and the preeminence of the creative work in philosophy and poetry, it is easy to think of Athens as the

137

intellectual centre of the Hellenic world. In fact, that centre was Alexandria. From about 250 B.C. to 400 A.D. not only was Alexandria the most important centre of mathematics and astronomy in the ancient world, it was also a major centre of literature, especially because of the collection in the Alexandrian Library. The first critical literary scholarship in the Western world – the editing of texts, the analysis of style, and the compiling of bibliographies – took place in the Alexandrian Library. This revolution in education consisted not simply of having in one place a large number of papyrus manuscripts but in the organization of large bodies of learning. Scholars from all over the Western world came to Alexandria to study and to talk to others.

Substantial libraries existed also in other major cities of the ancient Mediterranean cultures and in China, India, and Korea.

Printing

The third innovation of great historical importance in education was the move from written records to printed books. In the West, the printing of the Gutenberg Bible in 1452 marks the beginning date of this innovation. It is important to recognize, however, that block printing was used extensively in Korea and China three or four hundred years earlier. Nearly half a millennium later, it is difficult to have a vivid sense of how important the innovation of printing turned out to be. No more than five major libraries existed in the ancient world of the Mediterranean. In 100 B.C., the Alexandrian Library had few competitors; it was impossible for many copies of manuscripts to be reproduced when all copying had to be done tediously by hand. The introduction of printing in the fifteenth century produced a radical innovation – indeed, a revolution – in the distribution of intellectual and educational materials. By the middle of the sixteenth century, not only European institutions but wealthy families as well had large libraries.

Once again, however, there were definite technological side effects that were not uniformly beneficial. Those who know the art and the beauty of the mediaeval manuscripts that preceded the introduction of printing can appreciate that mass printing was regarded by some as a degradation of the art of reproduction.

It is also important to have a sense of how slow the effect of a technological innovation can sometimes be. Not until the end of the eighteenth century were books used extensively for teaching in schools. In arithmetic, for example, most teachers continued to use oral methods throughout the nineteenth century; appropriate elementary textbooks in mathematics were not available until the beginning of the present century. Fortunately, the scale of dissemination in the modern world is of an entirely different order from what it was in the past. Perhaps my favourite example is the estimate that it took more than five years for the news of Julius Caesar's assassination to reach the farthest corners of the Roman Empire. Today such an event would be known throughout the world in a matter of minutes.

It was not unusual for methods of recitation to be used in the elementary school until the nineteenth century; the same was true at some universities. According to at least one account, the last professor at Cambridge University in England who insisted on following the recitative tradition, which dates back to the Middle Ages, was C.D. Broad. As late as the 1940s, he dictated and then repeated each sentence so that students would have adequate time to write it down exactly as dictated.

Mass Schooling

The fourth innovation, and again one that we now accept as a complete and natural part of our society, is mass schooling. We have a tendency in talking about our society to put schools and families into the same category of major institutions, but there is a great psychological difference between the status of the family and the status of schools. The family is an integral part of our culture. The evidence that families in one form or another have been our most important cultural unit goes back thousands of years. Schools are, by contrast, a recent innovation in our culture. In 1870, for example, only 2 per cent of young people graduated from high school in the United States. One hundred years before that, only a very small percentage finished even third or fourth grade.

In most of the world, less than 1 per cent of the population completed secondary school as recently as fifty years ago. During the upheavals of the "cultural revolution" in China, the elementary schools, as well as colleges and secondary schools, were closed for several years. In contemporary North American society, closing elementary schools for such a period of time is unthinkable. From a Chinese historical perspective, however, it was not such an important matter; for Chinese culture extends back continuously several thousand years, and there is in that cultural tradition no salient place for mass schooling. In many developing countries today the best that can be hoped is that the majority of young people will receive four years of elementary school education. Until population growth is controlled, it will take all available resources to achieve that much.

The position of the United States as a world leader in education is sometimes not adequately recognized, though U.S. leadership in creating a society with mass education is one of the most important aspects of American influence in the world. As recently as the late nineteenth century, the British philosopher John Stuart Mill despaired of democracy's ever working anywhere in the world for one reason — it was simply not possible, he believed, to educate the majority of the population. In his view, it was not possible to have a significant percentage of the population able to read and do arithmetic. The revolution in mass schooling is one of the most striking phenomena of the twentieth century.

Testing

The fifth educational innovation is testing, which is in many ways older than the concept of mass schooling. The great tradition of testing was first established in China; testing there began in the fifth century A.D. and became firmly entrenched by the twelfth century A.D. Tests were used continuously from the twelfth century through the nineteenth century in the selection of mandarins, the civil servants who ran the imperial government of China. The civil service positions held by mandarins were regarded as the elite social positions in the society. The literature of various periods attests to the importance of these tests in Chinese society. In examining the literature of the fifteenth or sixteenth century, for example, one is impressed by the concern expressed over performance on tests. Literary tales often focused on the question whether sons would successfully complete the tests and what this would mean for the family. (In those days women had no place in the management of the society and no place as applicants for civil service positions.) The procedures of selection were as rigorous as those found in a contemporary medical school or a graduate school of business in the United States or Canada. In many periods, fewer than 2 per cent of those who began the tests, which were arranged in a complicated hierarchy, successfully completed the sequence and were put on the list of eligible mandarins.

Although the history of testing goes back hundreds of years, in many ways it is proper to regard it as a twentieth-century innovation. Scientific and technical study of tests began only in this century, with a serious effort to understand and to define what constitutes a good test for a given aptitude, a given achievement, or a given skill.

The five innovations I have discussed — written records, libraries, printing, mass schooling, and tests — are the very fabric of our educational system today. It is almost impossible to contemplate a modern educational system without each of these innovations playing an important part.

Of these five technologies, the effect of none was adequately forecast at the time of introduction. Of course, a few individuals foresaw some of the consequences and had something to say about them, but the details were not accurately foreseen. No doubt the same will prove true of technologies now developing.

What Computers Offer

What I have to say about the use of computers in education in the twenty-first century will also probably fall in the category of inaccurate prognostication. The technology and its applications are changing too quickly for one to make accurate predictions for the next century. In a certain sense, it is easier to talk about the computers that will exist one hundred years from now than about those of the next twenty years; it is reasonable to assume that any technical problem we have today will have disappeared or have been so radically transformed by 2085 that there is little use in trying to foresee the exact configuration of solutions. I shall try, therefore, to create a general picture for the hundred-year prediction and leave it to the reader to interpolate for the dates between.

The argument for computers having a central role in education one hundred years from now is the same as the classic argument for hiring the services of a tutor in ancient Athens. The computer, like the tutor, it is argued, adapts instruction to the idiosyncratic characteristics of a single pupil and interacts with the pupil.

In addition to this argument for individualism, I shall pursue the expected arguments about the accessibility of information and about the augmentation of technical skills. These are in essence very curriculum-oriented topics. I shall then move to the broader institutional setting of education and the way in which I think it will be transformed.

Individualization

It is both vivid and accurate to think of the model of a tutor in ancient Athens, but it is not sufficiently conceptual or abstract. What are the arguments for the individualized instruction computers can offer? First, and above all, computers offer immediate attention to individual responses. Second, computers can correct these responses and convey information about their character, especially when the student's answers are incorrect. Third, computers can adapt the pace of instruction in delicate and subtle ways to the individual student's pace of learning. Relatively simple computer systems can give us these three features, together with the virtue of the student's actively participating as opposed to passively listening.

About one hundred years from now we expect from computers something more like what we expect from sophisticated tutors. First of all, and of greatest importance in the Greek conception of instruction, is dialogue between tutor and student. Plato's *Dialogues* are not really good models of instruction but are meant to serve a different purpose. Socrates is always talking, and others are giving relatively short answers; good instructional dialogue should feature much more talking by the student and listening by the tutor. Listening by computers is very undeveloped, but there is no reason to think that the present formidable technical problems of constructing good listening computers will not be solved in the next hundred years. Good instructional computers should, above all, be good listeners; but they also need to be good talkers, for the young learn how to talk by listening to talk.

The problem of designing instructional programs for computers that can conduct intelligent dialogue with students is not primarily the technical problem of understanding spoken English or any other natural language. The real problem is understanding how to conduct a dialogue. All of us are used to conversation, and some of us are capable of good instructional conversation as well; but we do it naturally, without really understanding how we do it. The theory of dialogue is as yet undeveloped and must certainly be high on the agenda of future instructional theory. Very likely we will have good instructional dialogue by computer in many areas without fully understanding how the programs have been built. I have great confidence that in a hundred years we shall have computers that do an excellent job of giving tutorial instruction in a wide variety of subjects. It is important to emphasize that good interactive instruction, of the kind we expect from a good tutor, could in some respects be rather limited and still be effective. That is, one does not have to be a marvel of psychological understanding, wit, and rhetorical elegance to do a first-class job of teaching another person physical optics, organic chemistry, or the classical economic theory of the marketplace.

Our ambitions for good computer instruction will not stop with the phenomenological features of a good tutor; we want more. We want good instructional programs also to have a good cognitive model of the student and his learning problems. A good tutor intuitively has a sense of what is going on in the head of the student, but ordinarily a good tutor does not have an explicit cognitive theory of how the student is solving problems and why he is getting stuck in his problem-solving efforts. Some aspects of the process seem extraordinarily mysterious, but we should be able to make significant progress on such a cognitive model even if some questions still exist a century from now.

Finally, a good tutor is also able to motivate a student, to make the student want to continue learning. We do not now know all that we need to know about motivation, and again there is no reason to think that we will solve all the mysteries in a hundred years; but we will be able to understand matters much better than we do now. In fact, I often like to draw the parallel to physical and musical skills. Even though we do not theoretically understand students' motivation in learning physical skills or in performing music, in many cases we do seem to be much better at providing proper motivation to make a serious effort. In the next hundred years, our understanding of how to motivate the exercise of cognitive skills should begin to catch up with our practical methods for motivating the development of physical and musical skills.

There is an important point to make about this rather abstract discussion of dialogue between tutor and student, cognitive models, and motivation. We can very well put this analysis in the framework of general problems of education, but I want to emphasize that I see particular headway being made on these important problems just because of the availability of sophisticated computers. We shall have both the means and the challenge to develop instructional techniques far beyond anything that we have done thus far, because of what will be available to us as rich resources for the best possible sort of individualization.

Accessibility of Information

The transformation of learning that will take place because of the increased accessibility of information will be greater than that which occurred with the creation of the Alexandrian Library more than 2,000 years ago. Scholars of the ancient world properly stood in awe of the resources at Alexandria. The kinds of resources that were brought together there in one place will be available through computers in every nook and cranny of the land. The greatest potential effect of this availability of information by electronic means is the decentralization of our society, a topic that I shall examine at greater length later in this essay.

Augmented Technical Skills

We are all familiar with the kinds of problems that can be tackled with current computers that were simply out of reach even thirty or forty years ago. These problems range from massive computations about the weather to linear models applied to every sort of problem from medicine to economics. Students in undergraduate classes now routinely perform numerical calculations that were unheard of thirty or forty years ago and that were impossible fifty or sixty years ago. Such numerical power will continue to increase, but what is at least as important is that the number-crunching computers of today will be joined by the symbol-crunching computers of tomorrow. We shall expect symbolic analysis at our fingertips, whether it be applied to the structure of DNA, to a complicated mathematical equation that has to be transformed, or to a mathematical proof that needs completion of its combinatorial parts. We shall become, both in instruction and research, as dependent on symbol crunchers as we now are in many parts of science on number crunchers. The effect of these two in combination will be to augment our technical skills, and the sophisticated instruction we expect in technical skills, far beyond anything we have seen up to the present. There is some reason to think that scientific development in many disciplines will become increasingly complex. A thesis that science will keep unifying and keep simplifying is, in my judgement, much more a romantic hope than a conclusion supported by the actual development of science over the past fifty years. If my view is at all close to the truth, the problems of instruction will become ever more difficult. We will need every possible resource to augment our technical skills, and computers will be by far and away the most important means for doing so.

Changes in the Institutional Framework of Education

Even harder than forecasting the developments in computers for instruction is forecasting the ways radically new information technology will change the institutional framework of education. These projections about the distant future (which may, of course, in 2085 be seen to have been mere fantasy) I have organized into three parts: first, the elementary and secondary schools, or what will be their equivalent; second, post-secondary education divided into college and continuing education; and, third, future education in the home.

Elementary Schools

Elementary schools have the greatest stability of any of our educational institutions. They are the most widespread and will, I think, remain the closest to their current appearance a century from now. I believe that the greatest agent for uniform socialization in the world is the first-grade classroom. These classrooms are everywhere remarkably the same. A teacher is in charge of twenty to forty-five youngsters ranging in age from five to eight years, and the curriculum in most first grades emphasizes reading, arithmetic, and the beginning skills of writing.

Elementary schools may well change in two major ways by 2085. First, there will be a tendency toward decentralization and teaching in smaller groups. Even when the schools have several hundred children, as they do now, the ratio of students to teachers should decrease. It is one of the ironies of North American education that the student-teacher ratio is greater in the elementary school than in the secondary school in almost every school system; if any conclusion can be drawn from diverse research on this question, it is that the smaller class sizes should be for the younger children, not the older ones. This insight will, I think, gradually come to have some force in the span of a hundred years. There is no reason we should not have a student-teacher ratio of ten to one, rather than the current ratio in North America of approximately twenty to one. A second aspect that will help this ratio is the declining birth rate; children will be seen as even more important and deserving of even more attention than is the case today.

The second main change will be the vast array of information technology available to the teacher. Much of the routine instruction in reading, writing, and arithmetic can first be given by computer. The teacher can be there to keep a close eye on the sources of difficulty, to reassure and to help the child that is having momentary emotional or cognitive problems, and to engage in that free flow of talk between adult and child that is so important for the sophisticated development of children. The purpose of the computer technology will be to relieve the teacher of onerous routine and to free him or her for more focused attention to individual youngsters. Above all, I emphasize, there should be no sense of competition between the technology and the teacher, just as there is no competition between books and teaching staff. The computer technology is there to help, not to hinder, the education of the child.

The introduction of computer technology in the elementary school will permit teachers to give attention to the individual history of learning and of learning difficulties of each child, attention that is simply not possible today. The teacher will be given resources and immediate analyses to help in overcoming the difficulties of individual children. The technology will also be there to make rapid progress possible for those students who feel squelched by the uniform regime of the group moving together through a given curriculum. The student who can go quickly in one subject, be it reading or mathematics, will be permitted to forge ahead; the technology will provide all the tools for exceptional progress, and the teacher will be trained to encourage the student. We know from individual testimony how much certain gifted individuals have learned by the age of twelve or so, mainly because of the extraordinary personal environment in which they happened to be placed. It should be an item high on the agenda of education for the twenty-first century to provide that kind of rich environment for every gifted student. Let us remember also that being gifted does not mean being gifted in every respect. For almost all students, as John Dewey pointed out many years ago, there will be areas in which their gifts shine forth, and they should be encouraged to develop them as rapidly and as thoroughly as possible. Technology above all can help do this.

Secondary Schools
Technology should be used to decentralize secondary schools that are too large, too bureaucratic, and socially too complicated. The move from the little red school house of the nineteenth century to the comprehensive high school of the twentieth century is one of the great triumphs of mass schooling and an educational achievement that will have a permanent place in the history of education, but it is time now to move on to new opportunities and better things. We are in a position to return to the analogue of the little red school house because we can bring to the decentralized secondary school of fifty, one hundred, or two hundred students all of the educational resources that have been the glory of the comprehensive high school. It is important to emphasize my claim. The only real reason not to decentralize the large secondary schools of today is the problem of providing sufficiently individualized instruction, in this case, individualized subject matter, so that one student can study calculus, another photography, and another auto mechanics. I am not trying to say what the diversity will be. We currently tend to emphasize basic academic subjects in high school, but whether that will be the case in one hundred years is difficult to say. We will have the technical capacity to decentralize, to bring

to small teaching units any degree of diversity desired in instruction. A secondary school for a hundred students could have stored library resources equal to the current Library of Congress, the largest library in the world. The problem will not be having the resources; the problem will be understanding how to use them. We will need sophisticated instructional programs to guide the students and to help them learn the great range of possible subjects that may engage them.

There are also strong economic arguments for decentralizing secondary schools. A hundred years from now, it will be even more evident than it is today that moving information is much more economical than moving people. Schools will be close to where adolescents live. Teachers will be like tutors, but not like the tutors in ancient Athens in that they will not carry the full load of instruction. Teachers in secondary schools will be counselors and trouble shooters, not just counselors about future careers or emotional problems, but cognitive counselors, able to help when a student has not found the right mix or the right approach to instruction in the wealth of technological offerings. The demands on teachers will be greater than they are now. They will need to be more professional and more thoroughly trained, and they should be paid much better than they are now. The teachers needed for the technological setting of the secondary school in 2085 must be technically expert and intellectually sophisticated. They should be compensated accordingly.

Colleges

Some who may favour decentralizing and decreasing the size of secondary schools may balk at the idea of colleges going through a similar reduction. After all, the story of higher education in the second half of the twentieth century is one of an increasing concentration of students on campuses. We can already see, however, the signs of decentralization in local community colleges near Stanford, California, for example. It is now the practice to have off-campus centres to which students may go for courses. In fact, for many courses, it is only necessary to appear on the campus twice, once to register and once to take an examination. One hundred years from now a college of several thousand students may be the largest to be found anywhere. This will happen only if we see a degree of specialization that we do not now have in colleges. I am less certain about this prediction for colleges because there is a certain importance to the commingling of graduate students engaged in research. Highly sophisticated laboratories will not be easily decentralized, and so it may not be possible to decentralize college campuses as much as secondary schools. I could, however, be quite wrong about this, for we see in North America today a stronger tendency to decentralize community colleges than high schools.

I would like to comment as well on the college curriculum apart from any questions of decentralization. One of the technologically most efficient ways to teach young adults is to have them listen to a stand-up lecturer talking to two or three hundred of them at a time. I do not think we should abolish this classical form of lecturing, but I do think it is an inefficient form of learning from the student's standpoint. It is too passive, and it is too rigid in its pacing to accommodate individual differences in learning. Still, it should not be abolished because some matters of style and viewpoint are not easily conveyed in other ways. In our modern age of television, we have a sense of intimacy and closeness of perception of speakers that is simply not possible in a large audience but that is easily replicated in teaching by means of video technology. Thus, even what I say about large lectures may be wrong, but I am conservative enough to see some value in the diversity of approaches and the retention of this classical form.

For the past ten years I have not given a lecture course myself; I teach my undergraduate courses by computer or videotape. My personal teaching is entirely confined to seminars, of which I teach a great variety. This is the model I would urge for 2085. Students should acquire the standard skills or knowledge in a sophisticated technological setting, mainly using computers and associated video devices. With appropriate preparation, students should then enter seminars ready for discussion and, above all, ready to talk. What I am describing for college education is a transformation of current teaching methods, one that will be agreed to by people of differing attitudes about the promise of technology. Without the technology, however, it will not be possible, in practice, to use a skilled academic faculty entirely for seminars. It would be too expensive to cover the bulk of teaching in this way.

Continuing Education

Continuing education is already following the pattern I have mentioned of the community colleges, namely, off-campus centres and home-centred learning. The proportion of the adult population involved in continuing education in some community college districts in California is staggering, as much as 40 per cent in some places. There is no reason for continuing education to decrease, and many reasons for it to increase. One hundred years from now, continuing education of an organized systematic kind may very well be the norm for all adults until very late in life. How will this vast panoply of continuing education be arranged? It would be a mistake to have some monolithic single model of how it will take place; such a model does not describe the enterprise today and certainly will not a hundred years from now. There are, however, two identifiable tendencies in continuing education. The first, and most important, is decentralization, which will continue. The second is the use of information technology to make continuing education much more independent of the immediate presence of a human teacher than is now the case. This increasingly sophisticated use of the technology will increase the possibilities of decentralization to that ultimate point, the individual's home.

The Home
The most dazzling and intriguing prospect is the return of education to the home. Will this happen in a hundred years? I think it will. For many reasons much education should return to the home, and that return should accompany the return of work to the home. Let us consider a forecast of the home as a place of work and of education a century from now.

As many futurists describing life in the twenty-first century have observed, we have already entered the post-industrial era. This is the age of information, and the handling of information can be conducted as well from the home as from the office. The choice will be before us. Individuals of the next century will not work totally in isolation at home, but they will have a pattern of work that is much more flexible and interesting than the pattern so customary today of going to an office forty hours a week. An individual could work at home three or four days a week and perhaps go to the office one or two days a week. The parents of a family of one or two children could always arrange for one parent to be home, and the children could be educated at home as much as the parents liked.

The education of the young will not move back to the home to become as it was in the nineteenth century, or, for most of the world, the twentieth century. Instead, I can envision a pattern something like the following for a family with two children between the ages of five and fifteen. The father goes to the office only on Mondays, and the mother only on Wednesdays. The younger child, who is in elementary school, goes to school in the morning and then works at home another couple of hours a day, using appropriate computer technology, under the parents' supervision. The older child also spends mornings at school, perhaps for a slightly longer period than the younger child, but the older child also spends the afternoons at home, continuing the educational program under the parents' supervision and also possibly helping the younger child. The entire household is a learning environment. The mother and father are involved in complicated programs of continuing education in their own areas of specialization. The children are learning a wide variety of things and are very sophisticated about looking up a bewildering array of information in the enormous resources of the hundred giga bytes of storage available to them in optical form at home. Because of such innovations, it is possible that the family of he next century will be much stronger and more closely knit than is the family of today. Though many people have been predicting the end of the family for the past 150 years, I shall be boldly optimistic and predict its renewal.

There is one further point I want to make about this return to the home. Some of the mothers who have recently moved from home to workplace may not like the idea of the drudgery they see facing them as the most responsible agents for managing the household. Here, too, I want to be optimistic. I cannot think of anything that would sell better than smart robots designed for household work. We will not have really good ones even in twenty years; but with the market impetus to develop such a product, the rush to produce excellent robots for household work, once a few technical problems are solved, will be unbelievably strong. Surely in a hundred years we will all have superb, highly reliable, electronic servants. It will be a point of conversation in 2085 that as recently as the twentieth century educated, affluent people did not have such servants.

Conceptual Questions and Problems

I will close by mentioning three issues that will characterize the developments of the next hundred years.

Privacy versus sociability. Although I have emphasized the enormous potential for decentralization in our society one hundred years from now, especially as it affects education, I do not think that all education should be private and that learning is always best engaged in a private setting. Many aspects of group learning should be a part of everyone's experience. Social instincts are a natural part of human psychology. What we face in the future is the possibility of new mixes of privacy and socialization. Much of the world's population until the last two hundred years lived in small social groups in rural settings. It is this ancient social pattern that will be technically and economically possible in the future once again. Many people, I predict, will want to return to it. Those who prefer a crowded metropolitan environment, as did many people in the days of ancient Babylon or Alexandria, can continue to live in urban areas, but even then varying degrees of privacy will be possible. What the norm will be is hard to say from this distant point.

Commonality versus diversity. One of the great problems for education one hundred years from now, with all the rich information technology available, will be the mix of common and unique elements in the education of each person. How much of the education of the young will be devoted to a core curriculum and how much will be a matter of diverse choice? My crystal ball is cloudy on this point, but I predict greater diversity, if only because of the exponential growth of knowledge that will take place throughout the next one hundred years.

Freedom versus control. The final issue to be mentioned is the place of individuality and human freedom in the kind of modern society we can anticipate for 2085. There are Luddites now, and I am sure there will be Luddites then that preach the danger of men becoming slaves of machines. This is an extreme and romantic way of expressing what can be regarded as a real danger, namely, the use of high technology by one group of people to enslave another. These dangers and many others lie before us in the next hundred years, but we have also the hope and the promise of a society that is more intellectually sophisticated and materially affluent than any that preceded it. The use of computers can, through the elimination of drudgery and an effective emphasis on individuality, be a key element in creating a better world than we have ever known before.

UNIVERSITIES IN THE INFORMATION AGE

TONI CARBO BEARMAN

Introduction

We are now a mere fifteen years from the twenty-first century and on the brink of the Information Age. The way information is permeating and transforming all aspects of society is better expressed in French as "L'informatisation de la Société." Increasingly, we recognize the value of information in decision making, in productivity, and in improving the quality of life. The cliché "information is power" has taken a new meaning as we treat information products and services as valuable commodities to trade and protect, like gold or hog bellies. Universities are undergoing major changes as they move into the Information Age, as are most other institutions.

The past *is* prologue and, in examining the implications of the emerging Information Age for universities in the new century, it is useful to look at the developments that are bringing us into the Information Age. The major technological changes affecting universities early in the twentieth century were, of course, advances in telecommunication and transportation. Major social changes include demographic changes, an increased participation by women in all aspects of education, a loss of some autonomy by universities because of increased regulation by government and financial support from outside sources, a shift in emphasis from liberal arts to the preparation of students for professional occupations, and some movement toward more specialization.

One major change pushing the university into the Information Age has been the increased pressure on universities not only to transmit knowledge through teaching, but also to create knowledge through research, and to disseminate this knowledge to improve society. Throughout this century, universities, "believed to have a special understanding of society... were called on to bring about its improvements."[1] Two major events, the land grant movement and the alliance between universities and the federal government in the United States, have led to a change in the American university, reinforcing the involvement of the university in the daily life of the nation. These events have emphasized the public aspect of the university's role in society and have enhanced the public's involvement in the affairs of the university. In response to the nation's rapid industrial and agricultural development, the land grant movement called on the universities to extend the benefits of education to all segments of society and to develop more practical applications of education. The Morrill Act of 1892 provided land to the states, which used the proceeds to teach in agriculture and mechanical arts. Subsequent legislation provided federal financial support for research and the operation of the land grant colleges. These colleges contributed to the democratization of higher education in the United States.

The second event in the United States, the alliance between the federal government and universities, began before World War I, when the United States began to challenge the hegemony of the German chemical industry. At that time, the federal government entered into a series of agreements with academic and industrial science and technology interests to foster research and development designed to make the United States a world power. In 1980, for example, Congress enacted legislation to provide funding for basic research in land grant universities. During World War I, the United States pioneered the cost-plus research and development contracts, which have continued to support numerous high-risk technological developments. Support for academic research in science was dominant until World War II, when the need for radar, encryption, and weapons shifted the emphasis to applications. During World War II, most of the scientific community was mobilized under the Office of Science Research and Development for the war effort. This close relationship between national policy and the needs and interests of the academic community, especially in science, continued until the early 1970s.

Both the democratization of education and the partnership between the academic community and the government were furthered by conscious programs to increase the diffusion of information. U.S. agriculture is the most productive in the world in large part because of public policy actions assuring the continued flow of information from the university to the farmer. Similarly, the academic community has asserted the importance of communicating the results of research, and these results often lead to innovative application. It is the links among research, information, innovation, and productivity that are essential. In a recent article, Gerald Sophar of the U.S. National Agricultural

Library describes these important links as the key to success for American agriculture. He states:

> The key to this almost unmarred success story is the nearly universal understanding and acceptance in the agricultural community, that increases in productivity result from research and the transfer of the results of research through a change agent.... In other words, the change agent introduces information resulting from research to an individual, who then may take the risk of adopting the new idea or innovation. If the decision to adopt proves successful, the innovation spreads rapidly throughout the entire community and there is usually an increase in productivity. So in this one area of production, the links between research, information, innovation, and productivity are well established.[2]

Concerns about the decrease in the growth of productivity continue to be significant, and the need for industrial policies is being debated throughout the government. Although this policy objective is shared by the academic community, in the past decade we have seen many national policy objectives moving away from the interests that were shared by the research community to other areas. In the United States during this decade the government has cut funding for non-military research and development, differing priorities have developed between the two groups, and, not suprisingly, tension between national public policies and the needs of the academic community has increased.

In addition to this tension between policies and needs, the university in North America has had to respond to demands for it to take on a wide range of new responsibilities that have affected academic programs and the actual structure of the university. These new responsibilities include: (1) providing a liberal education to people from all segments of society; (2) striving to solve societal problems, rather than focusing only on those problems of specific interest to the scholarly community; (3) preparing individuals to practise a number of professions, replacing preparation through apprenticeship and experience with academic preparation; and (4) providing a centre for culture to serve the community as a whole, rather than simply the students and faculty.[3] Each of these new responsibilities has expanded the scope of university activities, both enriched the amount and kinds of resources available and put new strains on these resources, and has added to the importance of the university in society. During the past decade, individuals in government and in business have begun to question these functions and responsibilities, asking whether they are still necessary and appropriate and whether they are worth the cost. Projected decreases in student enrolment, shifts of graduate students from traditional departments into professional schools, rapid technological developments, and reductions in funding exacerbate the pressures on universities to continue to adapt and change to meet emerging societal needs.

As society moves from the Agrarian and Industrial ages of the twentieth century into the Information Age, we can expect to see changes in academic programs, in the balance between research and teaching, in methods of teaching and learning, in structures for academic administration, and in the understanding of the importance of the management of information resources. This paper attempts to describe the emerging Information Age, to highlight implications of developments in information technology and the management of information resources for universities, and to identify some issues for universities to address in the emerging Information Age.

The Information Age

The Information Age, or the Information Society as it is sometimes called, is a popular description of a society transformed by information technology and by an increased emphasis on the importance of knowing how to find and use information effectively. This transformation has brought problems as well as opportunities, and its consequences are poorly understood. As R.L. Stanfield and Gordon Robertson have noted:

> The label "Information Society" correctly encapsulates the concept of the vast flow and speed of information which inundates us all. But it fails to reflect the fact that our ability to store, manipulate, and transmit enormous quantities of information, of itself, does not improve our capacity to make good judgements or to act wisely. Moreover, civilization has always been dependent on the transfer of information from one person to another and from generation to generation. Only techniques for the transfer of information change because they are tools, means, but the process remains and is as necessary as life.[4]

How information is handled both depends on and determines the quality of decisions people make. Both the academic community and the government must be alert to the changes taking place and must jointly, with the commercial sector, accept the responsibility for leading society into the Information Age. Several key characteristics of the Information Age have been described in earlier studies. The U.S. Domestic Council Committee on the Right of Privacy, in its report *National Information Policy,* identifies the following seven characteristics: (1) an exponential increase in the volume of information flow; (2) a shrinkage of time and distance constraints upon communications; (3) greater nationwide dependence upon information and communication services; (4) an increase in the interdependence of previously autonomous institutions and services; (5) conceptual changes in economic, social, and political processes induced by increased information and communications; (6) a decrease in the "time cushion" between social and technical changes and their consequences; and (7) global shrinkage and its consequent pressures on increased international exchange.[5]

Thus, we are living in a world in which we are inundated by huge quantities of information and are relying on interdependent information and communication services that transmit data instantaneously without regard to distance. We have much less time to cope with the major conceptual changes in economic, social, and political processes that are brought about by an increased volume of information transmitted at a higher speed of communication. We are moving rapidly into an Information Age. Just as we used our knowledge from the Industrial Age to bring about innovation to improve productivity in agriculture, we should apply our knowledge from the emerging Information Age to improve productivity in industry, and, more important to improve the quality of life around the world.

Information Technology and the Management of Information Resources

The computer revolution is changing the way society functions even more dramatically than the Industrial Revolution did. Its long-term effects are yet to be fully understood. Although the computer is only one of the major information technologies, it is the single technology that is having the greatest effect on universities. Universities participated in the creation of the computer and have been among the most active users of computers, especially for research. The computer and other related information technologies were used primarily in support of research, but information technology is beginning to affect all aspects of information transfer for the university, from its creation, through its management and organization, to its dissemination.

As an increasing number of university faculty, administrators, and students acquire computers and as more universities wire their campuses and develop computer systems, we can expect that virtually all universities in North America will actively be using information technology by the year 2000. Most members of the university community will use the technology to acquire information, conduct research, and disseminate the results of their research. All aspects of publishing will be fully automated, and the teaching-learning process may well change dramatically.

Acquiring, Preserving, and Disseminating Information

In order to conduct research, keep current on the literature, and prepare for lectures, professors spend considerable time seeking and gathering information. The university library system has been the primary source of publications and related materials for centuries, providing references and information needed by scholars and students. The library in many universities was among the first components of the university to introduce information technology, and now many university libraries have automated circulation systems, acquisitions systems, and on-line catalogs. In addition, in the past fifteen years library and information networks have been developed, providing mechanisms for libraries to pool resources, thus eliminating unnecessary duplication of costly effort and improving access to collections of materials around the world. Participation in these networks, which provide within minutes access to tens of millions of references to publications, will continue to grow. By the end of the century, all universities in North America, and most in other countries around the world, can be expected to participate in these networks, which will be greatly expanded and improved. In addition to the services currently available, which provide lists of books, journal articles, dissertations, audio-visual material, and other publications, the improved networks will provide intelligent gateways to a series of different databases and systems through one easy-to-use terminal. The material searched will be easily manipulated, integrating data with text into remote databases and information from the user's own files and databases. Electronic delivery of the full text of articles, of photographs, and of other material will be provided quickly and at low cost. Software and other tools for personal and organizational information resources will also be provided, probably by commercial and not-for-profit organizations.

The library will continue to play an important role in sifting through the vast quantities of publications, databases, and audio-visual materials, including videodisks and videotex material, to identify those of most potential interest to the university community. Other important functions will continue to be: organizing and housing the material, preserving the cultural record, assisting in locating retrospective publications, training people to use the collections and systems, and continuing to serve as intermediaries between the users and the collections. The library's collections, in all media, will continue to be one of the most valuable information resources of the university.

Through the capability of satellites, we will see continued internationalization of research and communication. We may well see major strides toward solving the language problem, as machine translation continues to improve. International teleconferencing, already a reality, may well become far more widespread, permitting the instantaneous transmission of research results or, for example, demonstrations of surgical practices internationally. With the rapidly decreasing costs of satellite earth stations, even small universities around the world will be able to afford dishes and be able to receive communications via satellite.

Research and Teaching

Computers have been widely used in performing research since their beginning and will continue to be used. The advances in miniaturization and rapid developments in software design continue to improve the information technology and its applications for research. Improved graphics capabilities are also increasing the ease of using computers and their adaptability for research.

In teaching, media-based instruction and computer-based instruction are widely used in many universities today. Control Data Corporation's $1 billion investment in its Plato system has resulted in an effective and creative approach to new techniques for learning. The learning process is changing dramatically as freshmen with great experience in using computers enter college with their own personal computers and with years of experience with television and videocassettes behind them. What will be needed in the decades ahead are guidance, human assistance in adapting to computer-based instruction systems, retraining for some faculty, and a careful rethinking of the role of lectures and reading in a multi-media based educational system. Whether students will even travel to a "classroom" will be subject to debate. Many universities already have their own cable television channels; with home television sets capable of receiving more than one hundred channels, universities will need to determine how they will allocate their channels. Demonstrations of medical techniques, laboratory procedures, theatre performances, and musical events are already being transmitted via university cable networks. The possibilities for expanded use to provide international educational programs, discussions, multi-campus classes, interactive conferences, and other programs are virtually limitless.

The integration of information technologies to provide improved resources for research, access to a wide range of publications and other materials, and exciting possibilities for the use of many different media for teaching and learning opens an unlimited number of opportunities to a university.

Improving the Management of Information Resources

In addition to the library's collections, the university has a wide range of information resources, including its archives, files, research reports, laboratory notebooks, computer facilities, manuscripts, and other information assets. Most universities consider personnel, endowment, buildings, land, and other capital assets in their resources for planning, but few think of the information resources as a major component of their assets. Recent studies indicate that managers spend 50 per cent of their time in meetings and another 25 per cent of their time looking for information. Efficient management of information resources and the improved ability of managers to find information quickly can improve the productivity of the university. In all planning processes, the information resources should be considered as part of the university's total assets.

Some organizations are establishing a senior position to coordinate data processing, computer facilities, libraries, museums, archival collections, and other information resources. A senior official for information resources management has been named in each agency of the U.S. federal government, as a requirement under the Paperwork Reduction Act. The person responsible is often an assistant secretary for administration. Much more than the co-ordination of disparate collections of information and data is needed. Information resources management includes determining what information is needed by whom and in what form it is needed, organizing the resources so they can be found easily, ensuring that computer systems are compatible, providing mechanisms for linking systems to provide training on the use of the systems and collections, and planning for the continued growth and improvement of the system. Many universities have started programs to educate and train information managers, and these programs are located in departments of library and information science, computer science departments, and business schools. By the year 2000, the management of information resources is expected to become a popular career path with specializations in many areas, similar to the legal or medical professionals.

Technology and Publishing

All aspects of publishing from preparation of the original manuscript to the dissemination of the publication have already been affected by the information technologies. Authors compose their manuscripts on microcomputers, and the article is submitted electronically to a publisher who arranges for referees to read and comment on the article electronically. Changes are made on-line, and the text is incorporated with other articles into an issue that may be transmitted via satellite to another country for actual printing. Electronic forms of the printed publication, if there is one, are distributed to information systems and abstracting and indexing services, which make the full text of the articles, or the bibliographic references, with indexing and abstracts of the articles, available as part of their databases. The American Chemical Society, for example, has made the full text of several of its journals available for on-line searching by users through several different systems. The text of newspaper articles is often transmitted via satellite from several locations to a series of other locations for simultaneous publication in cities around the world.

The implications of these developments for universities are significant. Many authors may have difficulty adapting to preparing their manuscripts on a computer, preferring to continue to dictate or put pen to paper and leaving the input of the text to clerical staff. Those who do learn to use the new technologies, however, will find expanded opportunities, such as ease of revising text and increased opportunities for joint authorship. Joint authorship has traditionally been undertaken by individuals from within a single laboratory or university. Through computer networks, authors can correspond and compose their article on-line across state lines or national borders. The speed of publication can be vastly improved, placing even greater stress than before on the role of the journal article in laying claim to the author's discovery. Contests to see who published the results first will be measured, not in weeks, but in seconds. These possible benefits of improved communication and joint authorship across distance, coupled with faster speed in publication, must be balanced gainst the danger of losing what Warren J. Haas of the Council on Library Resources has called our "intellectual audit trail." What record will be left for future scholars, historians, aspiring writers, and others if all changes to a manuscript are made electronically on a microcomputer? How will we compare the third to the thirteenth draft of a play by a future Shakespeare if only the final draft disk remains? Universities must develop standards and procedures to protect this important record, as they have developed on-line preparation of journal articles. We must also develop standards for intellectual audit trails to ensure that the important record of the creative process is preserved.

Information technology is improving universities' ability to acquire, to preserve, and to disseminate information. It is providing exciting opportunities for new methods of teaching and learning, and it is helping to speed up and to change the publication process. Universities will need to manage their information resources more efficiently, giving the same attention to information resources that has been given to financial, personnel, and other assets.

Implications of the Information Technology and of the Management of Resources

The implications of the information technology and the improved management of information resources extend far beyond the use and dissemination of information within the university. The implications extend to significant changes in the university, itself, and within society as it moves into the Information Age. Universities in the year 2000 will be more information-oriented, educating individuals who are accustomed to finding information quickly and to using technology to organize it effectively. Both the producers and the users of information generated by individuals within the university community will not necessarily be located on a university campus. With the anticipated internationalization of the university, we can expect courses, demonstrations, and presentations given at a university to be transmitted via satellite or cable television to countries around the country, followed by discussions via multinational communication systems, utilizing video-telephone systems.

New types of communication centres will be needed in universities, and new turf battles may ensue, as departments and programs compete to house these centres. We have already moved away from traditional notions of departments organized by disciplines, speaking more frequently of interdisciplinary, or even multidisciplinary, programs. Communication centres for multidisciplinary programs will have to be designed, planned, and developed through co-ordinated team efforts, involving administration representatives, faculty, and information specialists. The challenges for libraries, department administrators, and faculty to re-think processes for teaching, learning, and communicating will be great. There will no doubt continue to be many who oppose the technology, in part because they fear it and find difficulty in adapting to it. We can expect increased emphasis, not on teaching facts, but on learning problem solving, on logical thinking and reasoning, and on finding and using information effectively. This shift has been aptly described as "learning to learn." Learning to learn in the Information Age is not acquiring a specific body of knowledge within a specific number of years in academic institutions. It is, and must be, part of an ongoing process from cradle to grave — lifelong learning, relying on many institutions, such as universities, libraries, the media, and the individual.

Issues for Universities as They Approach the Year 2000

These technological developments and their implications for improved management of information resources, internationalization, and a new emphasis on learning to learn raise issues to be considered and discussed by university leaders as they plan for the decades ahead. The following five issues focus on information-related concerns: (1) the role of goverment, (2) information and the economy, (3) the value of information, (4) protection of intellectual property rights, and (5) educating future information professionals.

The Role of Government

The commercial sector and representatives in government continue to raise the question whether information policies are needed to define the responsibility of government vis-à-vis the private sector in disseminating information. There is considerable disagreement over the role of governments, nationally and internationally, in the dissemination of information. Specific issues include the protection of privacy and proprietary rights, the right of citizens to know what their goverment is doing, the protection of national security, questions of national sovereignty, and support for (or competition with) the private sector. In the United States, one group argues that many types of information must be protected to guard national security and to keep other nations from competing with American industry by using technological information developed in the United States. A different contingent maintains that the principle of the unrestricted flow of information must prevail to ensure that U.S. industry can compete and argues that those who want the information will be able to get it anyway.

Concerns are also raised about the government's competing unfairly with the private sector by providing products and services at prices far below what commercial companies must charge to recover their full costs and make a profit. Users of government information contend, however, that if the goverment shirks its responsibility to disseminate information that the taxpayers paid it to produce, and relies on the market to determine whether a product or service should be offered, many citizens would be unable to obtain information products and services because either the price would be too high or the product would not make a profit and would be eliminated.

Universities need to examine these complex issues to help determine what the role of the government should be. The government's responsibility in supporting research, setting regulations for industry and universities, developing other policies affecting universities, and setting national policies and priorities should be discussed by universities. The academic community should lead in working to define and carry out these roles.

Information in the Economy

The second issue is use of information in the economy, especially in determining industrial policies. Like the government, universities produce and use massive amounts of information and educate students to use information effectively through conducting research and communicating the results of research. As countries move from an economy based on industrial growth to one based on information and information technology, it is essential that the scholarly community participate in the determination of how information can be harnessed to help improve economic conditions and develop industrial policies to reduce unemployment and increase productivity. Academics have made important contributions in the past in developing resources to achieve missions, such as improving agricultural systems and finding cures for disease. Their expertise is needed now to establish policies to develop and to exploit the valuable resources of information and information technology. As more of the gross national product is derived from information-related activities, careful planning for policies to continue to improve the economy worldwide must focus on information technology and information resources.

The Value of Information

As decision makers begin to understand the value of information for bringing about innovation and improving productivity, they also learn of the importance of finding and using information effectively. This ability is as important as the "three r's" and is essential for functioning in today's society. The cliché "information is power" takes on new meaning as the gap between the information rich and the information poor widens. Those who can find the information they need and make use of it quickly and efficiently do indeed have great power over those who cannot. The situation is analagous to the Middle Ages when those few who could read could exercise magical powers, such as "making" the sun disappear mysteriously, over those who could not. Universities are in a unique situation to be able to communicate the value of information and the importance of information skills for all aspects of decision making, increasing productivity, and improving the quality of life. Universities could require of all entering students that they have these information skills and provide remedial programs, as many now do for writing and mathematical skills, for those deficient in them. Also, as faculty teach students to learn how to learn and as they conduct their research and disseminate their findings using the new information technologies, they demonstrate by word and action the importance of information skills.

Protection of Intellectual Property Rights

In light of the rapid technological developments taking place, it is becoming increasingly difficult, if not impossible, to protect intellectual property rights. Serious ethical questions have been raised in recent years about violation of copyright through photocopying of printed publications. One university in the United States was sued by a group of publishers. Losses of revenues caused by photocopying of printed publications pale in comparison to potential losses from pirating of software or capturing the beaming of shows from pay television via satellites without compensating the owners. Several countries that do not honour copyright obtain copies of software packages and duplicate them in large numbers. Combinations of copyright law revisions, international agreements, lease and licensing arrangements, and encryption techniques are being used in attempts to protect intellectual property.

Many of the creators of this intellectual property are at universities. The moral and ethical questions about rights and responsibilities could benefit from discussion in departments of philosophy, law, and ethics. University administrators and faculty should consider the ethical and legal implications of this issue. Although it is discouraging to think that we must ask some of our best minds to turn their attention to developing methods to keep people from getting information, such efforts will be needed to ensure that the large economic and intellectual resources devoted to developing the products and services are not lost. Questions of how the property can be protected, who should be responsible for protecting it, who will pay to be certain that protective procedures are developed, who owns the intellectual property, how to protect against censorship, what legislation will be needed, and what international pressures can be brought to bear on all countries to respect intellectual property rights are a few of the important questions worthy of exploration by the university community.

Educating Future Information Professionals

The final issue is the developing of coalitions to determine what future information professionals need to know and how our educational systems can get the resources needed to educate and train them. It is extremely difficult to determine what knowledge, skills, and attitudes will be needed by future information professionals, yet our undergraduate and graduate programs are being called upon to develop curricula and work-study programs to provide them. The challenge today is similar to that of defining a computer science curriculum in 1955. New laboratory facilities, computer hardware, and funds for computer time for searching databases are needed. Resources are required to provide continuing training and educational programs for faculty teaching in information programs. The interdisciplinary nature of the information field demands close interaction with departments of computer science, management programs, communication schools, sociology departments, and other programs to provide the background and expertise needed. Large contributions from industry will be needed to endow chairs, provide faculty exchange programs, and student internships. The total needs for an emerging discipline are great and will require a combined and concerted effort.

University administrators can help to determine what they will require of future information professionals to work for the administration. By working with library directors, managers of computer facilities, and coordinators of research services, university administrators can provide the integrated team management needed to bring the university, itself, into the Information Age, through management of information resources and the use of information technology. Many universities are examining the importance of their libraries and other information resources in the automation of the university. As local area networks are established on campuses, administrators are learning how to make the most effective use of the available information resources. Deans of graduate schools of library and information science and directors of libraries now chair university teams to automate the university, improving the communications system and access to information resources.

Determining how to educate the future leaders in the information profession is very important in shaping the structure of the university in society as it moves into the Information Age. More than half the workforce in the United States is in information-related jobs. It is evident that the future information professionals will be major leaders in the information economy. Questions of what these professionals will need to know to lead us in the decades ahead certainly demand the attention of the academic community.

Conclusion

These broad issues should be on the agenda for discussion at every university and at every professional society conference. Answers to these questions cannot be left solely to government officials or to industry leaders; nor should they be decided by any single country. They are of international importance and could change future directions of the world economy and of international relations. The academic community must bring its wisdom and its unique perspective to these difficult, but challenging, issues as we move from the Industrial Age. The past *is* prologue, and to complete the quotation from *The Tempest*:

> And, by that destiny, to perform an act
> Whereof what's past is prologue, what to come
> In yours and my discharge.[6]

It is the responsibility of today's professionals in academic and in information technology to consider these issues, to work to answer the questions they raise, to help students learn to learn, and to participate in developing policies to lead the university into the Information Age. Through renewed partnerships between the academic community and governments and through

improved international co-operative efforts we can meet these
challenges.

Notes

1. United States Congress, Office of Technology Assessment, *Informational Technology and Its Impact on American Tradition* (Washington, D.C.: U.S. Government Printing Office, November 1982), p. 78.

2. Gerald Sophar, "Information, Innovation, and Productivity," *Bulletin of the American Society for Information Science,* vol. 10 (Oct. 1983), p. 32.

3. *Universities, Information Technology, and Academic Libraries: the Next Twenty Years,* ed. Robert M. Hayes, proceedings of the Academic Libraries Frontiers Conference, 13-17 Dec. 1981 (Los Angeles: University of California at Los Angeles, 1982), pp. 19- 20.

4. R.L. Stanfield and Gordon Robertson, "Popularization and Public Policy," *Annual Report of the Institute for Research on Public Policy, 1982* (Montreal: Institute for Research on Public Policy, 1982), p. 2.

5. U.S. Domestic Council Committee on the Right of Privacy, *National Information Policy* (Washington, D.C.: National Commission on Libraries and Information Science, 1976), pp. 5-6.

6. William Shakespeare, *The Tempest,* Act 2, Scene 1.

PART III

CONFRONTING AND REFLECTING ON THE NEW WORLD

TODAY IS TOMORROW:

HOW HIGHER EDUCATION'S PRESENT

SHAPES ITS FUTURE

LOUIS VAGIANOS

The fundamental purpose and task of education is not to teach people how to be, to be like their teachers in a world like their teacher's world. Rather it is to teach them how to become, become whatever they want in whatever kind of future world they live.
Bruce F. Goeller

The fundamental importance of education to the successful evolution and sustenance of a complex technological world is not debatable. Neither is the fact that complex social systems require sophisticated control mechanisms of appropriate structural depth to function effectively. What is debatable, and there is no paucity of material and no issue more worked over by iconoclasts and traditionalists alike, is whether the educational institutions entrusted with the responsibility for educating the individuals who are to develop, preserve, transmit, and guide our social and economic progress are in fact doing so adequately.

Although all levels of the educational community are undergoing savage attacks, none is under greater pressure for change than our universities. It is here that we send our children to explore the frontiers of knowledge and to examine and ingest our intellectual and cultural heritage. It is here that we expect them to cultivate their imaginative capacity to innovate and to discover what most thoughtful men and women of a given time believe that human beings should know. It is also here that we instil, in final form, the skills required for thinking and learning so that we can produce men and women prepared for a lifetime of learning rather than men and women with tailormade skills to fit a ready-made society.

Within this context the university serves as the intellectual template for the future because society will always be made over by the people in it. It is for this reason that the importance of higher education cannot be overstated and why higher education's falling from grace, thanks to a general public disenchanted with universities and no longer believing current

173

systems of learning work, is a matter of serious concern. Universities can ill afford a further loss in influence as they are forced to compete for funds with the pressing claims of other social services, such as pollution control, health care, and poverty programs.

There is another, more serious side to the loss of institutional influence: the continued weakening and possible collapse of authority. People can no longer rely on the common signposts culture develops to tell them where to go to get what they need. Worse still, it means that the identification of appropriate needs within society may not be subjected to challenge and debate.

In some circles it has become fashionable to blame external agencies for this falling from grace, but no thoughtful person can accept such a diagnosis. Even a cursory review of the present plight of universities highlights a state of affairs characterized by too many administrators and faculty who have failed to explore and exploit areas of co-operation, to demonstrate themselves the flexibility of mind they try to encourage in their students, and to define the universities' mission with a clarity and precision that can be understood by the public.

There is, however, a more hopeful side. One could argue that, far from being deplorable, the present situation was inevitable and is necessary and entirely normal during periods of great change. A consensus is growing that we are in such a period, even perhaps (to use Alvin Toffler's tired metaphor) between waves. During such times some drifting and confusion is unavoidable as we seek to find new bearings. For, as the old "saw" says, "Needs must, when the devil drives." At present, opportunities abound if we can rise to the occasion. Still, one difficulty remains: success rests on the requirement for institutional renewal; and although we know what the term means and can identify individual minds that practise it, we have not yet learned how to regenerate institutions within our present systems of governance. On one point, though, there is no argument: central to any process of institutional renewal must be planning.

The dictionary advises that planning refers to any method of thinking out acts and purposes beforehand. At its best, planning is based on the "anticipatory side." This means planning works most effectively when it is moderated by a clear vision of reality, some general agreement on probable futures, and a manageable set of goals. Planning cannot take place in a vacuum; any discussion of planning in higher education must deal with the environment in which it must operate. This essay will address three such areas: (1) the forms of anticipation toward which change should be directed, (2) the constraints within which planning for future changes must take place, and (3) the reality within which planning functions most effectively.

Since good planning must be directed toward some requirement, a definition of the role of higher education, together with some general guidelines, is in order. This is easier said than done. Aristotle perhaps best illustrated the complexity of the problem a few centuries ago:

> But consideration must be given to the question, what constitutes education and what is the proper way to be educated. At present there are differences of opinion as to the proper tasks to be set; for all peoples do not agree as to the things that the young ought to learn, either with a view to virtue or with a view to the best life, nor is it clear whether their studies should be regulated more with regard to intellect or with regard to character. And confusing questions arise out of the education that actually prevails, and it is not all clear whether the pupils should practice pursuits that are practically useful, or morally edifying, or higher accomplishments (*Politics*, bk. 8).

Despite the caveats, a suitable definition of education's function can be extrapolated from this quotation: education should prepare each person to develop his strengths as fully as possible within the context of the world in which he will live.

Robert Theobald has suggested that such a statement about education is essentially tautological. This is both apt and inevitable. Its strength lies in the fact that there is much room for disagreement and diversity, because different people will perceive different potentials in themselves and others, and there is certainly plenty of room for controversy about the world we will inherit or in which we wish to live. Its weakness lies in the certain knowledge that present systems of education fail to respect the foregoing implications. The most arresting contemporary example is the public's demand in North America to use public education as the principal mechanism for creating equality. This point, together with the problems involved, is clearly demonstrated in Diane Ravitch's recent book *The Troubled Crusade*. What all this suggests quite forcefully is that definitional problems have implications that go beyond mere words.

Positing a developmental function for higher education allows us to specify boundaries that can contain a discussion that would otherwise be infinite. A major analytic specification is implicit in the title of this paper: "Today Is Tomorrow: How Higher Education's Present Shapes Its Future." This underscores a major point: the present is the matrix of the future in that the problems to be resolved must be identified and described if the necessary technologies are to be readily available. To demonstrate this, however, we must examine the environment in which universities must function during this final quarter of the twentieth century. Environmental examination itself necessitates an inspection of some of the challenges we face, together with some major trends that will shape our future as we seek solutions, and the degree to which pervasive change will affect the limits forming the boundaries of the possible. What seems clear is that effective response will demand a double focus of analysis and projection to establish goals for the future along with timetables and procedures to ensure that desire and reality connect properly.

Another specification of analytic boundaries results from the recognition that effective planning to improve universities in the future must be rooted in the understanding that they are a part of a "system" of higher education. This will require relating analysis and projection within a dual focus: the external systems within which higher education functions and which will determine institutional responses; and the internal systems through which universities must effect objectives. This means the required solutions will be both substantive and procedural.

Put in another, more pragmatic, way: if the process of learning within a university is to be a "product" of appropriate utility within our society, will those who are in a position to define the needed product be able to do so in a manner and within a time frame that would permit sound institutional adjustment; and will those administering the systems that control the process of learning be willing (assuming they are able) to adapt to what will certainly be a revised schedule of needs?

If these questions are to have affirmative answers, we must start by recognizing that the ensuing "conversation" could be one of the most difficult educational debates of the century. It could also be acrimonious. The range of topics and vested interests involved are vast, because we are dealing at bottom with the total social fabric; for, as noted earlier, educational institutions are one of society's indispensable mechanisms for cultural survival, and institutional renewal is seldom an easy task.

My contribution to providing a manageable focus for this nexus of questions and discussion will deal with three topics: (1) the systemic and theoretical limits to future responses implicit in the present, (2) the present trends that act as instruments for shaping the future, including their educational significance, and (3) the current status of higher education as an effective mechanism for meeting future challenges.

These three facets of the effect of the present on the future — limitations in theory, limitation by trends, and limitations on capacity — form the armature around which we must plan. An exhaustive examination is outside the scope of this essay, but the following observations may precipitate a debate commensurate with the importance of this topic.

General Limits to Future Response

The principal effect of the present on the future is derived from a set of general constraints that will inevitably condition any individual or institutional response. These general constraints affect all contemporary systems to which they apply and cannot be removed by fiat, they constitute limits that inhibit but do not prohibit action. Because reality is self-enforcing, the results of indiscriminate or misguided effort to avoid them is merely waste. Nevertheless, the conceptual consequences of misguided action to the theoretical limits they represent can often be unpleasant.

The most "visible" class of such limits are *technical limits*. For the university this includes such things as the structural limitations of existing physical plants; the specific, specialized capacities of research equipment; the massive increase of intellectual and physical resources required for effective returns from research, including the expensive, quickly obsolete, but essential new equipment necessary to keep up with innovation or the frontiers of knowledge; and the finite capacity of support structures (such as libraries), which must cope with a vast increase in the required handling of artifacts. To some extent the university is suffering a "hangover" from past largesse, which resulted in the creation of a specialized technical base, much of which is now obsolete or decaying. The ever more specialized nature of our technical society makes effective redeployment of this base either difficult or impossible. Similarly, despite massive increases in the technical capabilities of communication and retrieval systems, it is still impossible to avoid duplicated effort. Regardless of desire or need, technical limits constrain the university's response to a changing situation.

A related technical limit that is extremely important to the university's capability to respond to change is the pace of diffusion of technological innovation within society. Diffusion is now faster than at any time in history, with estimates ranging from four to ten times faster. This introduces three interesting problems associated with implementation: (1) human beings and institutions do not adjust to change of such scale and speed very easily; (2) as the rates of diffusion quicken, it becomes increasingly difficult to predict the range of effects a single innovation will have; and (3) it is probable that no sudden developments of "magic" machinery are looming on the horizon, but sufficient innovations are waiting to be applied and absorbed.

Put another way: a wealth of examples (television, high-fidelity equipment, microprocessors, digital telephone networks, computers) indicate that it takes approximately a human generation (some twenty to thirty years) for a theoretical breakthrough in the laboratory to become established in society at large. If this is true, there are no new technological cures to the problems higher education faces, and no predictions for any current breakthrough of a sufficiently different prospect for the immediate future. The problem of the technical limits of educational innovation remains a microcosm of the general situation — how to determine the most appropriate use for technologies already available (or soon to be so) and how to diffuse them in practice.

A second class of limits is economic. *Economic limits* need little amplification in the university's current situation. The translation of protracted economic slowdowns throughout North America in the past decade into restrictions in university operations has been direct and permanent. The basic economic truism that resources are always finite while demands remain infinite continues to apply and has been reinforced by the general acceptance of finiteness in all areas, thanks to Buckminster Fuller's metaphor of "Spaceship Earth." This means, in the broader social context, that education must compete with many other programs for tax dollars and donations. Unfortunately, it also means competition among disciplines and functions within universities as they struggle in some cases for survival. (Classics department are an example.) Perhaps this was always so, but it was never so evident or acute. In the final analysis, diminishing returns place a limit on the degree to which expansion in one area or another will continue to be productive.

Economic limits also mean something else — something too often ignored but clearly demonstrated in the halcyon days of the 1960s: there is a limit to how much money can be absorbed efficiently by existing institutional operations without appropriate planning, even if economic alleviation is immediately forthcoming. "Throwing money" at a problem has never proven to be the best solution.

A third class of problems is ecological. *Ecological limits* in the broadest sense refer to the degree to which any disproportion in a given activity degrades the surrounding system. Since education is not physically resource-intensive, it escapes the image of "dark satanic mills" and might be considered exempt from ecological limits. But it should not. Ecology is the totality of things, and there is a sense in which higher education has caused its own form of "pollution." For example:

— To the extent that standards of certification were lowered during the years of educational expansion, the educational product was degraded.

— To the extent that pressure to "publish or perish" resulted in a flood of trivial publications, the signal-to-noise ratio was altered unfavourably.

— To the extent that higher education took on political or social roles (such as serving as a direct agent for trying to secure greater social equity) inappropriate to its fundamental nature, it was exposing itself to adverse opinion without any compensatory justification.

All these transgressions, which have severely tarnished the university's image, are activities contrary to ecological limits.

Another important ecological limit, which has been acknowledged without any clear prescription for its remedy, is the current demographic structure of the university teaching corps. One of the effects of explosive expansion in the 1960s was the creation of a disproportionately large cohort of younger faculty members. Most of these have now gained tenure and are at the halfway mark of their teaching careers. The subsequent abrupt reduction in the university's growth rate has sharply reduced opportunities for the recruitment of younger faculty. The internal ecology of the university cannot fail to be adversely affected by the overall aging of its faculty, particularly in critical scientific and technological areas. All systems wishing to remain vital need "new blood" from time to time to stimulate and regenerate them. Since "growing old together" is a condition that will persist for most of the remainder of this century within universities, this problem will become increasingly grave unless some ways are found to reduce its effect.

Ecological limits may also be seen as a subset of *social limits* that govern the capacity of the social system to respond to change, something Toffler neatly symbolized in the notion of "future shock." Many of the social traditions of higher education, such as collegial democracy, tenure, and certain forms of peer review, though individually of great intrinsic value, severely impede the capacity of the educational system to respond to change.

In addition, the relative amorphousness of academic decision-making structures in the past meant that decisions instigating a particular course of action were impossible to modify quickly enough in the light of altered circumstances. The replacement of these structures with the bureaucracy and the procedural structures of faculty unionization have made a bad situation even worse. Universities always demonstrated a rigidity to change, but with the advent of unions, an institutionalization of suspicion toward those who advocate change has been added. The result is a kind of social inertia that first causes universities to lag in responding to change and then to adopt strategies inadequate to an altered course of events.

A parallel situation exists in the relationship between society and the university where social limits have extremely important effects. Higher education is in general disrepute among the public because exaggerated claims for university education raised expectations to an unrealistic point. This in turn resulted in educational systems that the public views as inadequate to current challenges, let alone future ones. In Canada this could well lead to permanent intrusion by government in the administration of universities. Future scenarios should take into account the degree to which legal restraints, financial restrictions, and community sentiment will present obstructions to change within them. The current state of public opinion on higher education is an important social limit to future change simply because it has such pervasive effects throughout the control mechanisms governing the university system.

This leads directly to the final, most damaging and inuring class of current limits governing proper institutional response to future challenges. Alarmingly, this limitation is as prevalent within the academic community as without. This class comprises *imaginative limits*. Although it is true that only a minority of people seem able to think imaginatively about problems, the failure within universities to do so is particularly jarring. That universities are not alone in so failing is of little comfort. Perhaps the best example of such failure is the degree to which invention and production of computer and communications systems have outstripped functions or applications for them. How ironic it is that we have created a telecommunications network that allows each of us nearly instantaneous access to almost anyone in the world, yet we find we have little of importance to say. The "vast wasteland" of commercial television in North America is a tragic rejection of the beneficial capacities of this medium. We have, in fact, developed a superb system for realizing future change and utterly failed to articulate imaginative goals for it.

Failure to transcend limits to the imagination somehow seems more heinous in the university milieu, devoted as it is to the free life of ideas. One major cause may well be specialization – our attempt to know more and more about less and less. Initially this approach was not entirely bad, as shown by the remarkable output of useful results in the broadest sense. But success breeds its own brand of failure. These days we are witnessing within universities the way disciplinary binders prevent the cross-fertilization of disciplines required by current conditions. Even though interdisciplinary programs are on the rise, the current university system provides little incentive to create the capacity for integration of specialties, so its residents either have not cared to or cannot think of vehicles for exploiting such possibilities to the maximum.

Another imaginative limit with particular application to the university is the cult of the "expert authority." The "not invented here" syndrome has often caused academics to belittle or reject contributions to intellectual life offered by those outside the university or from universities perceived to be inferior. An important aspect of this syndrome is the cultivation of the intellectual equivalents of popular fallacies and fads – for example, rejection of productive profit-making industrial activity as invalid or pejorative, which in some cases became a required badge of entry to some areas of academic scholarship. Such attitudes give rise to parochial environments where risks are minimal. This impedes imaginative thought.

The significance of current imaginative limits to the future of higher education is plain when one considers the degree to which language and mathematics are enshrined as prima facie evidence that they are keystones of academic learning. To a great degree, proficiency in these areas is taken as a demonstration of the learning process. As Botkin, Elmandjra, and Malitza state in a report to the Club of Rome, however, this by no means exhausts the list of key elements in the learning process. They point out the degree to which tools, values, human relations, and images are important components of the intellectual process and therefore of the educational process as well. Yet many universities fail to accord these elements their proper place in academic activity, thus foreclosing the considerable creative and imaginative potential they entail. One of the reasons our system of information technology continues to fail in delivering what has been promised for it is precisely the failure of those in charge of the system, including those in universities, to imagine functions beyond ones traditional to the academic process. Our new tools have not been created merely to duplicate traditional teaching.

The consequence of these limits to change is simple: no system can be wholly re-made; therefore, the potential future of the university for the next twenty or so years is well established by present events. This does not discount the power of novelty and surprise. Knowing the factors influencing the future is not the same as knowing how these factors will affect the future. We can be sure there will be surprises, usually unpleasant ones. Yet considerations of entropy and "Murphy's Law" mean there is little chance of improved conditions occurring spontaneously. The general conclusion, then, is both simple and crucial: to deal effectively with future possibilities that will affect universities, we must understand the extent to which these remain rooted in or obscured by the dead hand of the present.

Through a Glass Darkly: Trends as Constraints on the University's Mission

Given the foregoing, we cannot escape the fact that progress in university education will depend in great part on the educational system's capacity for change through basing future implementations on current practices. The general limits to change such practices represent are realized in future outcomes through trends. Put another way: trends are a set of activities filtered through the general limits to change. Trends evolve from a confluence of perception, desire, capabilities, and activity, which is sometimes dimly seen but which forms part of an ongoing social response. Trends are the immediate past reacting with the present to provide catalysis for future developments. One other determinant to remember about futures and trends was nicely put by Dennis Gabor in 1964: " . . . the future cannot be predicted, but futures can be invented." The result may be a future radically different from the present, but its specifications remain firmly grounded in current realities.

There are always many trends, making it difficult to discern beforehand which amongst them are the most important. A consensus is evolving, however, about the identity of leading trends governing the evolution of North American society. A good example of current trends that have implications for educational requirements has been developed by Arthur W.

Combs. He has identified four existing certainties that will shape the future and suggests the educational consequences of each:

1. the information explosion, which changes the relationship between intellect and facts;
2. the increasing pace of change, which makes the objective of a universal standard for education impossible, demands intelligent problem solving, makes process-oriented education essential, requires an emphasis on values to form a framework for decision, and demands lifelong education and retraining;
3. the developing primacy of social problems as envelopes for technological applications, which is an outgrowth of the complex system problem; and
4. increased importance of personal fulfilment as a goal, because social binding institutions such as religion and family have ceased to have much effect.

In many ways the last issue is the key to healthy social development in the future and the one that is gaining momentum among the public. Overcoming the social limits to prescriptions as they affect personal fulfilment is a crucial task, which higher education can fail to address only at its peril. To address each of these trends and the issues involved in complete detail is impossible within the scope of this essay. It is possible, however, to sketch the implication of these and other trends for the planning of higher education's future.

An example of a major trend that encapsulates all four of Combs's trends is the emergence of what Edward S. Todd, among others, has called "steel collar" industries—the introduction of comprehensive robotics into manufacturing processes. Robotics is generally considered the leading edge in our society's evolution into a high technology future, one with vast implications for higher education's form and function. Why? Because robotization of manufacturing processes has introduced a number of serious problems, not least of which is the concept of productivity. This explains why Leslie J. Chamberlain is just one of a growing group of authorities predicting that by 1990, 15 per cent of all assembly systems will be robotic, 20 per cent of the auto industry, and 50 per cent of the small-component assembly industries. Moreover, by the year 2000, technological bootstrapping inherent in the reinvestment of the resulting capital wealth will accelerate this trend enormously. Although superproductivity brings superprofits, it also brings radical social changes as a result of the changing employment structure of nations. The degree to which rational and apposite social response to this and related developments is possible can be strongly conditioned by higher education's effectiveness.

Bruce F. Goeller has identified several other industrial and social problems now evident in trends whose resolution will also shape the future. They involve the ongoing computer and communications revolution, of which industrial robotics is only one facet that devalues acquisition and retention of factual information as valuable human attributes. (In fact, this is an adaptive response to the information explosion trend.) This revolution also devalues skills and techniques that can be computerized, such as instrument set-up and bibliography preparation, substituting instead an increased emphasis on mathematical models and simulation techniques using large databases and increased symbiosis between people and machines. The educational implications of the computer revolution are quite similar to Combs's objectives: we must emphasize the artistic over the technical, concentrate on synthesis rather than analysis, teach problem solving more formally, and employ varied methods to improve creativity.

The trend toward increased importance of self-fulfilment and the employment-displacing trend of industrial robotics create a requirement for both a leisure revolution and a new type of educational experience. Although recent economic setbacks have delayed any further reduction of the work week, increases in structural unemployment indicate unmistakably a necessity to devalue the work ethic and cancel out identification of one's work as the central value. Norman N. Goble has expressed the pith of this development in arguing, "The essential and most formidable fact about work in the next decade or two is that, in part because of the microprocessor, there will not be enough to go around." Goeller detects a twofold implication for education in this case — to educate people to the reality of this social shift and to expose them to things that will be recreational in the largest sense, thus permitting a situation that would encourage learning as a lifelong process.

The interaction among all these related trends produces a meta-trend toward the high technology society: more complex and more powerful than that of today, yet more vulnerable and more dependent on individual attitudes. In this regard we will need a new type of citizen, at once both able to cope in such an environment and able to make important judgements about differing interpretations of technological issues. Among other things, this may require the creation of a scientific/ engineering/technological elite who are also well-schooled in the so-called "soft" subjects of the humanities. They will be needed to help in the management of government and to be major participants in the political process. As Goeller says: "Government of a complex, technological society is too important to leave to the lawyers." This phenomenon would be the most revolutionary outcome for the future of education implicit in current trends one can possibly imagine.

The set of trends governing the future of high technology society gives rise to three general desiderata: (1) to better educate all citizens to use and to evaluate technology; (2) teach people to learn on their own so they can keep abreast of significant knowledge shifts; and (3) to restore the arts within all programs, which will enable students to develop backgrounds that permit richer lives through understanding and appreciating society and civilization.

Would that it were all so simple. As noted earlier, one of the major obstacles to success is that educational institutions cannot merely "will" to start anew in implementing revised educational objectives. They must start to regenerate their institutions.

To make matters worse, there are some added hurdles, not least of which is the requirement not only to educate a new cadre of people but to provide retraining for those already "out of work." Capital for and human tolerance of retraining and relocation are limited. More important, the capital-intensive nature of industrial robotics and developments in artificial intelligence means that universities will have to run as hard as they can just to keep their present place, because the high technology world of the future will provide no respite. Displacement will continue; it is estimated that eventually only 10 per cent of the population will be involved in production-related activities. The rest will have to provide services, consumption, diffusion, and application of high technology. A.P. Carnevale has drawn an arresting parallel between the situation of farmers after the Industrial Revolution and that of industrial workers after the information revolution. It is not that either class of workers is unimportant (far from it!); it is just that there will not be very many of them left.

Other factors that will have an enormous effect on universities can be seen in four additional trends.

1.   The campus is no longer the only location for education (the "university without walls" will become a reality).

2.   Training, the pursuit of knowledge, and general research will not be the exclusive franchise of educational institutions (hundreds of non-academic centres, including many agencies dissatisfied with the competence of present graduates, have entered the game).

3.　The advent of lower levels of general employment may mean the need for a return to labor-intensive activities, requiring a restoration of craftsmanship and an extension of the time required in the education system to hold people out of the market (this could mean the restoration of the apprenticeship system as part of the education process).

4.　There is a need for a permanent, integrated program of continuing education.

The extent to which the present educational establishment, and especially post-secondary institutions of which universities are a part, can meet these requirements will determine their futures. Those hoping the solutions to these problems rest in high technology better guess again. High technology, like any other technology, is a *means*, not an *end*. The key to a high technology society rests in the degree to which its production outputs are applied as a tool and a resource for both social maintenance and educational renovation. In this context, production will create the wealth, but that will not be enough. A new social philosophy is required. Technology can help, but the final answer lies in people. This leads directly to the consideration of the degree to which the present higher educational system is capable of responding effectively to the demands such people will impose upon it.

Can the Spirit Will More than the Flesh Allows? The State of the University Today

When we turn from the complex demands the university's environment is placing upon it to consider its ability to respond, the picture becomes bleak and depressing. I say this because throughout North America, universities face a decline in their traditional enrolment, weakening public support, and a loss of prestige in the corridors of power. This is no passing, temporary phenomenon. The causes of this malaise are reflected in problems that have emerged as we evolve toward a post-industrial society and that are rooted in accelerated economic, demographic, and social change. Let me outline briefly some of these major changes.

As a start, we must disabuse ourselves of the notion that the size of the university will any longer be directly related to the traditional "university age" cohort. Reasons for this include the baby boom, the growth of continuing education, the recession, and the increase in female students. But when all is said and done, however, a different truism emerges: until a major attitudinal change is brought to bear on our society, the participation rate within universities will remain wedded to the individual perceptions of the value of university education to one's future. Of late, universities have not done a good job preserving standards or explaining the true value of their wares. The "human capital" argument has supported the expansion of education in North America since World War II by claiming that investment in education was the social equivalent of capital formation. Its weaknesses were exposed in the late 1970s as employers complained about the quality of the graduates and thousands of graduates were unable to find work. Unless individual perceptions of the economic advantages of higher education turn from the negative, the student population will continue to diminish.

Four external factors about the recent fluctuations in demographic participation rates are worth noting:

— the almost universal acceptance of formula financing based on headcount rather than program, thus ensuring any enrolment drops or program changes would be exacerbated by negative external consequences

— the escalating wage demands (frequently union-driven) within universities and rampant inflation in all classes of consumable and capital goods

— the sharp shifts among established programs (for example, extraordinary growth in computer science and business science enrolments) which produced inefficiencies within universities

— the developments in technology, particularly in computer-assisted design and manufacture.

The result has been a general decline, prolonged for more than a decade, which has led to a vitiated higher educational establishment. The question remains: will the situation continue regardless of what universities do? Perhaps not, but the problem remains, and will not be solved easily, of establishing a more relevant programmatic sanction for the university's activities that will allow universities to resume a renewed and constructive role in society. This brings us face-to-face with the real problem: how to articulate the true value of higher educational institutions in a manner that will be creditable to both its external and internal environments.

Universities, no less than any other institution in society, must pre-select the framework within which this question will be engaged, recognizing the key to any answer rests squarely with the question of purpose. Specifically: toward what goal should curricula and efforts be directed? One simple example. If, as current trends suggest, much more emphasis has to be given to the process of self-development as divorced from vocational requirements, should the issue of "jobs for university graduates" become less relevant?   At present, our major benefactor, government, thinks not.

In the past, universities have been slow to react constructively to this and other questions and so have suffered popular (and therefore political) loss of esteem (not least of which resulted from the loss of control to students in the late 1960s and early 1970s). As a result, the university's fiscal viability remains uncertain, with many of its educational functions impaired or not adequately supported (for example, computer literacy).   This leads to diminished relevance when society has no broadly based, alternative social institution to fill the void.   Interestingly, this makes the implications for funding as unpleasant for parsimonious governments as they are easy for them to ignore. Yet without an infusion of revenue, higher education cannot keep pace in this increasingly technological world.

The result is a vicious circle: as universities are seen to be increasingly irrelevant, priority for external funding slips; as their fiscal state deteriorates, so does their capacity for keeping abreast of technological change; as the university is seen to slip further behind the current state of reality, it is seen to be increasingly irrelevant.   The alternatives to higher education that might step in to help take up the slack (corporations, the military) do so on an ad hoc basis because they have different goals or raisons d'être, thus compounding the difficulties to be overcome.

An arresting paradox emerges from these considerations. On the one hand, the wider technological future and its requirements are as clear and certain as prediction can allow; one can bet money on them (and the Japanese are).   On the other hand, the current trends shaping our short-term future are both irresistable and powerful.   Given the time that must be allowed for any system to react, the pattern for future activity within our social system has already been determined by current initiatives. This explains why we know what we have to do with a great deal of precision.   Yet the modus operandi within the contemporary university system is such that it lacks both an appropriate administrative structure and adequate resources to respond either quickly or properly to this challenge.   Sadly, the more exactly we see what it is that has to be done, the clearer it becomes that we cannot do it within our present institutional framework.   This is a far cry from the usual state of planning where one is expected to react in the face of inadequate data.

Turning to Our Task:
How Shall We Design for the Future?

The foregoing suggests that effective response will be difficult. This should not, however, deter us from making the effort; it was ever thus in education. Fifty years ago, Robert Hutchins summed up the problem of educational reform nicely when he said:

> I concede the great difficulty of communicating the kind of education I favor to those who are unable or unwilling to get their education from books . . . the answer . . . is not that some people should not have it, but that we should find out how to give it to those whom we do not know how to teach at the present. You cannot say my content is wrong because you do not know the method of transmitting. Let us agree upon content . . . and have faith that the . . . genius of America will solve the problem of communication.

The only way higher education can regain the prestige necessary to restore it to the pride of place it once enjoyed is to adopt a posture that demonstrates how vital its tasks are and to try to illustrate why universities are capable of discharging them. This requires a more precise definition of what higher education must do. A useful first step might be to consider how to implement the agenda for the twenty-first century developed by Thomas M. Stauffer, a leading practitioner deeply involved in education's future:

— shift emphasis from quantity to quality,
— take the lead in accelerating the shift of the North American economy to high technology production,
— address social problems with appropriate university expertise,
— emphasize the enrichment of the educational process at all levels,
— establish high standards for student performance and graduation,
— focus attention on problems of North American youth,
— develop innovative means of ensuring educational equity for minorities,
— formulate a clear mission concept and keep to it,
— provide a degree of program internationalization so as to reflect a more diverse, complex, and interdependent world, and
— develop an institutional emphasis on what students are to become, including citizenship preparation, proficiency in

communication, lifelong education, scientific and technological literacy, and computer skills.

Another issue is educational relevance. This remains a hot topic, as capable as ever of producing divisive debate. We can find a way out of this impasse and develop the appropriate course "content" if we can agree on the qualities the future world requires. Five measures suggested by Herbert Striner seem appropriate: (1) to focus thinking on logic and relationships; (2) to allow sensitive judgement to operate in applied situations; (3) to break down overly narrow disciplinary boundaries; (4) to tie application and reality firmly together as criteria for testing theories; and (5) to accept adjustment both inside and outside educational institutions.

These are not radical ideas, but they constitute a direct challenge to the comfortable status quo. A number of issues must be explored and effective methods of dealing with them evolved. These issues involve problems of:

— Pedagogy. We cannot assume that people can teach simply because they have degrees. Nor can we assume machines, that is technology, will improve teaching if they take over part of the educational process. Bad teaching by machines is still bad teaching; therefore pedagogy is vital. Current evidence suggests the pressure will increase for university teachers to demonstrate competence (just like garage mechanics, barbers, doctors, and lawyers).

— Certification standards for graduates. Nothing damaged the credibility of North American higher education more than its production of a flood of graduates who could neither communicate effectively nor think efficiently.

— Intellectual freedom. Intellectual freedom rests on tenure. Of late, tenure has often proven to be counter-productive. Any solution must preserve the principle of intellectual freedom as a prerequisite of university life, but the whole question of security and order versus creative ferment must be carefully considered.

— Process and product in education. Education as a process must be refined so as to make clear the degree to which the "continuing process" is really the only product universities have to market. Universities must not lose sight of the difference between process (the potential for a life of learning) and product (the grasp of a specific skill).

— Technology. Technology may help us in our attempts at institutional renewal, thanks to the many educational prosthetics provided to improve both learning techniques and to simplify our daily lives. In the final analysis, however, it can be neither the solution nor the problem. Rather, it is a powerful means to a desired end, but only if that end can be defined. The real issue to be dealt with by the educational establishment is definition of goals and the development of the "software" needed to reach them.

Conclusion

In many cases, the simplest things can be the hardest to do. In principle, what we have to do in planning how to educate the twenty-first century's leaders today is simple enough to specify. We know what general limits exist, forming the boundaries of the possible. We know that the major trends that will shape the future are already established and discernible in present conditions. We know what many of the consequences of continued high technology development are, and we know that the only way to escape these consequences is to suffer something worse. We also know that the present resources and volitional fibre of the current university establishment seem inadequate to the task of coping with future changes.

Sitting still will not help our paradox. We must act boldly but in diverse ways within differing environments. Universities are important for the well-being of society, so it is imperative that they make the contribution needed for the development of a twenty-first century society worth living in. Action is required, but action to be effective must be planned. We have to get down to specifics now. This means effective, constructive planning soundly based on the realities of the present. Let us remember, to paraphrase Robert Hutchins, that a university must be more than a collection of independent departments linked by a common heating system.

Bibliography

Barzun, Jacques. *The House of Intellect*. New York: Harper, 1959.

Botkin, James W.; Elmandjra, Mahdi; and Malitza, Mircea. *No Limits to Learning: Bridging the Human Gap; a Report to the Club of Rome*. Oxford: Pergamon Press, 1979.

Bowen, J.R. *The State of the Nation and the Agenda for Higher Education*. San Francisco, Calif.: Jossey-Bass Inc., 1982.

Carnevale, Anthony Patrick. "Higher Education's Role in the American Economy." *Educational Record* 64 (Fall 1983): 6-16.

Chamberlain, Leslie J. "Facing Up to Robotation." *USA Today* 111 (Nov. 1982): 30-32.

Combs, Arthur W. "What the Future Demands of Education." *Phi Beta Kappan* 62 (Jan. 1981): 369-72.

Dede, Christopher and Allen, Dwight. "Education in the 21st Century: Scenarios as Tools for Future Planning." *Phi Beta Kappan* 62 (Jan. 1981): 362-366.

Ferguson, Marilyn. *The Aquarian Conspiracy: Personal and Social Transformation in the 1980s*. Los Angeles, Calif.: J.P. Tarcher Inc., 1980.

Goeller, Bruce F. "Engineering Education for the 21st Century." Santa Monica, Calif.: RAND Corporation, July 1980.

Hesburgh, Thedore M.; Miller, Paul A.; Wharton, Clifton R. *Patterns for Lifelong Learning*. San Francisco, Calif.: Jossey-Bass Inc., 1973.

Jay, Timothy B. "The Future of Educational Technology." *Educational Technology* 22 (June 1982): 21-23.

Kierstead, F.; Bowman, J.; Dede, C. *Educational Futures: Source Book I*. Washington, D.C.: World Futures Society, 1979.

Schroeder, Timothy D. "Comprehensive Planning for Higher Education." *College Board Review* 122 (Winter 1981/82): 14ff.

Shane, H.G. *The Educational Significance of the Future.* Bloomingdale, Ind.: Phi Delta Kappa, 1973.

Stauffer, Thomas M. "Higher Education in the Year 2000." *Educational Record* 64 (Winter 1982): 60-61.

Striner, Herbert A. "The Changing Economy and Its Implications for Postsecondary Education." *Educational Record* 64 (Fall 1983): 36-39.

Todd, Edward S. "Impacts of the 'Steel Collar' Revolution and Robotics Upon Higher Education." Paper presented at the 23rd Annual Forum of the Association for Institutional Research. Toronto, Ontario, 23-26 May 1983.

Vagianos, Louis G. "Today is Tomorrow." *Library Journal* 101 (1 Jan. 1976): 147-56.

Vagianos, Louis G. "Cultivating Continuing Education." *Policy Options* 4, 5 (Sept./Oct. 1983).

THE UNIVERSITY AS A LEARNING SYSTEM

DONALD A. MICHAEL

Introduction

A key determinant of an organization's ability to engage its circumstances effectively is the characteristics of its culture: its norms of conduct; styles of personal relationships; reward systems; structures; modes of intercourse with its internal and external stakeholders; and its expectations and beliefs about its purposes and reasons for existence. This culture is the product of both the unique history of the organization and the cultural characteristics of the surrounding society. The latter are expressed inside the organization through its members who are also representatives of the external culture. Given these sources, an organization's culture is, in important degree, the residue of *past* learned successes and suppressed failures. It is not surprising, therefore, that in these times of turbulence and rapid change, most organizational cultures are drastically unfit for meeting the challenges confronting them as they move toward the twenty-first century.

This is especially so for organizations that must operate at high levels of uncertainty. For such organizations the options are: trying to muddle through or trying to change their culture so it is appropriate for the changing circumstances. On the face of it, the latter is more likely to preserve organizational vitality. The problem is that, under conditions of high turbulence, there are no time-tested directives pointing to *what* the new culture ought to be. There is no fixed culture to attain because circumstances keep changing. Instead, in view of this state of affairs, the appropriate culture is one that sustains a learning approach to organizational development. In this mode the organization is designed to ask continuously the questions: where do we want to go; how do we get there; are we getting there; do we still want to get there in light of what has now emerged, and what can we now anticipate, having gotten to where we are? Unremarkable as that might sound, only now and haltingly are some organizations beginning to experiment with such an approach. Learning what the unique characteristics should be for an organization that is designed to be a learning system and then learning to *be* that kind of system requires radically different values, operating norms, organizational structures, and personal relationships from those of conventional organizational cultures. The tasks are so different and so demanding that they would hardly be worth attempting if there were another way to remain vital. I do not believe there is. The remainder of this essay explores why this is so and, in that light, describes some of the fundamental characteristics of an organization – in this case the university – as a learning system.

First, I will describe some characteristics of the developing societal context in which the university must discover and pro-actively, rather than reactively, plan for its functions, for its values, and for the human and financial resources for realizing them in the next decades. Next, I will describe some issues pertaining to the purposes and conduct of the university that can be expected to preoccupy its stakeholders in the years ahead because of the societal context. Given the conflicting values and demands of these issues, I see no ready answers to the challenges they will pose in the university. Instead, coping constructively – that is, asking new questions and discovering new responses – will require a university culture that sees itself and is accepted and performs as a learning organization. Finally, I will describe some of the main attributes of the learning culture that characterizes a learning organization, the necessary (but probably not sufficient) condition for a resilient university moving into the twenty-first century.

The Societal Context

The developing societal context of the next few decades will display serious underlying divergences that will manifest themselves in political, social, and economic conflicts over purposes, policies, programs, and evaluations, some of which will impinge directly on the university. Unavoidably and unrelievedly, the university will be crunched between powerful outside demands and expectations and those inside, each force comprising traditional perspectives that conflict and compete with newly evolving ones. In other words, it does not matter much which scenario of the next few decades one embraces. Unless one subscribes to a scenario in which one set of values, norms of conduct, and societal purposes coheres everything into a new order – a scenario for which, for reasons I will describe, I see no grounds at all – what will characterize all likely situations is conflict, turbulence, and uncertainty about everything from self to society ... surely including the university. Such will be the persistence, complexity, and novelty of these forces for change and for stasis, that coping constructively with them will require unconventional norms, structures, and ways of relating to one another.

Perhaps the broadest overriding observation to be made about the societal context is that the dominant myths, that is, that which gives coherence, meaning, direction, and drive to a society, are disintegrating or at least undergoing deep change and multiple challenges. Traditional economic, political, and spiritual values, all expressions of earlier myths, are under question or direct attack in many cultures and most dramatically in the West. In the West, even the sufficiency of rational, scientific reason for understanding and coping with the big issues of human purpose and quality of life is being questioned. This is not to say, however, that the once-dominant myths no longer are able to define reality: for many, they are still powerful indeed, and they are likely to remain so. Many people subscribe to other myths or at least seriously question the traditionally dominant ones because they do not seem to "fit," to deal adequately with the consequences and conduct of the world of problems, opportunities, and predicaments that are the products of the traditional myths. Two pairs of mythic divergences are especially relevant for the culture of the university.

First is the deepening clash between the myth of the past three hundred years that sees causes and effects, ideas, organizations, persons, programs, things as independent and separate, and the other, much older myth that sees the world as systemic, holistic, interdependent, and interactive with causes and effects mutually creating and transforming each other. One emphasizes competition, self-interest, individual rights, and control; the other, co-operation, community interests, interpersonal obligations, and resilience. These two myths embody opposing principles: survival of the fittest versus being one's brother's keeper; autonomy versus spaceship earth; we/they versus us; "one thing at a time" versus "you can't do just one thing."

A second major clash in world views grows between those who see humans as predictable and therefore controllable, subject to the workings of laws analogous to those of Newtonian physics; and those who see human behaviour as emergent. In this view, what emerges in the human realm is not predictable from the characteristics of what has preceded it just as the meaning of a paragraph is unpredictable from the words it comprises, or a new theory, or art form, or stage of history is unpredicatable from what precedes it.

There is another vantage for viewing the context in which the university will have to work out its ministry. Cutting across these different mythologies, or world views, of what is real "out there" and, hence, how it can or should be dealt with, will be the persisting divergences of persons and groups that arise from differences in demography and experience. Very different motives, needs, and styles will be expressed by the young and the old; the illiterate, the poorly educated, and the well educated; the violent and the nurturing; the alienated and the engaged; those who hold to fundamentalist spiritual values and those who do not; and those who live in a cosmopolitan world and those wedded to parochial perspectives. These divergences will eventually bring powerful conflicting pressures to bear on the conduct of the university. More must be said, therefore, about the place of growing amounts of information in the emerging societal context.

> More information can result in more control but it also creates circumstances that reduce or defy control. It clarifies some issues but it obscures and complicates others. It enlarges the opportunities for participation in decision making and in doing so it both increases and reduces the incentives for adversarial confrontations in the courts and on the streets. It brings more ideas into the market place but at the cost of raising the noise level to where nothing can be heard clearly. Unprecedented amounts of information can be brought to bear on issues of policy and action but the persons who must use the information to make decisions become overloaded and everything gets muddled. In some cases one feels more information really gives an understanding of a situation. In more cases more information deepens a feeling of uncertainty. Information gives some ever greater access to a more complex world while condemning others to deeper isolation and alienation. It facilitates the coherence of groups and, at the same time, helps groups to splinter anew. It can make for both centralization and decentralization of power. In such ways information entices some into ever more demands for information and others to turn away from more information because it upsets habits of mind and action.[1]

More information, therefore, especially about the human condition, is more likely than not to increase uncertainty. The availability of more information will reinforce one norm that will continue to be widely shared among otherwise contending stakeholders in the university's ambit: their insistence on participating in policies and decisions perceived as affecting their welfare (whether it be through membership on appropriate committees, civil disobedience, violence, injunctions, or legislation). In the absence of shared perspectives, more information increases the likelihood that enough information can be marshalled to promote or defend almost any position on the university's ministry, according to whatever mythologies and values provide the incentives to do so.

Such a contentious and information-rich societal context is certain to face the university with multiple claims about priorities, services, opportunities, and claimant legitimacy. The university will have to plan for issues whose resolution will require unfamiliar, perhaps unique, decision-making criteria and will alter the university culture. How to create and to use these criteria will constitute a major part of the learning agenda of the university as a changing organization.

These issues will engender new ways of planning, funding, decision making, evaluating, monitoring, governing, relating to external stakeholders, and organizing internal activities. In the process, statuses and internal organizational structures will be altered along with the norms that define appropriate performance and responsibilities.

Basic Issues Disrupting the Conventional University Culture

I begin with the observation that the university (at least those arising out of the Western European tradition) has seen itself as autonomous, separate from the rest of the society. That has been its special value, and it is symbolized in the institution of tenure and in the unwavering commitment to freedom of inquiry. Moreover, this emphasis on separateness is dramatically demonstrated by the very norms and structure of the university with its implacably autonomous departments, schools, disciplines, and rigorously defended distinction between the realms of administration and those of scholarship. The traditional campus itself reinforces the impression of its insulation from the turbulent society. Nevit Sanford describes today's university as follow:

In my more despairing moments, it seems to me that
the modern university has succeeded in separating
almost everything that belongs together. Not only
have fields of inquiry been subdivided until they have
become almost meaningless, but research has been
separated from teaching, teaching and research from
serving action and, worst of all, thoughts from human
feeling.[2]

Contending with this tradition of isolation, however, is the
university's increasing interconnectedness with the rest of
society, so much so that, at least for the United States, university
"service" to its community is frequently deemed a responsibility
equal in importance to those of teaching and research. This
increasing tension between autonomy and interdependence
mirrors that in the larger society between the two world views
described earlier.

The university can be expected to continue to justify its
existence through teaching, research, and services. But it will do
so in what proportions; for what kinds of persons; under what
conditions; where, given the dispersion made feasible by
information technology; and to what ends? In other words, to
advance what values? Moreover, who shall decide these profound
matters, or, if left undecided, who shall be responsible for what
follows from that state of affairs?

A second issue is that one world view holds that knowledge
is value-free and that values are subjective and knowledge
objective, especially if derived from research. That view is under
powerful and sustained attack. What, then, should be the place of
values in teaching those subjects directly impinging upon human
lives? What of the appropriateness of maintaining the image of
the scholar or scientist as value-free regarding his or her
material? If values are recognized as perfusing knowledge, even
information, are there "right" values to be taught? Who says so?

Here, rising to new intensities in a splintered world, is the
tension between the conserving function of teaching and that
which encourages radical questioning of the condition and
purposes of life. The tension will grow as the university becomes
more dependent on funds from establishments favouring the
status quo, be they government or private enterprise. What then
is the obligation of the university as an entity for *acting out* its
values in the way it conducts itself and engages the rest of the
world?[3] What of the rights of faculty or administrative
dissenters? Are only tenured members entitled to go their own

way? Indeed, *may* tenured members do so? Who decides? On the basis of what values?

Whatever other values created and support that of freedom of inquiry, it was, I believe, rooted in the myth of a world of separate parts in which knowledge is separate from use. (Consider the oft-repeated, "technology is neutral; it's what men do with it that makes it bad or good.") The myth included belief in the objectivity of knowledge: it was or could be value-free if based on scholarly norms of investigation. The myth also included a belief that the overall effect of knowledge would necessarily be good, that somehow the transient bad effects could be dealt with or, at any rate, were "worth" it. Moreover, knowledge was believed to be created by those whose very dedication to the task separated them from worldly ambitions and circumstances. Whatever the past utility of that separatist mythology about the creation and status of knowledge, it will be increasingly under attack in the years ahead and so too the idea of unrestricted freedom of inquiry, by those who believe in the myth of an intensely interconnected world.

The question who gains and who loses from unrestricted inquiry is one way this issue will press heavily on the university. Who decides, therefore, who will be subject to what in order that some might gain? The questions accumulate power because, directly or indirectly, taxes support research. What are my rights to protect myself from the results of inquiry or research, or to have the benefits? Power, equity, responsibility all enter into this because, in many areas, research has affected people quite differently. Consider, for example, who gains and who does not when medical research emphasizes high technology cures for the few rather than health maintenance for the many. Or, as in the United States, agriculture research chiefly benefits agrobusiness rather than small, independent farmers.[4] An example from my own area, behavioural science, illuminates why this issue promises to present universities with serious challenges to freedom of inquiry as an unquestioned norm and pervasive shaper of its culture.

Even as in the past, today many behavioural scientists believe they do value-free research, that their responsibility is to contribute new knowledge through professional publications, "and that's it." In recent years, however, this research community has had to begin to wrestle with the fact that the selection of research topics and its funding are unavoidably value-laden, hence productive of results that give only a selective description of human and social reality. Geoffrey Vickers explains the problem this way:

It is clearly true that both science and philosophy, by
the concepts of human nature which they use and
propagate, can powerfully affect men's views of
themselves, their possibilities and their limitations
and may thus alter what human nature effectively is.
A mistaken view of planetary motion, though held for
centuries, had no effect on the motion of the
planets. . . . A too restricted view of human nature, on
the other hand, even though briefly ascendant, can
significantly alter the expectations and hence the
behaviour of men and societies and may thus provide
its own bogus validation.[5]

Consequently, there is a deepening preoccupation in the research
community over what research under what conditions is ethically
acceptable and what are the responsibilities of the researcher to
the subjects before, during, and after the research. As a result,
review committees for behavioural research are a new and
influential factor in some university cultures. The same kinds of
questions may well be raised about inquiry in other areas that
may result in technological or biological benefits for some at costs
or risk to others.

Another set of emerging arguments will challenge the
university norm of freedom of inquiry. The question is, why
should scarce moneys be allocated to indulge the curiosity and
irrelevant creativity of university people while the tasks of
teaching and service lack funds, or when other parts of the society
are in need? Why indulge historians, philosophers, and academic
economists who, as the inventor of input-output economics has
said, contribute hardly anything to understanding real life?[6] All
these pure researchers and what they teach, so goes the
argument, are a luxury, and funds for such studies must be
carefully allocated, not made an entitlement.

In sum, for reasons of consequence and for reasons of
irrelevance, those who pay directly or indirectly for research and
those who represent them will claim the right to question and to
influence how their money is allocated, thereby interfering or
attempting to interfere with freedom of inquiry. Under these
circumstances, the university will have to learn new ways to
protect its old norm or learn new norms. Either way, the task
will be difficult but necessary.

Another topic, sure to wrack the university with deep
conflict inside and outside its "walls," will be the appropriate
balance between specialized and general knowledge.

Increasingly evident is that, contrary to the conventional mythology, specialized knowledge seldom solves social problems.[7] The cry for expert generalists grows ever louder. University faculties devoted to and rewarded for creating ever more specialized knowledge and passing it on to specialized students who then move into the world as "experts" are ill-prepared, structurally or psychologically, to meet this growing demand. Preoccupations with personal status and administrative turf insulate departments and schools. The rewards of publication go chiefly to the specialist. Departmental support for interdisciplinary research is notoriously fickle.

Few universities have begun to think about the reconstruction of teaching, service, and research to respond to problems as much as to disciplines. There are problem-oriented institutes and centres; but the dominating status of departments, as reflected in the composition of academic senates and university budget line items, along with inattention to value issues and to the development of interpersonal skills in faculty members or students, make it quite clear that the cultivation of problem-oriented knowledge and problem-oriented students is hardly first priority. It seems equally clear, however, that societies will press ever harder on universities to forgo departmental and scholarly purity and to put ever more effort into problem-oriented theory, research, and practice. The cultural change, not to say personal changes, required to meet this demand will be upsetting. Finding a balance and a constructive relationship between insulated, neat disciplines and sprawling, grubby, real-world problems will be difficult. But the task of seeking that balance will, I believe, be unavoidable.[8]

The last issue that almost certainly will disrupt the organizational culture of the conventional university is, who shall govern the university? As described earlier, both acknowledged and self-proclaimed stakeholders in the university's activities will claim the right to participate in decisions that may affect them. Because of their multiple allegiances, there will be intense differences *within* the university membership about who, within and without the university, is entitled to participate.[9] Outside the university, there will be corresponding arguments, accompanied, no doubt, by shifting alliances across this organizational "boundary." In the United States, the preferences of public funding sources and the implementation of judicial decisions increasingly intrude on the traditional culture that defined the conduct of the university whether it be the composition of the student body, compliance with affirmative action, or the emphasis in subject matter, research, or service. Recently, corporations have begun a new approach, sponsoring research and jointly owning its products. Occasionally in the United States, the city in which the university is located has attempted, sometimes successfully, to participate in decisions pertaining to the conduct of research, notably about weapons development and recombinant DNA. Wherever large organizations and their incumbent leaders are largely distrusted (as is so in the United States, for example), their legitimacy will be questioned, or at least the sufficiency of conventional decision-making processes will be.   Therefore, universities can expect to be pressed to reconsider who is entitled to participate in university decision making and policy formulation.

Attributes of a Learning Organization

The key to appreciating the virtues, or indeed the necessity, of becoming a learning organization is to recognize that the combination of societal issues reviewed earlier presage a world of turbulence, change, and multiple circular interactions and interdependencies that will make it impossible to know with any certainty what is cause and what effects can be expected. In other words, in a world where uncertainty is pervasive and unrelieved, the ability to control outcomes becomes less and less. Under such conditions, organizational survival and development will depend, not on the ability to control but on the ability to be resilient — to discover what is going on inside and outside the organization and to adjust to and to influence events. An organization needs the ability to unlearn and to relearn successfully, much as one does being an artist, navigating "white water," or raising a family. Being resilient is at least as much a matter of being feminine, that is, receptive, mutually supportive, and context-oriented, as it is a matter of being masculine, that is, intrusive, independent, and focused (at least as these traits pertain in Western cultures). Being resilient means responding to the world as if it were *both* this *and* that rather than *either* this *or* that, though often actions must be taken that are interpreted to be either this or that. Being resilient means being a learner as a person and as an organization.

Becoming a learner either as a person or an organization is a difficult task. Just as other organizations are finding radical change necessary, so too must the university change if it is to develop appropriately. Frank Friedlander presaged the difficulty of the task:

Although identity is the source of an organism's sanity, its preservation is the enemy of learning. Identity is conceived here as an organization of knowledge among the interdependent parts of the organism. As conditions change, this organization of knowledge must also change. Thus, adaptation calls for modification in identity. Yet identity modification is invariably threatening to the consistency and competence of the organism. The organism will consequently go to great lengths to fend off changes in its organization of knowledge. . . .

A strong sense of self is crucial to the well-being of an organism. A sense of self provides the individual or organization with boundaries, conviction, purpose, values, beliefs, and a guide for action. Furthermore, a clear sense of self allows the person to know how to behave with others in order to receive confirmation and affirmation. Similarly, the image an organization presents to its publics and to its own employees provides it' with a sense of mission, values and boundaries – its guide to action. . . .

But identities may also be tender and vulnerable, so that we build castles around them for purposes of defense and fortification. . . . Defenses then become embedded in the very composition of identity. . . .

Recent studies have shown that people manage knowledge in a variety of ways to promote the selective availability of information that confirms judgments already concluded. . . . People tend to reject messages contrary to their prior opinions, while being accepting of messages that reinforce existing opinions.[10]

In what follows I shall refer to both individuals and the university organization. Learning to become a learning culture involves much more than described here.[11] I shall highlight crucial attributes to give a sense of what would be involved and of what demands such changes will make on the individual psyche and on the organizational culture it inhabits and sustains. Note, however, that, in compensation for the difficulties of changing to a learning culture, unprecedented opportunities for personal and organizational development become available; one finds new vistas, new discoveries, new opportunities to teach, to research, and to be of service to self, to the university, and to others.

The combination of attributes that characterize a learner I call the "new competence," that is, the competence appropriate for performing resiliently in the turbulent, uncertain environment inside or outside the organization. It bears emphasizing that, in keeping with a both/and perspective where cause and effect create each other, both individual behaviour and the norms and structures of the culture, in this case the university, must be redesigned to sustain learning — hence the learning *organization.*

The most fundamental attribute of the new competencè, of being a learner and empowering others to learn, is the ability to live with and to acknowledge high degrees of uncertainty. Usually this does *not* mean throwing up one's hands and lamenting, "I don't know what the hell is going on.'" It does mean being able psychologically and cognitively to recognize what specifically it is about the situation that one does not know. Uncertainty does not pertain to probabilities; uncertain situations are those in which, in the dark of the night, or in the light of the mirror, one has to acknowledge that one honestly does not know the probabilities. Perhaps the needed information is unavailable or perhaps one lacks a definitive sense of what information is needed or what actions can be taken. Or perhaps there is too *much* information. Of course, this state of mind encompasses the acknowledgment that there may be aspects of the situation about which one does not know one does not know.

Courage and commitment are prerequisites for acknowledging to self and to others that one is uncertain. Our conventional definition of the competent person is one who *does* know — school grades depend on knowing the answers. Being certain is what engineers, the constructors of our technological world, are privileged to be and are rewarded for. Or so we are told, and others emulate them. Besides, acknowledging uncertainty jeopardizes "turf," subjecting it to potential invasion by those who claim they *do* know. Then, why wash such dirty linen in public? Why take such risks?

In the first place, acknowledging what one is uncertain about is necessary for learning. Otherwise there is no benchmark for defining informative feedback or for evaluating it so programs and actions can be readjusted. It is the knowledge of uncertainty that shapes learning.

If other stakeholders are to learn to make responsible demands, and if they are expected to share the risks of any benefit, they must understand the uncertainties inherent in the issue at hand. They cannot learn or shoulder part of the risks attached to the uncertainties if one or one's organization acts as if there were no uncertainties in concept, decision, or the consequences of actions.

In the second place, sharing uncertainty increases the capacity to sustain uncertainty. It is unclear how much uncertainty persons or society can usefully sustain; there are limits. It is clear, however, that we can manage much more when others share it with us who also share their uncertainty. Misery loves company; shared, it can also increase capability.

A third reason to acknowledge uncertainty, one approaching political practicality even within the old system, is that the present norm, according to which leaders act as if they knew what they were doing, simply increases distrust. This is because the evidence is accumulating that assertions about the future ever more result in problematic outcomes at best. A critical requirement for governance, including that of the university, is some kind of shared belief, a basic if qualified *trust* in the capability, reliability, and responsibility of the leaders of an institution and its components to assess their situation realistically. This is not the prevailing state of mind. The very act of leaders acknowledging uncertainty — which, even if they wish it otherwise, increasing numbers recognize is the case — could greatly help to reverse this trend. Increasing trust would make it easier for all parties to take chances in learning, in discovering, in developing new potentials in the self and in the organization. When we trust we are more energetic, supportive, and innovative. In a word, we are more productive.

Embracing error is another critical attribute of the new competence. It is the operational consequence of learning by acknowledging uncertainty. We learn from errors. In the conventional organizational culture, however, as true of non-scholarly activities in universities as of the conduct of corporations or governments, one is rewarded for not making errors; or if one does make an error, one is rewarded if the error can be hidden or, failing that, blamed on someone else. If that is not possible, then the rewards go to the person or organization that can argue that the error was not important to begin with. The result: no learning — or the wrong learning. This tendency to shoot ourselves in the foot arises because, conventionally, we equate error with failure.

Our tendency to equate the two arises from our belief that the competent person, being in control, does not make errors. The assumption is that the knowledge possessed by competent persons allows them to discriminate causes and therefore control effects. If one errs, therefore, one is not competent; one is a failure. Because the emerging societal setting of the university requires, however, that it must innovate in the midst of acute uncertainty, errors will be much more likely than not. The only way to learn, then, is to make the most of the errors; that is, to reach out, to anticipate, to embrace them; to use specified uncertainties to plan error-detecting arrangements so that learning from errors can occur quickly and pervasively and be rewarded. The competent person (and organization) then establishes the ability to discover what is not going as anticipated and then uses those discoveries to learn, to revise, and to experiment anew.

Note that embracing error does not reward those errors produced by slothful or indifferent performance in routine tasks. These remain reprehensible. By this very standard *not* to embrace error, given a routine environment of uncertainty and innovation, would be a reprehensible error, an incompetent performance. Moreover, embracing error must apply as well to learning appropriate norms and methods for embracing error.

As with the acknowledgment of uncertainty, embracing error engenders trust and the gains that accompany that kind of relationship. Cost will accompany the benefits in any experiment in the governance or performance of the university. Stakeholder understanding and collaboration in such experiments will be necessary, and trust will be prerequisite. To gain that trust, stakeholders will need to participate in the learning process. Therefore, embracing error must extend across agencies, divisions, departments and offices out to other stakeholders. Logical as this is, from the standpoint of the conventional organizational culture with its emphasis on autonomous turf protection, this is a profound and radical requirement.

Being responsive to the future is a third requirement for becoming learners seeking to discover how to cope with the challenges facing the university. Studies and concern about the future must become central and persisting components in the definition of the present. Conventionally, studies about the future were expected to reveal what lies "out there" and hence what adaptations are required. They were expected to reduce uncertainty. But, as recognition grows that the future is multiple and unpredictable, the true value of such studies becomes more apparent.

First, they provide a mythic context of problematic futures, which, just because they are problematic, compel us to choose what to seek or to avoid in order to respond to specific challenges in the present.

Second, well-done and well-used studies of the future confront us with the ethical issues abiding in what we are aspiring to or avoiding by the ways we act *now*. These studies temper our satisfaction with how far we have come by exposing how far we yet have to go, thus informing and evaluating the ethical and operational sufficiency of present actions. Correspondingly, responsiveness to the future strongly discourages frivolous or hypocritical goal setting.

Because this responsiveness forces attention to who we are, to what we are doing, and to longer-term, more systemic consequences, it can also engender community building, trust, and openness, all prerequisites for resilience in self and organization. In the process of arriving there, however, responsiveness to the future can also engender much pain. For both reasons, universities have much yet to learn about how to act responsively toward the future.

Being responsive toward the future is a special case of another central attribute of the new competence: the personal ability and cultural undergirding required to span information and normative boundaries. This responsiveness spans temporal boundaries; there are interorganizational and intraorganizational boundaries to be spanned as well. Spanning boundaries is a difficult task even in organizations with "obviously" interdependent subparts. In the university, with its traditional separation of school from school, department from department, and of administration from many scholarly activities, spanning boundaries will be a special challenge.

All attributes of the new competence and all strategic planning and methods of systems design depend on much more sharing of information, goals, and perspectives than typically pertains across boundaries. Yet, university subdivisions, like those in most traditional organizations, jealously defend their boundaries from intrusions that might challenge academic and intellectual purity, administrative procedures, and evaluation standards. All are worthy criteria for defending and maintaining subdivision autonomy and subdivision culture to further their purposes. But organizations, especially vulnerable ones, cannot develop felicitously essentially as an aggregate of subdivisions, each intent on pursuing their separate ambitions. Systems problems require systems approaches, not the autonomous pursuit of special interests based on laissez-faire norms. Creating a connection between the university and society that is appropriate for the future is most certainly a task of systemic synthesis.

An important example of this task is the reconstruction of system and subsystem boundaries in time and space so the university can better accomplish its ministry with the aid of the new information technologies. As another example, training generalists and creating knowledge relevant to social problems will require more permeable departmental and university boundaries and revised and shared university norms and goals than has typically been the case.

Interpersonal competence is a fifth requirement for becoming learners. Our incompetence at listening, speaking, supporting, coping with value conflicts, nurturing, role playing, and empowering, all contribute monumentally to the appalling inefficiency and ineffectiveness of task groups, committees, staff meetings, and the like. As one who both teaches these skills and facilitates task groups, I must observe that most task groups are spectacularly, heartbreakingly incompetent when it comes to making joint use of their substantive knowledge, insights, and feelings for defining or solving problems. University task groups are among the worst, especially those composed of academics. Yet, most of us could learn these skills once we recognize we need them and risk learning them.

Most of us — the products of a disjointed view of ourselves and of the world, organized and rewarded for seeing and performing this way — do not listen well. We are too busy coming up with our *own* statement. Nor are we skilled — compassionate, empathic — at supporting one another as we take risks in expressing our hunches, our intuitions, our doubts, our feelings, our values. All these expressions will be imperative contributions to understanding, innovating, and acting in the university's turbulent, uncertain, and often unfamiliar context of the next decades.

We are also inept at creatively managing value conflicts, a major reason why we excise values from substantive issues and focus on the "data." By pretending the issue can be managed without attention to intense feelings in ourselves, or other stakeholders, we inadvertently convince ourselves and everybody else that we are not sincerely committed to the task since, somewhere in each of us, we know those values are essential. We know the facts have meaning and direction only in light of underlying values that transcend the cost-effectiveness equations. Some significant part of our depression and exhaustion results from the consequential guilt and cynicism.

Reactions to the observations in this essay usually follow one of two patterns. One, fear, resentment, and finally withdrawal into the comforting belief that either the world will settle down, or the organization (in this case, the university) can prevail doing things in ways that proved successful in the past or at least resulted in its survival. The other pattern is to recognize that the context of the university is indeed undergoing fundamental changes and, thereby, so too must the university;

apprehension at the magnitude of the task is compensated by a cautious excitement about the positive potential seeded in the change.

These are the two classic responses to the invitation to undertake a true learning experience. Undeniably the engagement is risky, undermining existing self-images and organizational culture. But the challege, if engaged, does open new possibilities. Not all organizations die that resist change. Not all those that attempt change become newly successful. But it would be ironic, indeed, if that organization most dedicated to the creation and transmission of the products of learning withheld from itself the potential benefits of that approach to life.

Notes

1.	Donald Michael, "Too Much of a Good Thing? Dilemmas of an Information Society," *Vital Speeches of the Day*, vol. 50, no. 2 (1 Nov. 1983), p. 38.

2.	Nevit Sanford, "Foreword," in John Whiteley and Associates, *Character Development in College Students* (Schenectady, N.Y.: Character Research Press, 1982), p. xiii.

3.	See John Maguire, "The Role of the University in the Search for International Value Consensus," *Rockefeller Foundation Conference Report*, Bellagio Conference, 1-6 July 1980, pp. 1-11.

4.	See Marjorie Sun, "Weighing the Social Costs of Innovation: A lawsuit against the University of California challenges farm mechanization research and its consequences," *Science*, vol. 223, no. 30 (Mar. 1984), pp. 1368-69. The article also touches on parallel issues in other areas of university research.

5.	Geoffrey Vickers, *The Art of Judgement* (New York: Basic Books, 1965), p. 17.

6.	Wasilly Leontief, "Academic Economics," *Science*, vol. 217 (July 1982), pp. 104-7.

7.	See Seymour Sareson, "The Nature of Problem Solving in Social Action," *American Psychologist*, Apr. 1978, pp. 370-80.

8.	Intimations of the complex ramifications for university culture of new demands are nicely evidenced in David Dickson's " 'Science Shops' Flourish in Europe: Organizations intent on focusing more university research on social problems have gained important political and financial support," *Science*, vol. 223 (16 Mar. 1984), pp. 1158-60.

9.	See Donald Michael, "Who Decides Who Decides?" in *The Recombinant DNA Debate* (Englewood Cliffs, N.J.: Prentice-Hall, 1979), pp. 261-78.

10. Frank Friedlander, "Patterns of Individual and Organizational Learning," in Suresh Srivastva, ed., *The Executive Mind* (San Francisco, Calif.: Jossey-Bass, 1983), pp. 208-13.

11. For a detailed description of and rationale for these and other attributes of the new competence, see my *On Learning to Plan — and Planning to Learn* (San Francisco, Calif.: Jossey-Bass, 1973).

NEW STUDENTS IN NEW BOTTLES

K. PATRICIA CROSS

The distinctive characteristic of the university in the twenty-first century is that it will be increasingly difficult to tell where the university ends and the so-called real world begins. Universities are just one part of the learning society that lies ahead, and students will move freely in and out of the universities throughout their lives. Instead of spending four years of full-time study in the glass bottle of the university, students will spend forty years of part-time study, moving in and out through the permeable membrane through which society and students mingle. Universities, for their part, will have to get used to thinking of students as a permanent student body. This will be a significant departure from the present image of the university as opening the bottle to admit a new class each year, shaking that class of students well, and pouring them forth into society four years later.

The trends toward lifelong learning and a learning society are already well under way, and they are changing dramatically the role of the university in society—at least in those domains of university function that involve teaching.

There are many ways to define the learning society, but for the purposes of this essay I shall define it loosely as a society in which most people are engaged in organized learning throughout their lives. Many organizations and corporations, profit as well as non-profit, are engaged in organized instruction. It is, in short, a society in which teaching and learning have escaped from the confines of designated institutions, times, and personnel to pervade the entire society.

Since I wish to think about education in this broad societal context, I shall go beyond the role of the university qua university to consider the total concept of post-secondary education and its changing role in society. To do so, I have divided this paper into two parts. In the first, I touch briefly on the egalitarian pressures for equal educational opportunities that led educational services to expand to broader and more representative segments of the society. In the second part, I set forth six propositions that illustrate the current pressures for change in the role of higher education in the society. In both cases, the pressures for change come largely from forces outside the university.

Egalitarian Pressures

Gradually, higher education in the United States has been shifting from a privilege to a right. Most students today are not especially grateful for the opportunity to attend college; they feel that it is their right and that sweeping away the barriers to college attendance is a responsibility of government. Thus, the first historical shift that I wish to illustrate is the shift in the stance of higher education from exclusiveness to inclusiveness.

Gradually at first, and then with increasing momentum, the barriers to college admission have been removed. In the early days of private colleges, criteria for admission were social and financial. Excluded primarily were those persons who lacked money for tuition and expenses. With the advent of public colleges, the meritocratic phase of higher education appeared, and education was offered to all students who "merited" it by virtue of their performance in school. Those excluded lacked the high grades and the test scores suggesting academic promise. Ultimately, it became clear that most barriers to higher education were highly interrelated, operating to exclude quite consistently certain groups of people. With that realization, the national picture changed abruptly, and one barrier after another was abolished in rapid succession. The call for equality of educational opportunity brought the establishment of low-tuition, open-admission community colleges at the rate of one per week throughout the late 1960s. Then higher education began actively recruiting previously excluded poor people, ethnic minorities, and women. Now colleges are looking for ways to abolish all other exclusionary practices, including discrimination because of age, part-time student status, and geographical isolation.

Most people want to learn, and they want society to provide the opportunities for lifelong learning. In surveys conducted in the 1970s, 75 to 80 per cent of the adults between the ages of eighteen and sixty said that they were interested in learning more about some subject, and it was found that more than one third are actually engaged in some type of organized instruction each year.[1] Although individual colleges may still exclude those deemed unsuited to their particular educational creed, the national picture is one of almost frantic activity to embrace everyone in the new learning society. In a relatively short time, the United States moved from a national policy of college for the few to college for the many, or from exclusion to inclusion in college admissions. Higher education in the United States today is largely non-selective; three fourths of all colleges admit more than 70 per cent of all who apply.[2]

This notion of offering education to everyone who wants it has a profound effect upon the design of higher education. Selecting those who are predicted to succeed in the type of college education that we happen to offer is a very different task from educating all who come. Under selective admissions, the emphasis is upon prediction. If a student fails, we look for more accurate measures of predicting success. The questions we ask are these: How can we enter measures of motivation into the prediction equations? Do admissions tests predict performance as well for minorities as for Caucasians? How can we recruit the kind of student who will succeed in college?

In the meritocratic era, we directed our research to improving the accuracy of prediction formulas about who would succeed in college. Today we are directing our attention to improving education for everyone. The big questions in egalitarian higher education are not how can we predict motivation, but how can we create it; not how well tests predict grades, but how well they diagnose learning strengths and weaknesses; not how to recruit those who will be successful, but how to make successful those who come. The new philosophy of higher education affects open admissions colleges directly, of course, but the new national mission of equality of educational opportunity has considerable effect on all higher education as well as on the national concept of educational systems.

The label that I want to apply to this concept is too simple to capture its effect on higher education, but for the sake of brevity I shall call it the trend toward student inclusiveness.

The move toward student inclusiveness was first fueled by the desire for social justice in the form of equal opportunity. Today, however, it is driven more by the demographics of the birth rate and by the desire of colleges to maintain enrolments in the face of the decline in the number of traditionally aged students. In the 1980s the number of young adults between the ages of eighteen and twenty-four will decline by 16 per cent. In contrast, the number of adults between the ages of thirty-five and forty-four will become the fastest growing age cohort, increasing their numbers by 30 per cent by the end of the decade. Although this market for educational services is largely part-time, it is nevertheless an attractive solution for many colleges threatened with extinction if they cannot fill the seats left vacant by declining numbers of eighteen-year-olds. Other demographic trends are also reinforcing the earlier social issues of making higher education more inclusive. The market for ethnic minorities, specifically blacks and Hispanics, will be increasing substantially, both because of the higher fertility rates of these minority populations and because more of these young people are completing high school and thus becoming eligible for college.

The second trend in the learning society I shall label campus-expansiveness. Geographically, as well as conceptually, colleges are reaching out to include a broader community. Early in the history of higher education, colleges were deliberately located in small towns away from the hustle of the city. Faculty lived around the campus, students lived on the campus, and college was a community unto itself — its geographical isolation a symbol of its removal from the worldly concerns of the masses.

Things are quite different today. Colleges pride themselves on being very much a part of the real world. College professors serve as mayors, and students run for city council; hotels abound with visitors from every corner of the earth, and airports bustle with professors off to consult with business and government about solutions to very practical problems. Not only have colleges moved from campus into town and more broadly into the world, but the new strategy is to take the colleges to the people either by locating them in population centres or by extending them into rural areas. This new geography of college location reflects not only the change from exclusiveness to inclusiveness, but also something even more fundamental to the learning society. It recognizes that universities no longer serve as the repositories of all knowledge. Great cities are conceded to have some of the finest educational resources available anywhere. Metropolitan libraries, museums, symphonies, trade centres, business offices, and government agencies combine with rich cultural diversity to provide learning experiences not available on many conventional college campuses.

Where off-campus learning facilities do not exist naturally, they are created through imaginative use of technology. Talk-back television permits isolated learners to join in class discussions conducted hundreds of miles away. Cable television is reaching into a majority of American homes, and videodisks and personal computers are spreading information more rapidly than we can absorb it.

The trend is as clear as it is steady. The college campus has burst explosively from its boundaries, and decentralization of learning is a major trend of our times. The demographics of the birth rate combined with the explosion of knowledge in the Information Age are pressing even thoroughly traditional colleges into looking for new clienteles to serve and new locations of operation. Thus, one of the consequences of the decision to include rather than to exclude people from post-secondary learning opportunities is the expanded campus that takes learning to the people. The two movements that I have described as people-inclusive and campus-expansive are now fully under way, and they pave the way for the events to which I turn now.

The Changing Role of Higher Education in Society

Most change in higher education comes from forces outside the institution-factors such as the demographics of the birth rate, migration patterns, directives from the state boards of education, sweeping court decisions, and shifts in job markets. These external pressures for change are sufficient now to call for a new lens through which to view higher education in society. That new lens might be likened to a wide-angle lens that includes a great variety of educational providers and an unprecedented diversity of learners of all ages. To look at the education industry through this wide-angle lens of the learning society, I will set forth six propositions derived from analysis of current trends and events in the United States.

Proposition One is that institutions of higher education no longer enjoy a monopoly on the provison of educational services. In yesteryear when college students were late adolescents whose primary occupation was going to school, if they were engaged in education at all, it was typically as a full-time college student. Colleges sometimes competed with one another for students, but students did not have many other options for obtaining higher education.

Today, the most rapidly growing population of college students consists of adult part-time learners. The enrolment of part-time students between twenty-five and thirty-four years of age increased 27 per cent in the past five years; for those over thirty-five years of age, the increase was 44 per cent. More than one third of all college students in the United States are now twenty-five or older, and 72 per cent of these students attend part time.[3] Adults who enroll in college classes voluntarily choose that option from a large number of possible alternatives, including courses offered by employers, labour unions, professional associations, community organizations, television, and a host of other providers. Higher education today provides slightly more than one third of the organized learning opportunities for adults; the remaining two thirds is provided by a vast array of schools and non-collegiate institutions, many of whom offer everything colleges do and more. They may offer credit, degrees, education leading to promotion, licensure, personal fulfilment, intellectual stimulation, and practical skills. Industry, for example, spends not mere millions but billions of dollars annually on the education and training of employees. Business currently allocates more money for education and training than all fifty states combined allocate for higher education.[4] Aetna, Xerox, IBM, and other corporate giants have built campuses with classrooms and residence halls that rival anything offered in our most exclusive and expensive colleges.

Professional associations, too, are becoming the builders of vast educational networks. The American Management Association conducts 3,200 programs annually, and enrolls 100,000 learners, but even they have no corner on the market for business education. It is estimated that 3,000 different providers, many of them private entrepreneurs, conduct some 40,000 public business seminars each year. Thus Proposition One is that higher education faces unaccustomed competition from other providers of education in the society.

Proposition Two, related to Proposition One, is that the roles of educational providers, once reasonably distinct, are increasingly blurred. It is no longer clear what courses merit credit, who may offer it, and who needs it. Indeed, the distinction that we used to make between the *education* offered by colleges and the *training* offered by industry is difficult to maintain – at least when applied to providers. Colleges today are heavily involved in training as well as in education, and the programs of many corporations contain as much emphasis on theory, research, and personal development as those of any college. Consider, for example, this description of IBM's Systems Research Institute:

> The Institute's educational philosophy is in many ways that of a university. It stresses fundamental and conceptual education and allows students to choose those courses that will best nurture their own development. The intent is to stimulate and challenge, to teach the theoretical and the practical, to discuss and argue differing viewpoints, to broaden the individual, focusing on his or her special skills.[5]

Contrast that broad educational philosophy with this course description taken from a college catalogue. The course is called

"Airline Reservations" and carries three academic credits. The description reads as follows: "Prepares students for airline employment opportunities through a familiarization of the procedures involved in airline reservations, the use of official airline guides, and airline route structures."

If one were given a blind sample of course descriptions today, it would be hard to tell whether they came from industry, colleges, museums, labour unions, or professional associations. A related blurring of educational functions occurs in the distinction between credit and non-credit learning. Within higher education the waters have been muddied by some shifting of non-credit, non-funded courses to the credit, funded side of the ledger. Institutions outside of higher education are beginning to offer not only fully legitimate credit courses, but full-scale degree programs. In the Boston area alone there are four new degree-granting programs founded by organizations other than colleges — a hospital, a bank, a consulting firm, and a computer manufacturer. Although the image of Bachelor's and Master's degrees offered by these establishments is still mildly sensational, the movement of collegiate institutions into the realm of non-credit instruction is now commonplace. Between 1968 and 1978, more than a thousand colleges introduced non-credit programs on — or more likely, off — their campuses. Today it is the norm rather than the exception for degree-granting colleges to offer non-degree instruction.

Whether a course was originally taken for credit is not especially important today. It is increasingly easy to convert non-credit learning into college degrees. Just a decade ago, only about a third of American colleges granted credit if students could demonstrate on standardized examinations that they knew the material; today 84 per cent of all colleges grant credit by examination. Ten years ago, only 14 per cent of the colleges would consider granting credit for experiential learning; today 41 per cent do.[6]

Historically, colleges have been reasonably generous in accepting credit from other colleges; today they are increasingly likely to endorse learning regardless of its source. The American Council on Education's Office of Education Credit lists over 2,000 courses offered by more than 180 corporations and government agencies that appear worthy of college credit to faculty members conducting on-site visits.

Illustrations of the blurring of once-distinctive functions for higher education could be extended, but my point is that the education frontier is very large, and higher education is not alone out there. Thus Proposition Two is that the roles of the various educational providers in the learning society are far from clear and that blurring of functions rather than distinctiveness is the trend.

Proposition Three is that higher education no longer has the full-time commitment of students – or, for that matter, of faculty. In the past decade, the proportion of part-time students enrolled for college credit has gone from 32 per cent to 42 per cent, and 52 per cent seems likely before the end of the decade.

While faculty of an earlier era may have complained that students were not giving undivided attention to their studies, traditional students were at least in the college environment twenty-four hours a day. They lived in an unreal "city of youth," and their full-time occupation was with the social and intellectual demands of college. Formal education is now changing from a full-time commitment for four years of a student's life to a part-time commitment for forty years. The first priority of the adult learner of today is not college, but job, family, and an array of other adult responsibilities that serve as enhancers, detractors, and sometimes inhibitors of education. Thus Proposition Three is that higher education faces unaccustomed competition for the time and attention of students. Education cannot do whatever suits institutional convenience and assume that students can or will go along with it.

Proposition Four is that learning has become a lifelong necessity for almost everyone. There are very few jobs left in this world that are immune from the necessity of retraining and constant upgrading of skills and knowledge. The development of human capital is now recognized as a fundamental and necessary component of progress in this era of technological change and labour-intensive services. In today's climate, the widening gap between the skills available in the work force and the skills needed for social welfare and economic productivity is nothing short of alarming. There is a growing gap between the supply and demand for educated workers.

Lifelong education for jobs is the most visible symptom of social change. In that change, from full-time education for a few years to part-time education for a lifetime, lie changes for curriculum, instruction, delivery systems, and lifestyles. So far in the history of industrialized nations, there has been a pronounced tendency to increase the separation between education, work, and leisure. The result has been termed the "linear lifeplan" in which education is for the young, work for the middle-aged, and leisure for the elderly. Authors of a study of the progression and influence of the linear lifeplan in the United States warn, however, that "there can be little doubt that many of our most serious and persistent problems stem from the ways in which education, work, and leisure are distributed throughout lifetimes."[7] The major social problem is unemployment. Although that problem is especially critical right now, it is not new. For the past fifty years, society has been unable to provide jobs during peacetime for everyone willing and able to work. A blended lifeplan in which education, work, and leisure are concurrent throughout one's life can address not only the urgent demands for lifelong education for the workforce, but also the personal and societal problems that are arising for youth, for the elderly, for two-career families, and for mid-career executives. More people are demanding a greater balance in their lives — more job-sharing, more part-time educational arrangements, more leisure.[8]

Proposition Five is almost Proposition 4 1/2, but the distinction between lifelong learning and adult education deserves its own space. In the United States, lifelong learning is equated with adult education. In Europe, and especially in the publications of the United Nations Educational, Scientific and Cultural Organization (UNESCO), it is quite clear that lifelong learning begins at birth and ends at death. The official UNESCO definition is that "the term 'lifelong education and learning' denotes an overall scheme aimed both at restructuring the existing education system and at developing the entire educational potential outside the education system; in such a scheme men and women are the agents of their own education."[9]

That definition contains, among other things, a challenge to schools and colleges to develop the educational methods that will prepare young people for their futures as lifelong learners. Ted Sizer, in discussing the needed reforms in high school programs in the United States, claims that "a self-propelled learner is the goal of a school, and teachers should insist that students habitually learn on their own."[10] That becomes especially important as we envision a future in which millions of adults are added to the ranks of learners. Schools and colleges need to develop self-directed learners who are motivated and capable of establishing learning goals and selecting from the many options available those which best meet their needs. The learning society will require sophisticated consumers of educational services.

Most traditional education, however, is still geared to the notion of teachers as experts and students as empty vessels to be filled. Alvin Toffler, futurist author of *The Third Wave*, claims that "the reasons schools are in deep trouble today is that they no longer simulate the future, they simulate the past."[11] Schools devised for the factory world emphasized virtues such as obedience, punctuality, and the willingness to do rote work because those were the demands of the Second Wave workforce. Despite the arrival of the Third Wave, dominated by electronics, telecommunications, and the information society, schools still simulate the standardized work patterns of the factory. Everyone arrives for class and departs at a common time; students move on to the next lesson en masse, whether they have learned the material or not, and there is still an emphasis on *absorbing* information, despite the futility of that mode of education in the era of the knowledge explosion.

New knowledge is created faster than it can be learned or taught. Between 6,000 and 7,000 scientific articles are written each day, and information doubles every 5.5 years. The problem for the future is not the *supply* of information, but the *selection*. People need to know how to select appropriate information from an overwhelming array available, and they need to know how to use it in conceptual thinking. Far more basic to education than technical and scientific training is the need for broadly educated people with the skills that will serve as the foundation for a lifetime of learning. That calls for fewer information-laden lectures and more active analysis, synthesis, and application of knowledge on the part of students. Teachers who see their role as providers of information can and will be replaced by machines. Teachers who nurture, inspire, and assist in cognitive growth and intellectual development cannot be replaced by machines. They are our greatest resource in the development of human capital.

Proposition Six comes full circle. It concludes that education will play new roles in the society of the future. There is widespread agreement now that we are facing a major revolution in society. It has been called the Third Wave, the Information Society, and the Technological Revolution. Whatever its nomenclature, the direction seems clear. Jobs, the economy, and lifestyles will be based on the creation and distribution of information. In 1950, only 17 per cent of the jobs in the United States involved the processing of information; today more than 60 per cent of all workers are creating, processing, and distributing information. Taking note of such changes, the Office of Technology Assessment of the United States Congress concluded that "the so-called information revolution, driven by rapid advances in communications and computer technology, is profoundly affecting American education. It is changing the nature of what needs to be learned, and who needs to learn it, who will provide it, and how it will be provided and paid for."[12]

The colleges and universities at the forefront of these changes tend to be those that are, by the nature of their curriculum or mission, closest to the changes taking place. The Department of Electrical Engineering and Computer Science at the Massachusetts Institute of Technology (MIT), on the occasion of its hundredth anniversary, issued a report called *Lifelong Cooperative Education*.[13] The title is significant; it suggests that the future of engineering education should be continuous throughout the working life of the engineer and that it will be provided by industry and education working in partnership. The report rejects the notion that a few years of formal education can provide an adequate foundation for half a century of professional work. They note that, in engineering, it is more than a question of keeping up with new developments. Recent technological developments have not even been based on the same scientific and mathematical knowledge that provided the foundation for earlier models. Thus, engineers who have been out of school for more than a few years face the probability that the very foundations of their knowledge are obsolete. Professor Louis Smullin of MIT was quoted in *Time* magazine saying that engineers "are washed-up by the time they are thirty-five or forty, and new ones are recruited from the universities."[14] As the MIT report observes, however, the demands of the 1980s cannot be met by replacing "obsolescent" engineers with new graduates, even if that were a humanly acceptable plan. Thus, they conclude that "the only apparent alternative is better utilization of the presently available engineering workforce through continuing education at the workplace, with the active encouragement and support of employers."[15] To the Centennial Study Committee, lifelong co-operative education is essential for three reasons.

1. Universities acting alone have neither the human nor the financial resources to carry out a lifelong education program on the scale required. . . .

2. Engineering faculties cannot by themselves keep up with the knowledge explosion. Close collaboration between engineering faculties and their industrial colleagues is essential if new knowledge is to be distilled from the literature and widely disseminated at the rate at which it is being generated.

3. Engineers in industry and their university colleagues need a supportive environment in which they can teach and learn from one another. A concerted effort will be required to bridge the many gaps — organization, social and temporal — that now separate "work" and "study."[16]

Although these recommendations for radical change in education come from an educationally conservative engineering school, they are a precursor of things to come across the wide variety of educational institutions. Thus Proposition Six is that the providers, the organization, and the role of education in the society are changing.

These six propositions taken together will, I believe, affect higher education profoundly. They raise questions about how higher education should respond to extensive societal and technological change. Educators should be thinking about more than new ways to deliver the standard curriculum, about more than convenient schedules and locations for new populations of learners, about more than increasing the accessibility of lifelong learning opportunities. The task is to reconceptualize the role of post-secondary education in the learning society.

That is not a task for the remaining few pages of this essay, but by way of conclusion, I shall illustrate how reconceptual-ization might affect one part of the university in the twenty-first century, namely relationships between the university and its students.

The learning society calls for thinking about students as permanent members of an extended academic community. The concept of a continuing *educational* relationship with students is far more exciting than the old alumni relationships that depended heavily on loyalty and money. Yet many colleges have been slow to capitalize on this potentially powerful turn of events. How can the university serve a permanent student body?

In the first place, students will be looking for on-going relationships with teachers and with the academic community. The adjective "academic" will come to refer to "the quest for knowledge" rather than to the university.[17] Indeed, as the MIT report points out, the extended academic community will have teachers and students in the workplace as well as on campus, and "the same individual may be both a student and a teacher, at different times or even simultaneously."[18] With the emergence of computer networks and telecommunications, it will be possible to participate in an academic community that extends around the world. Practitioners, researchers, and theoreticians will join forces in continuous learning.

Methods of classroom teaching will also change under the combined effect of lifelong learning, the information society, and the technological revolution. Classroom teaching has remained unchanged for centuries. The formula is simple. Professors tell students what they know. For many reasons, that formula is no longer adequate. In the first place, professors cannot keep up with the information explosion themselves. One estimate contends that a psychologist would have to read thirty to forty articles and books each day just to keep abreast of the current literature. Professors, as well as students, will have to become experts in the selection and retrieval of information rather than in its organization and storage in the human brain. A second change for classroom teachers has been known for some years; we just have not done much about it. That is, telling students about something is a very low-power learning device when far more powerful interactive methods are coming into existence via technology, but also via teaching techniques.

A third reality of the future for classroom teachers is that teaching and learning will have to be geared to the escalating pace of change. When the change is extremely rapid, it does little good to teach facts or skills that are quickly outdated. Content learning will be useful and necessary at any given time, but it cannot be the foundation of a college education. A foundation built on rapidly and constantly changing content will crumble under the demands of lifelong learning. Learning how to learn, which means gaining the cognitive skills and attitudes that characterize the lifelong learner, will be the task of students when they are "in residence" at the university.

Advising, career planning, and placement also take on new dimensions when viewed through the wide-angle lens of the learning society. None of these activities is ever "over and done with." Career planning is a lifelong challenge that changes with the life stage of the planner. Planning for an entry-level position with a twenty-year-old is a very different activity from planning a career change with a fifty-year-old. The professional knowledge and skill required of counselors and advisers escalate sharply with the need for increased understanding of the stages of adult growth and development. These examples of changing relationships between the university and its students just begin to scratch the surface of the changes that lie ahead.

Professionals in education, whether teachers, administrators, counselors, or researchers, will do their jobs differently when facing a student body that encompasses all ages and that comes from the workplace as well as prepares for it. Students of the future will be, in many cases, older and wiser in the ways of the world and of their jobs than those who teach and counsel them. Their interest in the institution will be based on this year's or last year's experience with it, not on what they remember from twenty years ago, which tends to be charitable in obliterating the petty annoyances and failure of educators to address their needs.

The learning society will be an exciting challenge to all of us who work in education. We will make many mistakes as we try to keep up with it, but the greatest mistake would be not to accept the challenge, not to respond to new times and new kinds of students, not to join with others in making the learning society all that it can be.

Notes

1. K. Patricia Cross, *Adults as Learners* (San Francisco, Calif.: Jossey-Bass, 1981).

2. George Keller, *Academic Strategy* (Baltimore, Md.: Johns Hopkins University Press, 1983), p. 17.

3. *Chronicle of Higher Education*, 4 May 1981, p. 3.

4. Ernest Lyton, "The Role of Colleges and Universities in Corporate Education and Training," discussion paper prepared for the Ford Foundation (Boston: University of Massachusetts, 1982).

5. *IBM Systems Research Institute Bulletin* (New York: IBM Systems Research Institute, 1981).

6. Verne A. Stadtman, *Academic Adaptations* (San Francisco, Calif.: Jossey-Bass, 1980).

7. F. Best and B. Stern, *Lifetime Distribution of Education, Work and Leisure* (Washington, D.C.: Institute for Educational Leadership, Portsecondary Convening Authority, 1976), p. 24.

8. Cross, *Adults as Learners*.

9. UNESCO, *Recommendation on the Development of Adult Education*. Recommendation adopted at General Conference, Nairobi, Kenya, Oct.-Nov. 1976 (Paris: UNESCO, 1976).

10. Theodore Sizer, *Horace's Compromise: The Dilemma of the American High School Today* (Boston: Houghton-Mifflin, 1984), p. 216.

11. Alvin Toffler, *The Third Wave* (New York: Bantam Books, 1981).

12. United States Congress, Office of Technology Assessment, *Informational Technology and Its Impact on American Education* (Washington, D.C.: U.S. Government Printing Office, 1982), p. iii.

13. MIT Centennial Study Committee, *Lifelong Cooperative Education* (Cambridge, Mass.: Massachusetts Institute of Technology, Department of Electrical Engineering and Computer Science, 2 Oct. 1982).

14. *Time*, 18 Oct. 1982, p. 100.

15. MIT Centennial Study Committee, *Lifelong Cooperative Education*, p. 6.

16. Ibid., pp. 6-7.

17. Ibid., p. 44.

18. Ibid.

HISTORICAL COMMITMENTS IN NEW TIMES:
THE RESTRUCTURING AND
REORIENTATION OF TEACHING
AND RESEARCH

E. MARGARET FULTON

Mock on, mock on, Voltaire, Rousseau:
Mock on, mock on: 'tis all in vain!
You throw the sand against the wind,
And the wind blows it back again.

William Blake
poem from *Songs and Ballads*

Prologue

The Canadian university in 1984, "repressed, unhappy, fallen from Grace, an anxious frown on its uptight face," struggles to grasp the cause of its fall, to gauge the motives of its enemies, to mobilize the resources of its friends, and to glimpse the outcome of its schemes.[1]

In this essay, I try to see into the future of teaching and research – the Siamese twins who form the basis of the academy. Many believe their separation is impossible; some nevertheless fear that one may be sacrificed in a vain and misguided attempt to save, or to strengthen or to liberate, the other. Whether the knife, when it cuts, will be wielded in the name of "Corporate R & D," "Skills Training," "Fiscal Restraint," or "Strategic Planning" by bureaucrats or business leaders or colleagues – who can say? But it is true that both twins, even before the knife has touched them, *are* dying. Something vital has already been taken from them, without which their death is as sure as if they had already been parted. That something is the spiritual component. And when death comes, we shall be culpable because while recognizing the outward signs of their illness, we ignored the root cause of the disease; preoccupied with the externals of image, we have missed the inner core of weakness.

I am reminded of a tale by Edgar Allan Poe of an artist who wished to capture the beauty of his bride. Day after day, in a tower, his brush strokes transferred her radiance to canvas. He did not see her features pale, however; he did not see the shadows deepen in her face. When at last the image of his bride was immortalized in paint, he turned to find his beloved had died.[2]

This essay is about the differences between the images of the university we cling to, and its reality; it is about the central core of life that has been taken from research and teaching. It is about the dark shadows on the face of the Canadian university that betray its self-inflicted ill health. Finally, it is about some tentative remedies that can mean a healthier academy in the twenty-first century.

The image we hold of the Canadian university and the reality are not the same. A particular example of the university's ill health is its treatment of women. Undeniably, the reasons universities discriminate against women are historic and systemic, but discriminate they do.[3] That the academy has discriminated in its hiring, salary, and promotion practices against women does violence to its antique self-image as a community of scholars seeking truth. This is but a single example of the disparity between the illusion and the reality of the university. Other illusions to which we cling include: the community of scholars, institutional autonomy, scholarly objectivity, and academic freedom.

I

The ideal current in Canadian universities until 1960 was of a community of scholars sharing in the pursuit of knowledge and becoming in the process an harmonious whole. The dominant educational ideology held that a university education should introduce students to a common historical and cultural background and should scrutinize the underlying ideas and assumptions on which society is based. It trumpeted its autonomy and its objectivity. Truth to tell, its objectivity was a fabrication, its autonomy non-existent. Male-dominated, elitist, sectarian or denominational, hierarchical, sometimes dogmatic, occasionally bigoted, the university indoctrinated, proselytized, perpetuated itself and the status quo, graduated leaders in its own image, and produced precious little social criticism, objective knowledge, or truth.

Then demographic forces undermined the ideal and its ideology. Population growth, swollen student numbers, the demand for faculty, and the trend toward specialization all acted to dissolve the "community of scholars." A new self-conception emerged. The campus was now perceived to mirror the outside world, to be a pluralistic society of competing interests. Disparate claims were to be resolved by the administration or faculty or senate on the recommendations of committees where all relevant interests were represented. Priorities were to be established by compromise. In effect, all interests became equal and so did all ideas. One subject was thought no more worthy of study than another. Random response to demand determined offerings, and a relativism of standards affected even the content of courses.[4] The multiversity was born.

The 1960s were heady times for the Canadian academy. Governments were only too willing to provide and universities seemed only too willing to accept enormous sums of public money for the purpose of "honing" a competitive edge to Canadian post-secondary education. It troubled the universities naught that governments viewed their contribution as an *investment,* an investment in Canada's industrial, scientific, and technological well-being; the universities chose to delude themselves into believing no such single-mindedness motivated their public support. Few university leaders were as clearheaded as Queen's University president J.A. Corry who described the Canadian university as a public utility in the employ of a political-economic system, which it persisted in thinking it was still free to criticize.[5]

New institutions were spawned and older institutions were retooled to qualify for public largesse. On the windy plains north of Toronto or atop Burnaby mountain, in a vainglorious attempt to capture the "Oxbridge" mystique or to shatter the conventional post-secondary paradigm, new multiversities rose. Not to be passed over in the scramble for public funds, older institutions severed time-honoured religious affiliations, jeopardizing in the process strong traditions, in the naive anticipation of greater autonomy and academic freedom. But to what end? Newer institutions discovered that without a sense of community, a pulse, centre, core, or soul the ideal of the multiversity becomes mediocrity, attended, as president Murray Ross has described, by disenchantment.[6] Similarly, older institutions found themselves in an academic vacuum, having bartered away their continuities, their connections, their soul. In exchange for what? For academic autonomy, illusory freedoms, mythic objectivity.

We are not autonomous; on the contrary, events have shown that we can be called to account by government for trends and conditions beyond our control. Nor are we free. Older faiths – Darwinism, Marxism, theisms of many stripes – may have been secularized; but the social structures, spawned by the linear, so-called rational male mind, which they support philosophically, remain unchanged – hierarchical and indivi-dualistic to the end. It is rampant individualism, in particular, that sickly modern obsession with self-gratification thinly disguised as self-knowledge and yielding only isolation and cynicism, which has become the dominant faith on our campuses.

No one would deny that individualistic, secularized, publicly funded universities have produced an avalanche of information. The achievement is laudable, but its implications for the academy and for society at large require scrutiny. A deeper question needs to be posed: is humanity the wiser for the agglomeration of new knowledge, or has the knowledge merely strengthened the oppressors of this world? Too many among us persist in the belief that the academy need bear no responsiblity for the application of our product, both scholarly and human. One is reminded of Milton's great lines, "Licence they mean when they cry liberty/For who loves that must first be wise and good."

The truth is that beyond accumulating knowledge in quantity, the university is but a small part of what it believes itself to be: we wrongly conceive ourselves to be the custodian of truth, the critic of society, the author of wisdom, the tutor of responsibility. Nor do we do, beyond conveying substantive knowledge and teaching verbal and mathematical skills, many of the things we believe we do: we mistakenly believe we foster intellectual integrity, wisdom, morality, and human sympathy toward individuals. We simply do not affect any ascertainable change in those dimensions of the human personality associated with excellence of personal character. Is it any wonder there is widespread concern about values in higher education.[7] How can we have become so deluded?

II

I suggest that the causes and the costs of our delusion began when we lost sight of the purpose of learning, which, in the words of Robertson Davies, is, was, and ever will be "to save the soul and enlarge the mind." In our misguided quest for autonomy and freedom we have lost sight of our moral responsibility. In our ill-conceived bid for objectivity, we no longer have anything to say. Under the cover of "pure" research, we have become non-judgemental. Even those disciplines traditionally committed to searching for a "central truth" — literature, theology, philosophy, history — sought objectivity as much as the sciences. William J. Bennett in an excellent article describes "the shattered humanities." He bluntly states, "The greatest threat to the humanities lies within — within the boundaries of current practice and doctrine, or more accurately non-doctrine."[8]

If a poll were taken of humanities professors across Canadian universities, I would wager the majority would deny the existence of the soul. What hope then for the teaching of the humanities in the future? We have all met those disenchanted students on campus who dropped out of courses in religion because the professor did not believe anything, or the courses in philosophy because the professor was not prepared to recommend anything, or the classes in poetry because the professor taught knowledge about the poetry and not the poetry itself.

Again, as Bennett has pointed out: "Students want and need to know where educated people stand, not on passing issues but on matters of enduring importance, matters that have always been the enduring concern of the humanities (but by no means their exclusive domain): courage, fidelity, friendship, honour, love, justice, goodness, ambiguity, time, power, faith."[9] We are not even inclined to try to establish or prioritize value systems.

The only reference to wisdom we seem willing to make is usually to be found in university mottos, mottos like Mount St. Vincent's "Truth Leads to God" or McMaster's "All Things Cohere in Christ." For research in the humanities to be as objective as that in the natural sciences, all commitment to doctrine or belief of any kind had to be denied, and with that denial died any hope of teaching students how to achieve that "coherence" mottos at least once espoused. Although Cardinal Newman and Karl Jaspers were still being read on university campuses, they were no longer understood — never mind believed. Newman's concern that a university education should nourish the "body, mind and spirit," or Jaspers's idea that any intellectual pursuit, to be meaningful, must be informed by a concept of spirit, was deemed, like the university motto, to be anachronistic.[10] An article by E.P. Sanders of McMaster University entitled "The Meaning of the Motto" serves as a perfect illustration of where objective scholarship in the humanities has led. After translating the Greek, and locating the passage from Colossians, there follows an illuminating discussion of the language of philosophy, a careful examination of authentic authorship (and it is *not* Paul), and an academic analysis of Christology. Finally, Professor Sanders ends his short but learned discourse by commenting somewhat lamely: "Our forebears doubtless saw in the motto a way of reconciling Christianity with the quest for knowledge in all its aspects."[11] The implication being that such a reconciliation, or such a coherence, or wholeness is no longer possible. Apart from knowing more about the motto, it would seem to be meaningless for McMaster's students today. Is, then, the whole quest for knowledge in all its aspects doomed to this kind of fragmentation? Are we to be left knowing all of the facts but lacking totally in any wholeness of vision?

If specialized scholarship raises concerns about the secular humanist, how much more disturbing is the objectivity of the secular scientist? Professor Bill Emery, of the University of British Columbia, when asked about applications of his research funded by the Department of National Defence and the U.S. Navy, replied, "We're doing basic research that I can see military applications for, but applications aren't my business."[12] Emery's Faustian "ivory-towerism" is not unusual. On the contrary, our labs and lecture halls are filled with individuals who, if funded, will serve the system — no questions asked.

My profound concern is aroused not merely by the secular scientists' apparent indifference to the applications of their work, but also by their lack of interest in maintaining a core of shared intellectual experience, in overcoming the fragmented nature of research in the sciences, as well as in the humanities. This lack of interest is attributable in part to the extraordinary history of modern physics. Did not Einstein's momentous discoveries, culminating in the splitting of the atom, establish that random probability rather than universal laws governs the universe from microcosm to macrocosm? An Einsteinian world view — characterized by the rejection of any notion of order, coherence, convention, or permanence — spawned changed concepts as diverse as situational ethics and new mathematics, anarchic politics and atonal music, "God is Dead" theology and Dadaism. The irony, of course, is that Einstein himself never ceased his search for a "unified-field theory" and never wavered in his belief that God has created an ordered, unified, lawful reality. Even so, few secular scientists today seek the coherence of knowledge in a central truth, once personified by Christ, a central truth that is the same "yesterday, today and tomorrow." But without it, what can tomorrow bring? Pollution of the mind, the devastation of the environment, the demise of human relationships. Has the bigotry and pedantry, once believed to attend religious affiliation and from which public funding was supposed to have freed us, merely recrystallized, this time attributable to the intellectual arrogance of that new breed of objective secular scholars?

Nothing has changed and nothing will, so long as universities disregard deeper spiritual and moral truths. We have exchanged masters, the patronage of the church for the patronage of the state. We have altered committees. We have not changed structures. They remain as they have ever been — patriarchal, linear, and repressive, fostering competition and conquest rather than sharing and nurturing. We persist in the mistaken belief that we severed our religious affiliations because the notion of a soul constrained and compromised scholarship. Our spiritual dimension never could constrain us. Failure to acknowledge our spiritual dimension can and does. Without realizing our own intent, we attempted to reject the oppressive, hierarchical church structures that supposedly shackled the spirit, but we succeeded merely in reimposing them under another name. What we require are concepts and symbols of the spirit, the soul, that will meet the needs of our age together with new structures that will support and nurture our total humanity. Without the restoration of the spirit to its rightful place in the life of the university, every other solution — either devised from within or imposed from without — will be incomplete.

III

Insights and opportunities to improve the university cross the minds of many of us every day. Knowledge about ourselves, however, is, for the most part, acquired retrospectively as the result of "myriad inadvertencies," to use Buckminster Fuller's phrase. Furthermore, it would be wrong to imply that none of the new scholarly breed is concerned about fundamental questions. Finally, we must acknowledge that the level of consciousness of students and their expectations of the academy will occasionally, and usually with shocking results, become markedly different from that of the academy itself — as it did, for example, during the turbulent 1960s.[13]

When university performance is challenged, however, either by one of our number, by students, or by an outsider, our response is always predictable and always the same. We excuse our mediocrity as the result of the permissiveness in the schools and society at large; "back to basics" we vaguely hope will provide a solution to the problem, but again, the larger societal solutions are not our task, our responsibility. The university, for its part, needs only to make "improvements" in its own teaching and research.

Of teaching, we claim to hold especially high expectations. According to Larkin Kerwin and Denise Michaud, its product should:

> be capable of disciplined, logical, creative and critical thought to enable the continued search for truth; [be] capable of enlightened cultural, social and moral concern required if a society is to preserve, defend, and enhance its civilization . . . have skills, fineness of

taste, social concerns, sound ethics, and freedom from prejudice.[14]

George Pedersen has concurred in the belief that the genuinely educated person is the product of quality teaching. We readily confess, however, that we fall far short of achieving so lofty an ideal. Indeed, Pedersen has described "excellence in teaching" as the missing link in the academic evolution of our universities. Again we faintly hope that we can improve our performance if only we correct an imbalance in our universities as to what is important. Research and publication as a precondition of promotion through our vertical rank structure has worked to replace the genuinely educated professor with the educational entrepreneur, the academic gamesperson. Pedersen urged that every member of the university community be "prepared to operationalize his support for quality teaching." "Every effort," he stated, "must be made, to escape from the hypocrisy of alluding to the importance of instruction while continuing to reward research scholarship disproportionately."[15] Perhaps our most daring response to criticism by government and private industry, who find fault with the product of our career-oriented programs, is to suggest we are not at fault for having been forced against our will to depart from "an earlier more noble commitment; the education of civilized human beings." Our predicament was pressed upon us by our critics who compelled us in the first place to offer the programs they now fault. Furthermore, suggests M.J.L. Kirby, we should be prepared to return to our "more appropriate role as process-oriented institutions" in which we shall once again "impart the heritage, the skills, and the mode of thought indispensable for a civilized society."[16] In short, if we had been left alone in the first place we would not now be in difficulty. This is a ludicrous assertion since we have only ourselves to blame for becoming "public utilities," as Corry called us.

As for the inflated opinion we hold of the research we actually do, no amount of abuse from outside the academy can budge us from that opinion. We remain convinced that the knowledge we generate by our efforts is both civilizing and objectively true. We accept no blame for the fact that governments have not been persuaded by our performance of the value of humanities research and so pare away at precious research funds. Nor will we be faulted when we turn around, setting principles aside, and accept research funds from corporations and the military, without reference to the consequences; we have no choice, or so we maintain.

Our claims to be blameless, to have been victimized, and to be able to restore our virtue by merely reinvigorating teaching, by restoring research funding or by re-entrenching a romanticized ideal of "process" have convinced few besides ourselves. We have not convinced many corporations. They charge that we have failed abysmally to produce the pool of trained graduates the economy requires, and the accusation becomes justification for competing with us. As Jerome Deutsch has suggested, corporations in the United States "are now self-sufficient in meeting their employee training and development needs."[17] They attach little worth to our cant about the development through teaching of the whole person. Nor is government fully convinced of the worth — never mind the morality — of our research effort. We must now compete with industry for the same government research funds to conduct the same research. Governments themselves have created a galaxy of specialized research facilities removed from the university sphere. Finally, millions of dollars of research we have done is described by the federal patents office as a wasteful duplication of research done elsewhere.

We have made monumental blunders in determining the right methods by which to re-establish our legitimacy and integrity. We were wrong to believe improved teaching, or more research, or both, would produce graduates who are better informed (never mind being as Larkin Kerwin described them "noble human beings") or knowledge that is civilizing. To begin with, excellence in either teaching or research is far more illusive than customarily acknowledged. University excellence must stem from an element of synergy rather than single-mindedness. In other words, professors and students alike must learn to do many things at once in order to do one thing well. Excessive specialization is a root cause of both students' and society's dissatisfaction with our performance.

We were wrong to believe the university is shackled in perpetuity to a pendulum that swings between two poles — variously described as process and product, elitism and egalitarianism, scholasticism and vocationalism, authoritarianism and permissiveness. We were wrong to think the academy can be governed only by Platonists with their hierarchy of values or by Sophists who relativize all values; back and forth, the power will shift, until, that is, we locate a third option, a substantially new philosophical position. It has been a mistake doggedly to support limiting structures and even more limiting material concepts. The university must remain a place for the examination and preservation of knowledge, but the naive belief that somehow knowledge is a good in itself is not the case. An old Japanese proverb states, a person who has only knowledge without wisdom resembles an ass with a load of books on his back. Early in this century, Karl Jaspers reminded us that university education was intended to mean universal education. John Stuart Mill, a century before, anticipated Jaspers's remarks when he wrote:

> What professional men [and, of course, women — since Mill well knew the subjection of women had to end] should carry away with them from a university, is not professional knowledge, but that which should direct the use of their professional knowledge, and bring the light of general culture to illuminate the technicalities of a special pursuit.[18]

For both Mill and Jaspers, general education was to be the catalyst in a renewal of the university. Today, a restoration of general education will not be sufficient. We shall still be required to do so much more.

Finally, we were wrong — terribly wrong — to disavow responsibility for the social consequences of the research we do, irrespective of the source of its funding.[19] We repaid society's overindulgence of the university with irresponsibility and indifference. As T.E.W. Nind, former president of Trent University, remarked bitterly,

> Material wealth has been so showered upon us . . . that we have in the past been able to thumb our noses at common sense and indulge ourselves without reaping the consequences. But our demands are becoming too great, and our lack of self-restraint, of honesty, and of courage, and above all, our lack of respect for others, are threatening to take their toll.[20]

How shall we re-acquire the qualities of self-restraint, honesty, courage, and respect for others? Certainly not through retrenchment, nostalgia, mere curricular modifications, or cancelling athletic programs. It may help, however, to recognize the inadequacies of the principles upon which Canadian universities have come to be based. Our universities, whether they are publicly or privately funded, are all predicated on the principles of exclusivity and vocationalism. Arnold Toynbee explains the problem thus. Our educational system is still faithful to a pattern that arose in Greece of the fifth and fourth centuries B.C. The purpose of the pattern was to educate boys to be citizens of city-states. The Roman Empire continued the pattern for the purpose of educating boys to be civil servants. Christendom modified the pattern for the purpose of educating boys to become Christian priests. Today, of course, we attempt to accommodate women in this same educational system, and with typical Western egocentricity we are trying to transport it around the world.[21]

In the main, this type of exclusive education was designed, and still is intended, to preserve the social system. Its goal has always been the employability of its product. It fails, if it ever intended otherwise, to make its students critical of the system, the professors, and the subject matter. It relies heavily on indoctrination rather than on education, which in the strict Latin usage means "leading out" – not "putting in" as we have defined it by our practice. We indoctrinate, instil ideas and reward students who regurgitate accordingly. We do not encourage students to criticize independently, to reason, to discriminate, and to make connections between the received wisdom of the past and the perceived reality of their present experience.

Such an antique and entrenched system of education is almost impossible to change because it perpetuates itself; hence, all the continuing problems of its elitism, its hierarchies, its false notions of standards, its patriarchal leadership, its egocentricity, and its burgeoning bureaucracies conceived to ensure that all the rest remains unchanged. Surely we should not inflict this system on the rest of the world. If the Western world is to contribute to the common heritage of humanity, we must evolve a university system that can adapt to the needs of a pluralistic, global, technological society for the twenty-first century. Endless committee meetings to refurbish and renovate outdated curricula, devising new texts to preserve those so-called standards – such tinkering with the past will not prepare the university for the future. We must bring about fundamental change in the entrenched system by creatively reordering the priorities of higher education, by examining the structures that lock us in and the attitudes of mind that resist fundamental change, and by restoring the soul to its rightful place in the life of the university.

IV

As is no doubt apparent, this essay is an attempt to capture insights and experiences from within the academy in a very brief form. It is neither systematic nor complete; it makes no claim to be. So in proposing remedies to the condition of the Canadian university that I have described, I caution readers not to expect a tidy plan of action but a call to commitment, commitment in four areas of endeavour.

First, we must radically alter our consciousness and our attitudes of mind. As a precondition, the university community should seek new images of nurturing to replace those of competing, confronting, and conquering. We must let go of myths and language that repress us. Our objective must be to re-enchant the world, as Morris Berman suggests, by first re-enchanting ourselves.[22] In this task, we shall find for our guidance an emerging discipline, the psychology of consciousness, of invaluable assistance; it has much to offer those who see the necessity of sweeping away the systems that perpetuate the vertical view of the world of the academy.

Research has shown that the two sides of the brain operate in radically different ways. The left cerebral hemisphere uses a linear, logical, verbal mode of information processing while the right hemisphere functions in a more intuitive mode. I suggest the Western educational pattern, of which Toynbee spoke, involves and is almost exclusively the product of the left cerebral hemisphere. In contrast, right brain processing – involving intuition, creativity, rapport, and bodily health – figures more prominently in the processes of altered consciousness. Greater willingness to develop use of our total human intelligence and less reliance on artificial intelligence – which by definition can never be more than artificial – is needed now to help solve our human problems.

There is reason to be hopeful; significant change in our consciousness has in fact occurred. Einstein stated: "When we released energy from the atom, everything changed except our way of thinking. Because of that, we drift toward unparalleled disaster." We have not yet arrested the drift toward disaster, but the consciousness-raising that has taken place since Einstein issued his dire warning – the students' movement of the 1960s and the renewal of the women's movement – has been nothing short of miraculous. Regrettably, both movements were misunderstood by the powers that be. Students asked for knowledge that was relevant and were given permissiveness. Women demanded equality and were given sameness. It is a measure of the incomprehension of the academy that women who have received some kind of equal treatment in the academy have had to learn to function as "pseudo-males." One would have expected the academy to recognize that the real challenge of the women's movement is the demand to change all systems and structures so as to accommodate both sexes in ways that will allow for and benefit the differences. It is apparent to me that in the past decade women have become the real catalysts in bringing about the new consciousness. The feminist perspective brings with it genuinely basic changes in the assumptions we make in all disciplines.

Second, then, both teaching and research, if they are to be restored to health, must evince the ability and the willingness to move in these new directions. Here again, the work is well begun. *Academe,* the prestigious journal of the American Association of University Professors, devoted its September-October 1983 issue to "Feminism in the Academy" and revealed very clearly that feminism is an accepted "analytical tool for the sciences." It is a perspective that can bring about badly needed new concepts to all disciplines.[23] The goal is to perceive all the specialized and fragmented knowledge we have amassed to date in such a way as to discover its unity.

Regrettably, much of the learning the new perspectives have spawned is deemed suspect or dismissed in conservative circles. The fact remains, however, that if teaching and research do not adopt a new perspective, reconstitute the lecture hall as a place of consciousness raising, and restructure the university as a centre of lifelong learning, then the traditional university will find itself replaced by more appropriate communications centres. New interdisciplinary research, making new connections to form new disciplines, and new technologies afford extraordinary opportunities for creative change in teaching. Even so, one feature of the traditional educational pattern will retain its honoured place in the pattern to come: a learner-centred method that enables the process of discovery and choice, the method of Socrates and of Jesus.

It should be the responsibility of the university to provide programs that give substance and meaning to the half-truths students often discover on their own. This is already the raison d'être of a daring breed of scholars currently engaged in the struggle to make others recognize that the classical educational paradigm is in a state of collapse. Daring they may be, disreputable they are not. Scholars like Willis Harman of the Stanford Research Institute, Paul Hawken, Hazel Henderson, Mark Satin, and others are committed to some form of "transformational change."[24] Their commitment to transforming the classical paradigm must become our own since no task is more urgent than the preparation of young graduates able to provide leadership in a new age.

Growing networks of very diverse groups committed to "new age thinking" exist across the country and around the world.

Ruben Nelson heads such an organization in Ottawa.[25] On the West Coast, the Communications Era Task Force has made a substantial effort to raise the consciousness of students and citizens to new ways of perceiving and imagining ourselves as humans.[26] If society is to design a new paradigm more suited to a planetary society, then, as David F. Noble has demonstrated, we must start with such fundamental issues as dealing with technology in the "present tense" rather than vaguely hoping that sometime in the future technology alone will make possible a better society.[27]

No writer gives us a clearer indication of how to prepare our graduates than Doris Lessing in *The Making of the Representative for Planet 8*. Throughout the series *Canopus in Argos: Archives*, she writes from the premise that chaos has come; she uses metaphor to show that while ultimate disaster may be unavoidable, hope remains and the human spirit may yet prevail, provided we rekindle the eternal, human abilities to endure and to transcend.[28] Endurance and transcendence are the essence of my last two challenges.

Third, if we are to avoid the chaos *Planet 8* endures, if we are to halt the slide toward Einstein's "unparalleled disaster," which an unexamined use of science and technology can cause, we must begin a progressive disengagement with the national, military-industrial complexes that control us and establish that the academy is genuinely global, genuinely universal, and genuinely all-inclusive. We must form links with one another to create a new world community of learners. New communications technologies already exist to help us accomplish this task. We should not avoid using them. Indeed, we should assert our control over them, enlist them in our efforts to order the possessions of our mind and to interconnect in the ways necessary to bring about a truly international synergy. In this era of global communications, no culture shall dominate; new styles of learning will emerge; new opportunities for scholars will arise. Above all, new styles of leadership must evolve that will provide all peoples of the planet with at least the chance to reassert control over their own destiny and avoid the disaster that Einstein warned would be the end of the age he himself inaugurated. Einstein urged us to adopt another course – which brings me to my final challenge.

We must transcend. Anticipating the nightmarish weapons of today, Einstein called for new ways of thinking and for a revolution in our system of values. His own search for the "unified field" was rooted in his very personal, very spiritual nature. Traditional religion becomes rather sheepish in the presence of such a personal perception of the spiritual. Unfortunately, the cults and subcultures are not similarly embarrassed. It is a depressing irony that the cults have become the haven of disenchanted students turned cold by professors without faith, without truth, with nothing to offer save sterile facts and barren knowledge. I recall my sense of quiet despair, nine years ago, when I read that Parsons College in Iowa had become the Maharishi International University. Western universities are so constrained by the classical scientific and educational paradigm that they cannot accommodate the spiritual and recognize the visionary.

William Blake recognized more clearly one hundred years ago than we seem able today the character and tragedy of our condition. In his painting of Newton with his calipers, Blake presented Newton as a symbol of the age that was to befall us, the age of rationalism and material self-sufficiency. He well knew such an arrogant age could not accommodate, indeed, would even reject the very necessity of a spiritual reality rooted in a central truth. The only reality Blake painted in his pictures or conveyed in his poetry was a spiritual reality. He had no use for any other kind; for Blake recognized that the Newtonian, or any other, soulless material reality enslaves people. In dramatic contrast to, and immediately after, "Newton," Blake painted "Albion Worshipping Christ." With moving simplicity, Blake captured the essence of Christ's message: "Jesus Christ did nothing but teach men . . . that they were slaves . . . and that he had come to deliver them. . . . " But we have ignored this message of freedom and spiritual deliverance. Most men, whether they were scientists or theologians or scholars, chose to follow Newton, who taught them to measure materiality. Not surprising, then, that the mottos on our crests that speak of truth have lost their meaning. We expect nothing grand of knowledge today. We use knowledge rather pathetically, to classify and rationalize and entrench systems that enslave us.

To continue to misuse knowledge so would be the height of folly. If teaching and research are to continue to govern the university, indeed if they are to have any meaning, then it is incumbent upon us to reorient our perspective to a more holistic view, restructure the university in new horizontal and circular modes, which permit free and creative exchange, as an example to the wider human community. Above all, we must cultivate our awareness of the spiritual unity that ties each one of us to every other. In the words of William Blake,

This life's dim windows of the soul
Distorts the heavens from pole to pole
And leads you to believe a lie
When you see with, not thro', the eye.

William Blake
The Everlasting Gospel

Notes

1. Quoted in Kenneth J. Reckford, "Teaching the Heroic Journey," in Thomas H. Buxton and Keith W. Pritchard, eds., *Excellence in University Teaching: New Essays* (Columbia: University of South Carolina Press, 1975), p. 12.

2. Edgar Allan Poe, "The Oval Portrait," in *The Complete Tales and Poems of Edgar Allen Poe* (New York: Random House, 1938), pp. 290-92.

3. Thomas H.G. Symons and James E. Page, *Some Questions of Balance: Human Resources, Higher Education and Canadian Studies, vol. III of To Know Ourselves: The Report of the Commission on Canadian Studies* (Ottawa: Association of Universities and Colleges of Canada, 1984), pp. 118-214.

4. Alston Chase, "Skipping Through College: Reflections on the Decline of Liberal Arts Education," in *Atlantic*, Sept. 1978, pp. 33-40.

5. J.A. Corry, *Farewell the Ivory Tower: Universities in Transition* (Montreal: McGill-Queen's Press, 1969), pp. 101-12.

6. Murray Ross, *The University: The Anatomy of Academe* (New York: McGraw-Hill, 1976).

7. Howard R. Bowen, *Investment in Learning: The Individual and Social Value of American Higher Education* (San Francisco, Calif.: Jossey-Bass, 1979), p. 220.

8. W.J. Bennett, "The Shattered Humanities," in *AAHE Bulletin*, Feb. 1983, p. 3.

9. Ibid., p. 4.

10. J.H. Newman, *The Idea of a University* (Garden City, N.Y.: Doubleday Image, 1959 [1852]); Karl Jaspers, *The Idea of the University*, ed. K. Deutsch (London: Peter Owen, 1960).

11.   E.P. Sanders, "The Meaning of the Motto," in *Ta Panta*, vol. 1, no. 1 (1983), p. 6.

12.   Pattie Flather and Jackie Charlton, "Renting Brains to the Military," for Canadian University Press, in *The Picaro*, 15 Feb. 1984, p. 7.

13.   See, for example, Claude Bissel, *Halfway Up Parnassus: A Personal Account of the University of Toronto, 1932-1971* (Toronto: University of Toronto Press, 1974).

14.   Larkin Kerwin and Denise Michaud, "The Pursuit of a Definition of Excellence: A Draft Position Paper for the Council of University Presidents' Conference on Excellence," June 1979 (Ottawa, Ontario: Association of Universities and Colleges of Canada, May 1979), p. 14.

15.   K. George Pedersen, "Excellence in Teaching: The Missing Link in Academic Evolution" (Unpublished paper, Burnaby, British Columbia: Simon Fraser University, 1979), p. 18.

16.   M.J.L. Kirby, "The Changing Demands Which the Public and Governments Will Place on Universities in the 1980s" (Montreal: Institute for Research on Public Policy, 4 June 1979), p. 14.

17.   Jerome M. Deutsch, "Retrenchment: Crisis or Challenge," in *Educational Record*, Winter 1983, p. 44.

18.   J.S. Mill, "Inaugural Address at Saint Andrew's," delivered 1867, reprinted in A. Levi, ed., *The Six Great Humanistic Essays of John Stuart Mill* (New York: Washington Square Press, 1963).

19.   Derek Bok, *Beyond the Ivory Tower: Social Responsibilities of the Modern University* (Cambridge, Mass.: Harvard University Press, 1982), pp. 169-94. See also Theodore M. Hesburgh, "The Moral Dimensions of Higher Education," keynote address at the First Joint Meeting of the Association of Universities and Colleges of Canada and the American Council on Education, Toronto, Ontario: 13 Oct. 1983.

20. T.E.W. Nind, *Trent University President's Report 1977-78* (Peterborough, Ontario: Trent University, 1978), pp. 14-15.

21. Arnold Toynbee, *Surviving the Future* (Oxford: Oxford University Press, 1971), p. 87.

22. Morris Berman, *The Reenchantment of the World* (Ithaca, N.Y.: Cornell University Press, 1981).

23. Carol Gilligan, *In A Different Voice* (Cambridge, Mass.: Harvard University Press, 1982); Evelyn Keller, "Feminism as an Analytic Tool for the Study of Science," in *Academe*, Sept.-Oct. 1983, p. 18.

24. Willis W. Harman, *An Incomplete Guide to the Future* (New York: Norton, 1979); Paul Hawken, James Ogilvy, and Peter Schwartz, *Seven Tomorrows* (New York: Banting Books, 1982); Hazel Henderson, *Creating Alternative Futures: The End of Economics* (New York: G.P. Putnam's Sons, 1978); and Mark Satin, *New Age Politics: Healing Self and Society* (West Vancouver, British Columbia: Whitecap Books, 1978).

25. Ruben F.W. Nelson is the author of *The Illusions of Urban Man* (Ottawa: Ministry of State for Urban Affairs, 1976, reprinted 1978), president of Square One Management Ltd., and founding president of Transformational Research Network, 302-100 Gloucester St., Ottawa, Ontario, K2P 0A4.

26. Communications Era Task Force, Box 52, Winlaw, B.C., V0G 2J0.

27. David F. Noble, "Present Tense Technology," in *Democracy*, Spring, Summer, Fall 1983.

28. Doris Lessing, *The Making of the Representative for Planet 8 (Canopus in Argos: Archives*, vol. 4), (London: Granada, 1982).

THE UNIVERSITY AND SOCIETY: HISTORICAL AND SOCIOLOGICAL REFLECTIONS

ALAN C. CAIRNS

Of the various vantage points from which the theme of the university and society could be approached, I have chosen sociological analysis, through which I will impressionistically explore the subtleties of tradition, vocation, community, and identity that are central to scholarship. Though I stress tradition, I am not interested in the past as such, but in the support structure for intellectual activity that has been bequeathed to us. This support structure resides more in the norms and behavioural attributes of scholarship than in such tangibles as research grants and laboratories.

The task of placing the university and scholarship in context is not a secondary activity. Put simply, it is impossible to understand universities and research if they are abstracted from the traditions they exemplify and if they are viewed in isolation from the social system of research and scholarship. The university brings together the traditions of the past and the resources required by contemporary scholars with the evolving disciplinary contexts from which research questions emerge.

The layman and the politician have a natural tendency to equate the world of universities and scholars with its tangible, physical manifestations—particular scientists in particular laboratories performing particular experiments or particular professors of Latin lecturing to particular students in particular classrooms. These bricks and stones and flesh and blood are real; that any cultural activity has to be undertaken by real people in actual places—museums, libraries, studies, laboratories, and classrooms—is a truism requiring no elaboration.

What does require elaboration is the subtle context of cues, values, and ambitions that motivates individual researchers and the system of norms, understandings, and constraints that, by the mutual adjustments it generates, produces a co-ordination of research superior to what anyone could have planned.

Max Weber's graphic and succinct statement of "Science as a Vocation," which portrays that mixture of anguish, personal

251

insignificance, humility, and collective pride characteristic of the true scientist, is a useful beginning.

> Every scientist knows that what he achieves will be outdated in 10, 20 or 50 years. Every scientific "fulfillment" raises new "problems" and should be "surpassed" and rendered obsolete. This is the fate — and indeed the significance of work in science, to this it is subordinated and devoted. This distinguishes it from all the other spheres of culture which also demand submission and devotion.
> Everyone who wishes to serve science must accommodate himself to this. Scientific achievements can, it is true, endure as "satisfactions" on account of their artistic quality; they can also remain important as a means of training for actual scientific work. But — it should be repeated — it is not only our fate, but also our goal that we should be scientifically transcended. We cannot work without the hope that others will go further than we have. In principle, this progress goes on *ad infinitum*.[1]

In this passage, Weber locates the individual scientist in time, building on and transcending the work of his predecessors, while preparing the building blocks for the transcendence of his own work by those who follow.

Scholarship not only exists in time in Weber's sense of a chronological growth in understanding. It also partakes of tradition, a perspective from which the past is not viewed as a sequence of imperfect efforts to be cast aside by progressive improvements of our knowledge, but is rather viewed as a rich and evolving practice, a heritage of norms, understandings, and revered predecessors from which each generation derives the courage, will, and perseverance to continue a daunting vocation.

Further, scholarship is not scattered randomly in space, but is concentrated in university settings. Nor is it an activity carried on by isolated individuals. It is a collective enterprise that unites classicists and mathematicians. At another level, it is organized into particular disciplines providing coherence and boundaries for intellectual activities. More subtly, especially in the natural and physical sciences, it is informed by a complex social system, the scientists' version of Adam Smith's market, which co-ordinates the activities of scientists around the world. Finally, it takes place in the midst of particular national, cultural, and ethnic contexts.

The preceding all come together in dimly understood ways to influence scholarship. They are not all that matters. The influence of organizational structures on scholarly activity, the relation of research to teaching, and other variables would all have to be considered in an analysis professing to be comprehensive. For the purposes of this essay however, they are enough. My themes are united by a common concern for the context, conceived from different vantage points, in which scholarship takes place. To attempt more would exceed both the time and the competence I can bring to the task.

Thus, in the remainder of this essay, I will explore four major themes: (1) the significance of tradition for universities and scholarship, (2) the compatibilities and incompatibilities between academic disciplines and universities, (3) a profound definition of the social system of science by Michael Polanyi – "a society of explorers," and (4) some recent illustrations of the influence of society on the social sciences and humanities.

I diverge in some parts of this essay from examining the university as a whole; some parts are more relevant to the social sciences and humanities, and some to the natural and physical sciences. This reflects, however, a reality of the modern university that cannot be wished away. Research and scholarship in the contemporary university respond to multiple imperatives differentially distributed across the varied intellectual pursuits of the faculty. In any event, I was encouraged in this view recently after reading that " 'intellectual and inconclusive discussions' are the very life-blood of the University."[2]

Traditions and Universities

The university is a historic institution deriving, in its modern form, from the early middle ages. Particular universities – Harvard, Oxford, Bologna, Paris, and others – have individual histories extending over centuries:

> By the fifteenth century the university was a recognized institution with a concern for its autonomy *vis-à-vis* Papal interference, with a supranational character and with concerns, customs and ceremonies which are recognisable in the twentieth century university institutions.[3]

This traditional aspect of contemporary universities is not merely of antiquarian concern, for the university derives significance and prestige from its lineage. History gives to the

faculty of universities and to those administrators entrusted with
their care a sense of participating in a transtemporal existence.
Many European universities have ancient chairs, which have
been continuously filled for more than three centuries.
Particular universities are identified with the historical
reputations of great scholars, Newton and Cambridge, Kant and
Königsberg. Universities inherit purposes and identities that
contribute to a certain detachment from contemporary concerns,
that produce a feeling of rootedness, and that thus encourage an
individual and a collective sense of responsibility for the
maintenance and improvement of a tradition. The tradition
constitutes a common resource, one that, fortunately, is enriched
rather than depleted by use.

Those who immerse themselves in the tradition come to
believe that their work is invested with unusual significance for
society and that they are the proud carriers of a heavy
responsibility. Consequently, many faculty privately feel, and
occasionally publicly say, that they have a vocation, a calling, not
simply a job. In the words of Edward Shils:

> A university is more than its stock of capital, its
> buildings, books, machines and instruments, and its
> monetary endowment. . . . It is a capital of
> institutional traditions as well as of intellectual
> traditions; every member and every action of
> discovery, interpretation and transmission benefits
> from these traditions. The intellectual traditions are
> the accomplishments of scientists and scholars,
> scattered . . . [around] the world and located at
> numerous points in the recent and remoter past. . . .
>
> A university . . . is a culture which is maintained
> by the traditions of many men and women of learning,
> living and working in each other's presence, sustaining
> each other, keeping intellectual wits and sensibilities
> alert and sharpened. The culture is the product of past
> achievements and it is sustained by co-presence of
> many individuals of different generations who keep
> this tradition alive and active. If the tradition is not
> alive and active, the performance of each individual
> suffers, some more than others.[4]

Academic Disciplines, Invisible Colleges, and Universities

The university is the major centre for intellectual pursuits that
unite segments of the scholarly community on a global scale

around common problems, models, styles of scholarship, and intellectual orientations. In a formal sense these linking mechanisms are disciplines and subdisciplines with their associations, membership fees, annual meetings, journals, and awards. More subtly, however, they are intellectual clusterings of geographically separated individuals who take their cues from one another, who feel they are engaged in a common enterprise, and who exchange and evaluate one another's scholarship in a well-understood and highly developed system of reciprocity. These invisible colleges, as they are called, focus on the research aspect of academic existence, rather than on the teaching role. They are central vehicles for the advancement of knowledge.

Several decades ago it was fashionable to contrast the spatially bounded individual university with the multifarious and differentiated disciplinary links of the faculty, and to suggest that the university was threatening to become like a railway station in which all were coming and going on disciplinary journeys and none was staying. In a closely related analysis the university was visualised as a mix of university careerists – the locals, interested in moving up the university administrative hierarchy, and the discipline-focused cosmopolitans, who had transcended parochialism, whose gaze was ever outward, and whose loyalties were to scholarly confreres scattered around the world. For such cosmopolitans, the university was a kind of academic hotel, good for short stays and selected for practical reasons such as teaching loads, research funds, and salaries.

In retrospect, those who saw the contrast between the spatially confined university, rooted in a few acres of buildings and grounds, and the intradisciplinary traffic of migratory academics as a structural contradiction with debilitating consequences for the university had exaggerated fears. In the 1980s when austerity has stifled mobility, our worries are different. We now fear the stagnation of stability and insufficient mobility.

The earlier fears reflected the simultaneous emergence of two related phenomena in the post-World War II era, especially during the 1960s and early 1970s. First was the dramatic expansion of universities in the Western world and in those parts of the third world emerging from Western imperial control. This generated an academic marketplace in which opportunities for mobility were extensive. Second, the past forty years witnessed an explosive burst of disciplinary development and specialization that tended to strengthen linkages within disciplines and across university boundaries at the expense of more traditional conceptions of university citizenship. In addition, the average faculty age was low, reflecting rapid expansion, and the young faculty member was fresh from the intense disciplinary socialization of graduate school when he or she arrived to take up a university appointment. Not surprisingly, these faculty were especially susceptible to disciplinary pulls that, in an expanding professorial market, were typically accompanied by salary increases.

The conjuncture of these phenomena stimulated disciplinary loyalties and identities to the detriment of university loyalties and identities. As Shils pointed out, the basic proposition of the supremacy of disciplinary identity over identification with the university "was intended to legitimate disloyalty to the university as an institution, to one's own particular university and to the university as a general category or ideal."[5]

The emphasis on the either/or aspect of discipline versus university led to a neglect of this basic compatibility. The overwhelming bulk of disciplinary work and scholarship in the past quarter-century has taken place in university settings. Mobility was overwhelmingly within the university system — those who moved to government or the private sector were typically considered lost to the discipline — and universities themselves in their efforts to build up new departments or strengthen old ones were catalysts of mobility as well as seeming victims of it.

The compatibility of universities and disciplines in a minimum sense rests on the elementary consideration that scholars have to live and work somewhere. In an era when the scholar could no longer own all the necessary research tools, there was no alternative to being located in an institutional setting that provided the complicated and expensive infrastructure of contemporary scholarship. With the exception of the occasional research institute not affiliated with a university, there was no practical alternative to housing disciplines in university homes.

The fact that alleged tension between disciplines and universities was overwhelmingly presented and discussed in terms of individuals was itself highly revealing. The message was clear. It was not disciplines that attempt to escape from the university system as a whole, but individuals who moved between universities within disciplines in pursuit of professional advancement. Those individuals typically remained committed to the general virtues of a university existence. They were like practitioners of serial marriage who did not reject marriage as such, but only the particular marriage to which they were ephemerally committed.

In the period after World War II, accelerated fragmentation of scholarship into differentiated disciplines, whose adherents unquestionably developed strong disciplinary identifications, was not as threatening to the universities as alarmists implied. In fact, the setting and traditions of the university were highly appropriate for disciplinary development. Flexible university structures proved capable of accommodating the demands of new intellectual specializations for organizational distinctiveness. The university of the past half-century has provided a congenial context for the fission and fusion of disciplines required by the growth of knowledge. Further, the university facilitated fruitful interdisciplinary exchanges, which worked against disciplinary ossification and kept alive the possibilities of future integrative tendencies across particular clusters of these mushrooming intellectual diversities.

More important than any of the preceding is the fact that the university, as a result of a historically evolved division of labour among institutions, has been given the primary responsibility for pursuing understanding and for finding patterns in man and nature. Universities are "corporate entities animated by a common spirit which transcends the boundaries of disciplines and specialties and divisions. . . . the university is . . . a spiritual and intellectual corporation."[6] Universities, in other words, provide an enriching context for disciplines. They are central meeting points for intellectual concerns. They concentrate, monitor, and sustain the task of inquiry, which spills over into innumerable intellectual communities whose members are scattered around the world but united in common enterprises.

None of the preceding is to deny that the nature of the university faculty as an intellectual community was transformed in recent decades by sheer growth in numbers and by disciplinary specialization, or to deny that the problems of governing the modern university were profoundly affected by those same factors. The point is simply that the tensions can easily be exaggerated, that the university has proven to be a highly flexible instrument, and that disciplines are enriched by their location in university settings, which, among other things, bring the supportive traditions of universities to the evolving traditions of disciplines.

A Society of Explorers: The Scientific Ideal

In one of his publications, the sociologist Robert Nisbet likened the work of a social scientist to that of an artist who seeks to unravel the mystery of a personality by subtle shadings on a canvas as he brings a portrait to life, or to that of a novelist who captures a prototypical character type of a particular era by the nuanced use of language. According to Nisbet, Marx's depiction of the bourgeoisie was such an artistic creation, which not only caught a social class in a sociological snapshot but by so doing, altered the phenomenon it described. To Nisbet such works by social scientists produce shocks of delighted recognition when a situation, a social category, or a process in society or nature that we may have been struggling to describe or analyze is captured and illuminated by the work of a colleague.

By a pregnant and evocative phrase, "a society of explorers," Michael Polanyi has brought to life, and hence to the possibility of intensive analysis, the decentralised, unplanned, and yet systematic process that co-ordinates the intellectual efforts of thousands of dispersed individuals who co-operate without meeting and without the guidance of superior authority. The explorers in Polanyi's society are the individual scholars engaged in experimenting, researching, probing, finding, and communicating their understandings of the portion of the puzzle of man and the cosmos that has attracted their curiosity. The society to which they belong is simply the relevant grouping of scholars with overlapping interests who are responsive to one another's work, although they are scattered around the world.

In Polanyi's words:

> In a society of explorers man is *in thought*. Man the explorer is placed in the midst of potential discoveries, which offer him the possibility of numberless problems. . . . scientists, scattered over the globe, respond to one vast field of potential thought. . . each finds in it a congenial area to develop, and . . . the results then co-ordinate themselves to produce a systematic expansion of science. . . .[Through] the principle of mutual control . . . each scientist independently plays his part in maintaining scientific traditions over an immense domain of inquiry of which he knows virtually nothing. A society of explorers is controlled throughout by such mutually imposed authority.[7]

Scientists with focused interests constitute a team, each member of which is exploring the unknown and is constantly adjusting his efforts in the light of the successes and failures of his colleagues. These teams, in Polanyi's sense, are not composed of contiguous colleagues working as a cohesive group. On the contrary, they are scattered, they do not engage in group activity, they have no common plan, and they play their part in the scientific endeavour, not in response to the hierarchical biddings of a superior, but in response to the cues of the system that guides them. They are a team in the sense that they share a common purpose in rolling back the unknown, depend on one another, have a sense of mutual solidarity, and inhabit the same intellectual worlds.

What Polanyi describes is a vast unplanned system that is nevertheless co-ordinated, is infinitely flexible, and consists primarily of the incentives and norms of the scientific community whose members respond to the constantly unfolding panorama of knowledge and discovery resulting from the efforts of their colleagues. To Polanyi, in the same way as a businessman responds to market signals in a free market society, a scientist responds to the research findings of other scientists in determining his own research plans.[8]

As Polanyi and others have pointed out, the evolution of the division of labour among social institutions has made the university the major institutional embodiment and locus of this never-ending exploration of the unknown, an exploration that is fragmentary, disjointed, unplanned, spontaneous, and yet, in its overall structure, is orderly. Shils writes of a "vast, unplanned collaborative undertaking, moving forward on many fronts at more or less the same time trying to understand the world in its infinite variety...[with] the university...[as] the institutional corporation of these movements possessing a common ethos and ideal."[9]

While a society of explorers is non-hierarchical, it is not without distinctions. The division of labour in such a scientific society must be made palatable to those practitioners working on some small corner of a problem, and to those who, by bad luck as much as by bad judgement, find themselves in a cul-de-sac. Since satisfaction cannot always come from personal triumphs, it must find a supplementary source in the overall scientific enterprise.

There are masters and apprentices in the scientific enterprise. There are the Nobel Prize-winners and the journeymen. There are those who publish and acquire fame and those who publish and perish, those who are cited virtually automatically in first footnotes and those who are never cited at all. A collective enterprise such as science requires the latter as well as the former, partly because their unsung labour may be building blocks for their more famous colleagues, and partly because it is impossible to predict in advance who will fall into each category. The whole enterprise must be kept going, not just those triumphant winners of the Darwinian process who sit at the apex of clusters of scholars. How is this achieved? Shils provides partial answer:

> The pursuit of particular truths would not last if those who carried it on did not in fact sometimes unwittingly conceive of themselves as parts of a wider engagement on a front as wide as all the objects which engage the human mind in its efforts for fundamental understanding.... The narrowest specialist—as many academics are nowadays—would be overpowered by the smallness of his undertaking if he were not carried forward by awareness that he is working alongside others who are, no less than himself, given over to the discovery of the truth about some part of the universe.
>
> Each specialist hears the click as he brings events, previously perplexing and exasperating by their randomness, into a pattern. He might be satisfied with a small pattern but he knows and draws strength from the simultaneous activities of others also seeking patterns which are consistent with his own, which are consistent within a large pattern. He is as dependent on the presence of these other pursuits in his marginal awareness as he is on the accomplishments of those who precede him. He is carried forward not just by his own motives as he perceives them but by the motives of others in the past and present. It is not always easy to perceive this participation of the individual in the larger tradition as it is inherited from the past and as it is cultivated in the present.[10]

The collective nature of science, sustained by tradition and kept buoyant by individuals constantly striving for integrity—each of whom is driven by the hope of discovery and vicariously encouraged by the discoveries of others—provides the moral and psychological sustenance without which the enterprise would falter.

The Influence of Society on the Social Sciences and Humanities: Some Recent Illustrations

Polanyi's society of explorers and the vast unplanned and yet co-ordinated order of scientific activity lovingly portrayed by Shils are ideal types passionately described by deeply committed scholars. They excite by the simplicity they bring to a chaos of particulars that otherwise threatens to engulf us. Further, they unquestionably contribute to our understanding of how intellectual communities work. Finally, the norm of universality implicit in these descriptions not only imposes obligations on all who "do" science, but also reassures us in its denial that scientists are time-bound or culture-bound. In Ziman's words:

> By its very nature, science is a co-operative activity, in which all who can contribute with observations, theories, concepts or criticism are free to participate. The transnational solidarity of science is thus strictly functional; Americans and Russians, Britons and Germans, Japanese, Brazilians and Nigerians, all belong to the same scientific community, and have a common interest in the welfare of all scientific institutions around the world.[11]

The image of a society of explorers washes out distinctions of culture, personality, and individual values. It logically follows that scientific personnel are interchangeable — that there is no scientific reason why those who pursue physics in Canada should be Canadians rather than Germans, Japanese, or Brazilians. Considerations of security, prestige, or career opportunities for citizens might dictate otherwise, but these would be seen as factors extraneous to science as such. That the *use* of science is subject to the requirements and capacities of particular societies would also be admitted, without affecting the proposition that pure science as an intellectual activity strains toward cosmopolitanism.

Does the same logic apply to the social sciences and the humanities? Are scholars in these fields as readily interchangeable? Are sociology and physics similar in the virtual irrelevance of cultural and national membership to the pursuit of understanding? Certainly in the social sciences and humanities, Polanyi's portrait of a society of explorers united around a common task that binds them into a single moral and intellectual community would not elicit universal recognition. The assertion that nationality and cultural background are irrelevant to the pursuit of knowledge and understanding is clearly not unanimously accepted in the social sciences and humanities. Perhaps the most passionate and emotional controversy in the social sciences and humanities in Canada in recent decades concerned an alleged Americanization of Canadian social sciences and the related issue of whether the extensive resort to American faculty would distort the development of the social sciences in Canada.

Social scientists are not neuters detached from the societies and cultures that formed them. Nor can we understand the nature of the contemporary social sciences as disciplines without examining the nature of the particular national contexts where they developed, and where they are now concentrated. From the third world the assertion is made that the unequal global distribution of social scientists results in understandings of the human condition that are partial and based on the differential capacity of rich and poor, large and small countries to support scholarship.

Many of the poor countries of the world lack not only the talent and funds to undertake basic scientific research, but even the more limited resource requirements of the social sciences and humanities, which are, consequently, weak, minuscule, or non-existent. Further, the political conditions and cultural climate in many third world countries are far from propitious for scholarship. Where possibilities for scholarship do exist in the third world, it is not uncommon for the Western university to be equated with cultural imperialism. Thus Mazrui asserts that the African university based on Western models is "the most sophisticated instrument of cultural dependency."[12] The social sciences of the West are denigrated as bourgeois and as presupposing roles for the state and norms of autonomy for the economy that are ill-suited for the task of aiding the major social transformation considered to be necessary in third world conditions.

The argument, in short, is for a high degree of specificity in the models, theories, and choice of problems that guide research. Much of the critique is based on practical considerations of the requirements of social engineering specific to particular societies at particular stages of their evolution. In that sense the situation may be said to differ little from the applied sciences.

The criticisms, however, go further to argue that the limitations of the social sciences extend to their fundamental assumptions about many in society. Malinowski noted that much of Freud was inapplicable to the Trobriand islanders. Such models and theories as Marxism and economic liberalism are value-laden and purpose-driven. They posit desired end-states and become weapons in political battles. A recent survey article noted that the contending approaches in international relations theory "basically reflect an Anglo-American-Eurocentric historial experience."[13]

It is unnecessary for our purposes to assess the larger question of whether the social sciences are intrinsically incapable of escaping from contingency into universality. It is enough to note that, in contrast to the physical and natural sciences, there is widespread resistance to claims that at their present stage of development they can fully take their place with astronomy and theoretical physics in Polanyi's society of explorers.

Another aspect of the critique of bias in the social sciences is also prominent in the third world and involves somewhat different concerns. This version focuses on the relationship between national and cultural dignity and the findings of scholarship. In its simplest form the argument is that they reflect the ethnocentrism of Western, capitalist, and formerly imperialist nations. In the post-imperial era, this elicits a historical revisionism by third world scholars that denigrates the imperial era as a negative interlude and that tries to project a more positive image of yesterday's colonized peoples.

As the preceding indicates, the social sciences and humanities are seen to be engaged in more than clinical examinations of a reality that is the same to all observers. In addition to seeking patterns, to searching for causal links to improve our policy performance, they also and simultaneously, both obliquely and directly, are engaged in providing descriptions and evaluations of a people, an era, an ethnic group, or mankind as a whole. Their task here is not photographic but creative. They are engaged in the creation of those collective images in which a people sees itself. They distribute status deliberately and inadvertently to blacks and whites, to men and women, to the West and the East, to capitalist democracies and to the guided, planned economies of Eastern Europe, Russia, and China. That this is a consequence of much work in political science, sociology, and history, especially when these disciplines engage in macro-descriptions and evaluations of third world societies and political systems is undeniable. That such descriptions and evaluations are significantly affected by the culture of the observer and by the passions and tensions of basic global cleavages is equally undeniable. From this perspective it is understandable that one of the psychological attractions of Marxism for third world scholars is that it externalizes blame for the indignity, poverty, and human suffering that surrounds them.

In their largest sense, these social science contributions help to construct the symbolic order in which we live, find meaning, fashion our identities, and look to see if we are included and fairly presented. For many, the answer has been "no." Dissatisfaction with unflattering portrayals of one's group is not confined to the former colonies of Africa and Asia seeking to escape from images and definitions that justified their subordination to outsiders; the dissatisfaction is also domestic.

Centrifugal developments within Western societies that have led to the erosion of traditional hierarchies and of customary deference have also had major effects on the social sciences and humanities. The women's movement, the revival of ethnicity, and the assertiveness of aboriginal peoples have affected universities and scholarship as well as the larger society. A proliferation of new journals and demands for academic representation, for new programs, for reinterpretations of the role and contribution of women, of ethnics, and of indigenous peoples, and for affirmative action in universities, as well as in the larger society, all are the academic and intellectual manifestations of societies in turmoil. Women's studies, black studies, ethnic studies, and native studies organized by clientele and employing holistic approaches hostile to fragmenting their constituencies among psychologists, economists, political scientists, and others are in themselves implicit criticisms of the more traditional disciplines.

The advocates of new academic orientations to raise the visibility of hitherto neglected or underappreciated groups in society recognize the role of universities and scholarship in fashioning the collective image a society has of itself. They wish to see themselves in that image. The African intellectual task according to Ali Mazrui is "not only to decolonize modernity, nor merely to participate in it, but also to help define modernity for future generations."[14]

The issues raised by the critics of hitherto dominant paradigms are not trivial. They reveal the evolving interactions of universities, scholarship, and societies. They testify to the increasing diversity of the societal influences that play on the university and on scholarship, especially outside the physical and natural sciences.

On the one hand, these critiques of dominant scholarship are salutary to the extent that they lead to recognition and rectification of biases in the intellectual construction of the meaning of the world. On the other hand, they have the potential of politicizing scholarship and the university. Those who seek change have some of the characteristics, at least for some transitional period, of social movements. Their desire to increase their representation on university faculties, to have their interests more prominently featured on research agendas, and to find themselves portrayed prominently and positively in published research injects political criteria into academic choices.

The situation is further complicated because of a tendency for the new research areas these pressures elicit to have a high proportion of their faculty from the group being studied. Black professors of black studies and female professors of women's studies reveal the social movement aspect of these new research fields, manifested in the tacit assumption either that only sympathizers are welcome or that the reality of the black experience or the female experience under study is unique and only insiders have the capacity to understand its nuances and subtleties.

The long-run consequences of these developments for the humanities and social sciences are unclear. In themselves and as portents for the future, they indicate the societal pressures playing on universities and scholarship. To the extent that the objective is the creation and dissemination of images of society consonant with the preferred self-image of the critics, they ultimately confront the problem of scarcity — that not everyone can have high status in society's pantheon without the currency of status being devalued. Ultimately, also, they must come to terms with the evidence.

A revisionism that does not adhere to the cannons of scholarship will be counterproductive, although even this observation is subject to the qualification from a feminist critique, for example, that mainstream scholarship is often malestream scholarship.[15] More generally, at least in their early stages, these movements to re-orient the academy threaten to institutionalize partisanship around the cleavages they stress. They bring with them the faint suggestions that the university should be a representative political system responsive to constituencies rather than a community of scholars responsive to disciplinary cues.

More positively, the global diversification of scholarly personnel to include increasing representation from the non-Western world, as well as greater diversification in the backgrounds of domestic faculty in the homelands of the Western university tradition, will increase the juxtaposition of divergent perspectives, which often produces creative intellectual work. This national and international social science community is a version of Gordon Tullock's thesis asserting the diseconomies of putting too many resources into a given line of research. The amount of overlapping and duplication of effort, he states:

> will increase exponentially with the number of men in the field. The marginal return on increased personnel is thus a declining function of their number, and it is therefore wise to keep scientific investigators dispersed in their interests. Concentrating them in one or a few fields will only marginally increase the rate of discoveries in that field, but will greatly reduce the rate in the fields from which they have been drawn.[16]

The future significance of the tendencies just described depends on whether they are minor eddies that will ultimately merge into a broadened, transformed community of scholarship, or whether they are indicators of a more profound change in the university's role in studying society. The possibility that the latter may be in store for us should not be discounted. The university is likely to live a relatively untroubled existence only when there is a high degree of social stability both nationally and internationally. Such a future will probably elude our grasp.

Yet, as I have argued in this essay, the university and academic disciplines are semi-autonomous domains that partly insulate scholars from society and relate them to one another in a social system with its own norms. The university has survived other turbulent times. As long as its central core of the traditional conception of the university and of the scholarly vocation remain intact, it will retain the capacity to assimilate those who enter its ranks and challenge its biases and will benefit from their presence.

Notes

I wish to thank Karen Jackson and Cynthia Williams for helping me with this paper.

1. E. Shils, ed. and trans., *Max Weber on Universities* (Chicago and London: University of Chicago Press, 1974), p. 61.

2. G.H. Bantock, cited in D.P. Leinster-Mackay, "The Idea of a University: A Historical Perspective on Some Precepts and Practice," *Vestes*, vol. 20, no. 3-4 (1977), p. 31.

3. Ibid., pp. 28-29.

4. Edward Shils, "Government and Universities in the United States," *Minerva*, vol. 17, no. 1 (Spring 1979), pp. 140, 168.

5. Ibid., p. 159.

6. Ibid., p. 151.

7. Michael Polanyi, *The Tacit Dimension* (Garden City, N.Y.: Doubleday, 1967), pp. 83-84.

8. John R. Baker, "Michael Polanyi's Contribution to the Cause of Freedom in Science," *Minerva*, vol. 16, no. 3 (Autumn 1978), p. 390.

9. Shils, "Government and Universities," p. 150.

10. Ibid., pp. 151-52.

11. John Ziman, "Solidarity within the Republic of Science," *Minerva*, vol. 16, no. 1 (Spring 1978), p. 11.

12. Ali A. Mazrui, "The African University as a Multinational Corporation: Problems of Penetration and Dependency," *Harvard Educational Review*, vol. 45, no. 2 (May 1975), p. 192.

13. K.J. Holsti, "Along the road to international theory," *International Journal*, vol. 39, no. 2 (Spring 1984), p. 360.

14. Mazrui, "The African University," p. 210.

15. See the articles in Angela Miles and Geraldine Fenn, eds., *Feminism in Canada: From Pressure to Politics* (Montreal: Black Rose Books, 1982).

16. Gordon Tullock, *The Organization of Inquiry* (Durham, 1966), p. 129. In "A Cooperative Multinational Opinion Sample Exchange," *Journal of Social Issues*, vol. 24, no. 2 (April 1968), p. 247, Donald T. Campbell cogently argues that

> when all of the hypotheses being tested or all of the structuring of inquiry come from a single culture, one can be sure that an undesirably narrow range of problems and perspectives are being examined. *Culture does have effects upon social scientists as well as upon other citizens.* It is of the essence of the resulting provincialism that those most provincial are least aware of this fact. For an optimal social science, contributions from all provinces are needed. The preponderance of any one province, no matter which one, is undesirable. (Emphasis in original.)

THE FUTURE OF A MEDIAEVAL INSTITUTION: THE UNIVERSITY IN THE TWENTY-FIRST CENTURY

IAN WINCHESTER

From the overthrow of the Roman Empire in the fifth century by the barbarian invasions to the capture of Constantinople by the Turks in 1453 and the subsequent Renaissance in Europe is a thousand-year span. It took roughly half of that time for the dim analogies of the Greek and Roman schools coupled with the monastic movement to work their way through the Karoline schools of France, the Palatine, and Italy, the Saracen schools of Baghdad and Cordova, and the professional institutes such as Salerno's school of medicine and Bologna's school of Roman law. These influences, together, perhaps above all, with the Paris lecture-rooms of the early schoolmen Abelard, Roscelin, and William of Campeaux, finally issued in the twelfth century into institutional form. It is now nearly eight hundred years since that institutional form was fixed and nearly a thousand since it spontaneously formed.

The university is our great mediaeval legacy, and in spite of vast historical change in the past millenium and in spite of national differences, the university retains a great deal of its mediaeval form. Indeed, the university as a movement as well as a collection of institutions is in many respects today more like its mediaeval counterparts than at any time in the past five hundred years. Of the mediaeval universities as such, we know most, perhaps, about Paris and Oxford. Paris serves to illustrate the astonishing parallels that have been preserved throughout the history of the university up to our own day. Let me dwell on a few points that distinguish our universities from other institutional forms.

— They are largely immune from the interference of the surrounding civil order, and sometimes they actually dominate that order.
— They are international in scope.
— They have a faculty and student body that reside nearby and often within the university precincts.

—   The university is internally organized into hierarchical and systematic educational machinery; usually a faculty of arts and higher faculties, including theology, law, and medicine (at least).

The University of Paris after a practical existence of perhaps one hundred years was granted a charter in 1200 by Philippe Auguste, which accorded it immunity from taxation and a jurisdiction of its own.   The international scope of the University of Paris was marked in the first instance by scholars from all over Europe wandering there and listening to the lectures of, for example, Abelard on topics such as nominalism and the Christian faith. The institutional form this initially took was the organizing of the faculty and student body into "nations" — in this instance into the "honourable nation of France, the most faithful nation of Picardy, the venerable nation of Normandy, and the most steadfast nation of England." This form survives today at, for example, Uppsala. Students from abroad were assigned to one or another of the various nations, thus, for example, Swedish students were part of the English nation. The internationalism was marked as well by the fact that the common tongue of the university was Latin.   Perhaps there will never be another common tongue to the university movement to rival Latin, but in our own day English plays a roughly analogous role.

In the Paris of 1200, the four "nations" formed the Faculty of Arts, the curriculum of which embraced the trivium (grammar, rhetoric, dialectic or logic) and the quadrivium (arithmetic, geometry, astronomy, and music).   Our own faculties of arts and sciences are direct descendants of these.   If there is a split between the arts and the sciences in our universities today (Lord Snow's "Two Cultures"), this split can be traced to the distinction between the studies of the trivium and those of the quadrivium. The character of a university during an era is largely determined by which of these is dominant during that period.

Going to "college," at least in the English-speaking world, is a near synonym for going to university.   This is not surprising since, as the mediaeval universities of Paris, Oxford, and Cambridge developed, a whole spate of colleges were founded as independent teaching and residential institutions that prepared students for degrees. Paris was by far the dominant "collegiate" university in terms of the number of such colleges, until the French Revolution closed it, leaving only the Sorbonne after the Napoleonic reforms of 1808.   The close connection between undergraduate teaching and colleges is perhaps most striking in the United States today with a vast number of religiously founded independent colleges from which a graduate might go on to higher studies in a university. One secret of the collegiate system that has never been passed on beyond Paris, Oxford, and Cambridge, however, is that in bad times an independently funded college can more easily weather the financial crises that weaken a university funded by a king or church or state. Indeed, in a university like Oxford today, it is rather hard to find the "university" in the North American sense, but the colleges are everywhere.

Besides library arrangements common to both mediaeval and contemporary universities, however, the most striking parallel between the mediaeval and contemporary universities are the hoardes of students. Oxford was said to have had between twenty thousand and thirty thousand students in the twelfth century, and Paris was known to have had twenty-five thousand at the time of the death of Charles VII in 1453. A mediaeval student transported to, say, the University of Toronto today would not feel out of place in the crowds.

In all sorts of superficial ways, then, the modern university is much like its early counterpart. There are, however, deeper ways in which the university today is still very much a mediaeval institution.

There are, I think, six features of modern universities that are continuous with their mediaeval counterparts and that have always been present whenever the university amounted to anything worth having. These are: its independence, its neutrality and impartiality, its bookishness, its concern for the advancement of knowledge, its interest in the passing on of knowledge critically, and, finally, its role as a cultural centre. Indeed, I think that these features might be described as the absolute presuppositions of the university as an institution in R.G. Collingwood's sense of that notion. I mean here that if you deny or remove any one of these things, while you may have an institution, you do not have a university-like one. The university has occasionally had to defend one of these presuppositions as explicit principles.

The most frequently challenged of these has been its independence. The independence of the university takes two forms. First is the independence of the university as an institution from the surrounding civil order. Since universities from their beginnings have almost always been located in some already existing town, this has usually meant independence from the surrounding town—and at an early period it usually meant hegemony over the town as well. Surviving in this tradition is the presence of a university police force independent of the town or city police in most universities today. Also, offences committed on university territory are not usually subject to civil or criminal action but rather to courts of university origin.

At earlier times, whenever the university's institutional independence was threatened, as it often was at Bologna or Paris, for example, in the twelfth century, the university used the very powerful weapon of cessation. It simply picked up and moved out of the town it was in, leaving the local economy in a state of complete collapse.

In the early days, universities had no property of their own so that portability was a central feature of the mediaeval university. The possibility of cessation depended upon another feature of institutional independence, namely, financial independence. The reason that the university could easily invoke cessation — and so have to be begged back to a town it had left — was that it was financially independent in a way in which the town was not. Students and masters brought wealth from external — worldwide — sources. Although there was never enough, and though the impecuniousness of both the teachers and the students was legend (and still is), the combined financial resources of the university were nonetheless, always a great temptation for a town.

The second form of independence that the university presupposes and ideally embodies is intellectual independence. By and large, cessation was not so good a means of maintaining this feature as was migration of teachers and portions of the student body, rather the movement and dispersal of the university as a whole. The intolerance for new and different ideas, although it has no place in the university, is nevertheless often found there. This is not particularly surprising since universities, in institutional form, have at least a minimal bureaucratic structure — and bureaucracies are conservative in their very nature. By and large, however, though there has always been the danger of an internal threat to the intellectual independence in a university, the greatest danger has usually loomed from without. External orthodoxy, either in the form of an overwhelming religious fixity, or of the demands of the nation-state, tend to pose a recurring threat to the free conception and discussion of ideas within a university. I need only mention the names of Galileo, Darwin, and Marx as illustrations. In each case, although each was of the university, none of them was in the university while freely conceiving and teaching.

In spite of the dangers from without and within, the university has, since the twelfth century, maintained forms that, in principle at least, ought to sustain the independence of the spirit – of science and scholarship – on which the advancement of knowledge depends. The disputation, the dissection, the public arguing of theses, the demonstration, in later ages the tutorial and the seminar, all are devices for the collaborative maintenance of the independence of thought by means of discussion and argument. Each can be and has been perverted, and the lecture perhaps most of all. But each can also be, and often has been, a recurring means for the maintenance of creative scholarship, creatively handled and presented in a public or quasi-public forum in which only the quality of the argument has mattered, and not who was delivering it. Abelard, that twelfth century genius who dominated the early logical and theological thought of the university movement in Europe, tells us of his response to the public pronouncements of a famous theologian at Laon called Anselm (a student of *the* Anselm) in these words:

> So I came to the old man, whose repute was tradition, rather than merited by talent and learning. Anyone who brought his uncertainties with him went away more uncertain still. He was a marvel in the eyes of his hearers, but a nobody before a questioner. He had a wonderful wordflow, but the sense was contemptible and the reasoning abject.[1]

The university has always tried to determine whether one was a somebody or a nobody before a questioner. In order to do this, however, the university has to invoke its second great presupposition – its neutrality and impartiality in the face of evidence.

Neutrality and impartiality, as the universities have practised it, is a vast and difficult topic. Like the other presuppositions of the university, it has its genuine uses and its perverted ones. The judiciary of our own time, in its neutrality, impartiality, and independence, owes much to the university tradition relating to the importance of soundness of argument, of fidelity to principles, and to the careful sifting and weighing of evidence that mediaeval forms of discussion and judgement took partly because of the classical ideal derived from Plato and Aristotle. It also owes, I suspect, a great deal to the crucial role university theologians played (particularly at Paris) whenever there was a theological dispute in the mediaeval church. In those days the University of Paris was called in as a neutral and impartial party to weigh the theological arguments of the disputes surrounding canon law and to arrive at a binding decision for the church.

Neutrality and impartiality before the evidence and the argument is just as important in the science and scholarship of our own time as it was at the dawn of the university in the twelfth century. Now, just as then, we can fool ourselves into an orthodoxy in the name of neutrality and impartiality. From Abelard to Galileo, while Aristotle held sway as "the Philosopher," the ideals of neutrality and impartiality before the face of evidence and the argument tended toward a kind of rigid obeisance or acquiescence in the end to the overwhelming convincingness of both Aristotle's evidence and his argument. Perhaps if it had been easy to find ways around Aristotle this would not have been so. But it was not, just as a matter of fact, easy to do so. Aristotle's neat and apparently complete science of logic was recovered by the thirteenth century from Arabic and Greek sources, and it was not until the late nineteenth and early twentieth centuries that Frege and Russell and Peano added something to it. It was not until Galileo and Newton that Aristotle's physics could be put aside, and then only because of devilishly difficult arguments in devilishly difficult books by these two men. In the brief period before the more or less complete recovery of the Aristotelian corpus — mainly the twelfth century — things were much freer than they were to be subsequently. From the early scientific work of Robert Grossetest and Roger Bacon, two twelfth-century Oxford men, we get a glimmer of the possibilities that might have flourished if Aristotle had not been so apparently convincing and so complete. Indeed, his very convincingness and completeness posed a great threat to the other great orthodoxy of the early period, namely, the tradition and theology of the universal church.

To make all of the learning of Aristotle and his Arabian commentators as well as the theology of their age available to the Latin world of the time was the life work of Albert the Great, Albertus Magnus, and his pupil Thomas Aquinas. It is to these two scholars, who flourished in the middle of the thirteenth century (circa 1240-1280), that we owe the greatest achievement of neutrality and impartiality of mediaeval scholarship. The task was to be neutral and impartial vis-à-vis both Aristotle and the traditions and doctrines of the church. This could be achieved only by embracing them both in a grand synthesis.

This brings me to the next great presupposition of the university movement, its essential bookishness, a feature that both Albert and Thomas Aquinas exhibit to an extraordinary degree. In constructing his great system of philosophy and sacred knowledge, Aquinas built upon the incredible bookish scholarship of Albert, who in turn had built upon the not especially bookish scholarship of Aristotle and his entirely bookish commentators and the vast bookish acquisitions from the mediaeval church. The tendency of this activity, the bookish bias, meant that throughout the mediaeval period until the Renaissance, looking at books rather than looking at the world tended to predominate. To some degree the effect of natural science on the university from Isaac Newton's day has tended to redress the overwhelming prejudice of the university in favour of the book, of the written word, of the idea imbedded in print or script. This prejudice does, however, have a real ground and is closely connected both with the university's independence and with its neutrality and impartiality vis-à-vis doctrines. Books and manuscripts are highly portable. Until the advent of the digital computer in our own age, no other way has been found for packing so much information into so light a burden as written or printed script rolled or bound on parchment or paper. A cessation or a migration, to be completely effective, must not leave the objective counterparts of knowledge behind. In our own day, were we to suppose a university of say, fifty thousand students and a library of five million books, a migration or cessation in which all of the books were moved could be done with each student carrying one hundred books. With modern means of transportation this would be no problem at all. Laboratories, however, are not so readily portable.

The essential bookishness (until now) of the university, is connected with the maintenance of this objective counterpart of knowledge — what Karl Popper and others have called the Third Realm (as distinct from the natural and the psychological order). The permanence, portability, and accessibility of books has always meant that the death of a scholar never meant the death of a discipline or of knowledge. It is also connected with the neutrality and the impartiality of the university, in a characteristically mediaeval way. Abelard probably started the habit that every doctoral dissertation today maintains, namely, the literature review. In this peculiar mediaeval form, the authorities for and against a particular answer to a question are placed in juxtaposition as they are in Abelard's *Sic et non*, with respect to a variety of theological questions. The very same form survives strikingly in works such as William Harvey's *Circulation of the Blood* and Darwin's *Origin of Species*, though here the review is not of received theology but received science. What has this method to do with the neutrality and impartiality of the university? Only this. It is the duty of the scholar to canvass faithfully and evenhandedly all previous received or expounded opinions before submitting them to scholarly scrutiny, whether of the logical or the observational kind. So the essential tradition of bookishness, here, is the tradition of using all of the relevant books (there were not so many in the twelfth century) available to illuminate a point of dispute before attempting to resolve the matter once and for all.

Beyond the essential independence, neutrality, and bookishness of the university lies its central interest in the truth, that is, in the advancement of science and scholarship. This interest, of course, is connected with the independence, neutrality, and bookishness of the place, but it certainly does not reduce them. Roughly, they are the conditions that make the advancement of knowledge, the furtherance of the truth, possible, but they are not in and of themselves that advancement. Also, it is the advancement of knowledge, the furtherance of truth, that makes the maintenance of its preconditions worthwhile. An independent, neutral, and bookish place might last a long time; but if it were intellectually stagnant, it would little deserve to last. One should not, of course, imagine that the university in its various embodiments has always been in fact actively engaged in the furtherance of knowledge.

One of the marvels of the university is that during the late mediaeval period, roughly from Aquinas to the Renaissance and Galileo, the universities, though stagnant on the whole, somehow survived. Here and there the flame of knowledge shone or at any rate flickered, but as a broad rule, it had gone out. The miracle of the seventeenth century is inconceivable, to be sure, without the universities. It was accomplished, however, as much in spite of them as by them. Descartes, Galileo, Huyghens, the Bernoullis, Leibniz, Spinoza, Newton, Locke, Boyle, Wren — to name but a few and to leave out most — all had fitful relationships with universities, if at all. Only Newton was centrally in the university during his moments of great creation and scholarship.

What had happened to make the universities between the fourteenth and nineteenth centuries, though places where knowledge was husbanded to be sure, not places where it was furthered? For the moment I shall remark only in passing that the splintering of Europe into both religious and national factions, thereby reducing the free flow of knowledge as well as the picture of its unity, played a central part. Also, the independence of the university was increasingly compromised and with it its neutrality and even its real bookishness, since it had earlier always been able to play off church and state against each other.

A university cannot maintain its interest in truth and the advancement of knowledge without its interest leading to the passing on of the knowledge already acquired, but not blindly, rather, critically. This is the teaching function of the university, and the fifth of our presuppositions to its possibility as an instituituion embodying an idea.

In my list of presuppositions I might have put the teaching function first. Certainly, the teaching function is historically first, both in the great student universities of the south, such as Bologna, and in the great masters' universities of the north, such as Paris and Oxford. At these places the universities spontaneously sprung up because there were students who wanted to know and teachers willing to teach. Also, the teaching function is arguably first logically as well. The embodying of knowledge in books, however well done, is not itself complete. There must be a next generation to read those books critically for the knowledge to be transmitted. The knowledge in a book, though objective, is only a means to future generations of knowers, not an end in itself. Also the teaching function, if defective or deformed, in itself spells the end to the university in the sense that all of the previous presuppositions are themselves transmitted in a defective or deformed fashion. It is crucial that knowledge be transmitted with the understanding of its dynamic and tentative nature. For what would be the point of independence, neutrality, and the attempt to further knowledge if this were not true? Here teaching and bookishness, unless they are both seen as essentially the maintenance of knowledge in a critical and tentative spirit, can come into conflict with each other — and often do. Finally, teaching is crucially connected with the last of our presuppositions to the idea of university, namely, the role of the university as a cultural centre — as *the* cultural centre.

Throughout the entire history of the university, from the twelfth century to the present day, the role of cultural centre has been uppermost not only in the universities' pretensions but in its accomplishments. When the culture was predominantly religious, it was the centre of that culture. When the culture was becoming increasingly secular, it was the centre of that secularization. As our culture has become more oriented toward science and technology in the past two centuries, the universities, led initially by the great research universities of Germany in the nineteenth century, have done the same. The universities have served as the training ground for all of the major professions that the general culture could devise, or demand. Until recently, the classical curriculum of the universities, the trivium and the quadrivium, locally modified, provided even the meanest lawyer, doctor, or theologian with a co-ordinated picture or map of the best of the past of human accomplishments, knowledge, and values. Specialization, while always present, was always subordinate to the demands of the Faculty of Arts, which was always the real cultural storm centre of the university. The Faculty of Arts, more or less intact until this century, is not, however, what it used to be.

There have been two main diagnoses offered us in recent years of the problem of the present weakness of the university as a cultural centre. The first is that of Lord Snow who, in his Rede Lecture nearly twenty years ago at Cambridge, suggested that our universities have lost their common culture and have split into two cultures: the culture of science and the culture of the humanities. The second diagnosis, by F.R. Leavis, also of Cambridge, was produced first in the 1930s and repeated in response to Snow. Leavis maintained that the university had ceased entirely to be a relevant cultural centre because of its inability to cope with the rise of the "technologico-Benthamite" civilization that has encompassed the world. Of the two diagnoses I am inclined to think that Leavis's is the deeper and explains Snow's observations in much the way that a diagnosis of a causative agent in medicine can account for the symptoms.

This brings us to the central question with which I wish to wrestle. Suppose it is true that in some sense the university is at the moment not able (or perhaps not willing) to play the role of cultural centre. If it is not, then has it a future in the twenty-first century? And if we wish it to have a future in the next century, what can we do to restore the university to its place of cultural centrality – as the cultural storm centre?

If the university ceases to be the cultural centre for an extended time, then I am inclined to think it has no future, because all of its defining features are interlocking and interdependent. There is no future for an institution that takes for granted independence from the claims of the civil order and freedom of the spirit. The university has weathered the feudal order and been its cultural centre. It has survived the transition to nation states and the decline of the Latinate culture and the universal church. It has had a central place in the rise of science and in the transition in the seventeenth century from the final shucking off of the mediaeval economy to the rise of capitalism. It has lived through the juggernaut of the Industrial Revolution and has survived its transformation, first in Prussia and in the Germany of Bismarck, to being closely allied with national linguistic and cultural goals. For most of this century it has struggled to come to grips with these two massive movements, which have not yet spent their force and in most of the world are only just beginning.

Culture, Teaching, and Research in the Next Century

Predicting the future is a very risky business, and perhaps it is our inability to see very much of that future, either individually or collectively, that makes living tolerable at all. With respect to the history of the university, attempts to predict the future from any of a whole series of vantage points in time would have been not only risky but almost certainly a failure. For example, suppose we could be transported back to the Cambridge of 1666. If we could visit the senior common room at Trinity College we might find the dons talking about the decline in enrolment and the long-term effect of the plague on the university. It would be most unlikely that conversation would turn to the young Isaac Newton who had matriculated in 1660 but had waited out two years while the plague was raging. Yet what Newton has meant for the history of the university cannot be exaggerated, while the plague and its attendant problems have been a minor triviality. Similarly today, we are inclined to worry about the present funding problems that beset our universities – at least in Western Europe and in North America. Yet there may be a discovery, a movement afoot, a series of fresh ideas, that will transform us indelibly in the years to come.

If one had visited the sleepy German universities in 1800, one might have been in a swordfight, or drunk a lot of beer, and perhaps had a conversation about a classical author. No one would have predicted that Von Humboldt would transform the Prussian educational system in 1808 and create a research university that would come in time to be closely allied with both state and industry. Nor would one have predicted that this model would spread to all the German universities that were to make such a great cultural and scientific contribution to the world in the nineteenth century. Nor, for that matter, could one have predicted how this model of a university system could be subordinated to linguistic, national needs for the better part of a thirty-year period in this century – thereby compromising its independence, its neutrality, its critical powers, and its role as a real cultural centre, if not its bookishness, or its scientific prowess.

The course of German universities is, I think, illustrative of my concern today. At no time in the previous history of the universities, except perhaps in the twelfth and thirteenth centuries, did any identifiable group of universities make such a contribution to human culture generally as did nineteenth-century German universities. Physical science, chemistry, archaeology, historical scholarship, classical studies, and biblical criticism were all transformed. Mathematics was furthered to an incredible degree. Between 1810 and 1914 the world looked to Germany, and this was all accomplished by a very small number of scholars and a very moderate student body when we compare universities of that time with those now. The largest university, for example, in Germany in 1878 was Berlin, which had 214 instructors and 2,834 students; Göttingen, the university of the great Gauss, had only 124 instructors and 909 students; historic Heidelberg had but 113 instructors and 461 students. Indeed, in 1878 the entire German university system of twenty-two universities had 1,887 instructors and 17,846 students — it would have easily fit into the University of Toronto twice and nearly three times over. Would that we could claim equal accomplishments!

The reason that I am dwelling on the German universities of a century ago is to point out how difficult it is to see what the university must guard against to retain its full integrity. Furthermore, it is no longer possible for a university — or a whole system of universities — to order a cessation or a migration in order to defend its integrity as the kind of institution that it should be. For the German universities, and for the remaining universities of Europe in the late nineteenth and early twentieth centuries, it was when things were going most swimmingly that they were in greatest danger as a cultural centre. As they became increasingly bound to Bismarck's alliance of German nationalism, state centralization, and industrial co-ordination, their role as a German cultural centre rose, and their role as a human cultural centre faltered. One should not imagine that it was better in Cambridge or Paris or Harvard or Bologna in those times either. Shortly after the outbreak of World War I, while the universities of Europe and America gleefully sent their best young men to be slaughtered for "cultural" reasons, Bertrand Russell was imprisoned in England for speaking out against the war. He lost his fellowship at Trinity College, Cambridge, as well, since concern for human culture was not appreciated in times of national fanaticism, a fanaticism in which university men had a large and inglorious part to play.

We can, I think, see in the role of the university in the first and second world wars and subsequently that the universities are in the grip of forces that they have not really understood, and so have only fitfully resisted. This is so in part because the Industrial Revolution is no longer confined to a portion of the planet, no more than are the universities. Also, we have no grand synthesis of human values that motivates the university movement as a whole, as it was perhaps motivated at the time of Albertus Magnus and Thomas Aquinas. Affecting universities also is our failure to assimilate the fact of our absolute aloneness as a species in this part of the universe, or of the horrifying possibility of our total disappearance in the course of the next century, if not in the next few years.

Here is a task that relates to the kind of teaching and research necessary in the university in the immediate future, and which can certainly keep us busy in the next century. I mean the task of unifying, through the university movement, our human culture.

Values in a Scientific Age

Ours is a scientific, not a religious aga — even if religious "revivals" are present here and there over the whole earth. Science, which was fostered and sustained in the climate of obsession with truth that characterized the religious era of the early universities, is now our dominant obsession. Although science in the earlier era may have been understood as displaying the rational glory of God in his natural realm, religion in our era is, ironically enough, not able to display the glory of science in the supernatural one. At best, then, in our own era, religion is seen as utterly disconnected from science; at worst, religious notions are seen as silly holdovers from a bygone era.

It was the passing of the dominance of the Christian religious obsession, which had energized the universities for so long and so dominanted European culture, that Friedrich Nietzsche labeled with the striking slogan "God is dead. We have killed him, you and I." Nietzsche did not, of course, mean that God himself is actually dead. On that point Nietzsche had no opinions. What he had noticed, however, was the overwhelming cultural fact that in the thrust of modern civilization, in which the universities played a central role, the dominant questions and answers were no longer given in the valuational terms of theology. We, and our entire civilization, were no longer directed by the older theological obession. The interrogation of God, as a dominant phase in the history of the university, was over; and the interrogation of nature, which had previously been but a minor way of interrogating God, was now the dominant activity obsessively indulged in for its own sake.

The passage from a religious to a scientific age has had important effects on the universities, some of them external, some internal. The most important external effect is that the university movement has spread more rapidly in our time than at any time since the twelfth century. Universities in our age are seen essentially as vehicles for producing the necessary intelligentsia for a technological civilization that has spread over the entire globe. Universities with Christian theological concerns and value judgements as their central interest would not have the appeal in non-Christian countries that the scientific-technological university possesses. So the second great international movement of the spread of universities is the main external result of the shift to the interrogation of nature, which was led by the nineteenth-century German universities.

Another important effect on the universities internally is the shift in the paradigm of what counts as research and scholarship. We have seen since the turn of the century, for example, the rise of psychology and the social sciences. In both cases the dominant effort has been toward the aping of the natural sciences, using experimental methods or observational methods, and slipping in a little elementary mathematics where possible. It has been said, not without some truth, that psychology has experimental methods and massive conceptual confusion and that sociology has mathematical methods and trivial results. Be that as it may, the effect has been increasingly to downgrade the humanities except where they are thought to ape the methods of the natural sciences. Indeed, for our era, to a considerable degree "research" has come to be understood to mean, perhaps is presupposed to mean, "doing things rather like one would if the subject matter was physics or chemistry," or, since most scholars are in fact ignorant of either of these, doing things as one imagines they would be done in physics or chemistry. Anyone who has filled out forms for funding agencies or had one's project assessed by neutral third parties also learns something about the assumptions of the scientific age. The categories and headings on the forms, the kinds of questions reviewers ask, the distribution of funding, each has its own message about our age.

Perhaps the clearest expression of the presuppositions dominantly in place in this century is given by Karl Pearson, the great pioneer statistician, in his book *The Grammar of Science*, first published in 1892. Pearson insists that there is only one method for arriving at knowledge, the scientific method. As a consequence, if we have any problems we wish to solve, the only appropriate strategy is to apply the scientific method to those problems. If we have problems to which the method apparently does not apply, then we must despair of their resolution, or else abandon the problems as pseudo-problems. This sort of thinking has been a constant temptation in our century, and, until Science is Dead, will be a constant temptation in the next century as well.

I shall shortly give what grounds I can for the pseudo-Nietzschean announcement that "Science is Dead," although that is not my present topic. What I am after is how the university in a scientific age can genuinely be *the* cultural centre. For whatever science is, it is not culture, or not the whole of culture since, other than the obsessions for order and truth, it embodies no specifically human values whatsoever. Even if science is dying, which I desperately hope it is not, the death throes are likely to go on for centuries.

Since the 1850s or so, the prestige of a country's universities has been largely dependent upon the scientific achievements of those universities. A century ago the learned quickened at the sound of Halle, Go"ttingen, Berlin, and today we gasp at the sound of Harvard, Stanford, Michigan, the Massachusetts Institute of Technology, Cambridge, and Cal Tech. Yet our scientific obsession is almost totally co-ordinated with such value judgements we as humans in this age have been able to sustain. Since neither science nor technology offers us any values in and of themselves, we find ourselves in the midst of an obsession that is leading us neither to heaven nor hell but to nowhere in particular.

Many disciplines in the university are still centrally connected with questions of value (outside of theology, which in any event cannot get a truly international hearing in our age); however much they have aped or tried to ape the natural sciences, they have failed in the impossibility and still retain their integrity. Among these are philosophy, history, and literary criticism. Music and mathematics are also quite unlike the natural sciences and undeniable in accomplishment, but are not centrally connected with value in the same way as philosophy, history, and literary criticism are. I take it for granted that questions of value cannot be addressed by scientific means, although, of course, ignorance of science is not useful for coming to grips with the great valuational questions of the age. So I pose the great research and teaching problem of our immediate future in the following terms: What kind of collaborative effort of research and teaching (and here I do not presuppose that this must be "scientific" research) can be made in our universities, worldwide, so that our scientific prowess is guided by humane values in a scientific age?

Something like this question seems to lie behind the thinking on the topic of universities and research by such diverse twentieth-century thinkers as Alfred North Whitehead, Karl

Jaspers, R.G. Collingwood, Ludwig Wittgenstein, and J. Robert Oppenheimer. It was a primary question for the great English literary critic F.R. Leavis, who at one point wrote:

> We have not to debate whether it is to produce specialists or the "educated man" that the university should exist. Its essential function involves the production of both — though to say "*the* educated man" is perhaps misleading. The problem is to produce specialists who are in touch with a humane centre, and to produce a centre for them to be in touch with; but this centre is not best conceived as a standard "educated man." There will be "educated men" with various stresses, various tendencies towards specialization. There will be — as happily there are — specialists who will be classifiable as "educated men."[2]

In another passage in the same work, he makes the same point in these words:

> An urgently necessary work . . . is to explore the means of bringing the various essential kinds of specialist knowledge and training into effective relation with informed general intelligence, humane culture, social consequence and political will.[3]

In one of Oppenheimer's essays entitled "Science and the Human Community," written when he was director of the Institute for Advanced Study in Princeton, he described the educational problem posed by the advancement of science to the dominant place in our universities:

> All the way from history to biology a great arc of science is about to catch fire. We have to be prepared to deal with this and to see that it does not throw us off balance and does not even further corrode the vitality of our society. . . .
> The receptacle of all the knowledge we have, the agencies to whom this knowledge is entrusted and who create it, are not individual men. They are communities of men. They are the specialized professions, often increasingly specialized. The world of knowledge is a world held together by little bands of people who know a great deal about some particular

field but whose relations with neighbouring fields, while warm, are not often very intense. As far as the world of learning goes, we live in a way in a kind of generalization of the old mediaeval guilds, a kind of syndicalism which is a cognitive syndicalism, a syndicalism in which true community, the true intimate collaboration of men, is best exemplified by groups of specialists who understand each other and help each other. Every scholar is in some sense or other a member of such a group. To use the image of a network again, these communities offer a picture of internal intimacy, cognitive intimacy, an intimacy of understanding and clarity, and usually of good will and cordiality; and these communities stretch through all parts of the world. One notices this fact with hope, but one notices it also with melancholy. For one thinks of these communities as networks holding the world together, and one cannot believe that these bonds are strong enough for the times we live in.[4]

Oppenheimer was writing more than twenty years ago, and at that time his argument was that "science by itself will self-destruct"; for the dispersal of knowledge among tiny, international, specialized groups in our universities (mainly) is coupled with two other obvious features of our age. The first is that the rate at which this kind of specialist knowledge is being produced (and so tiny specialist groups are being formed) doubles every decade or so. Second, very little of this knowledge gets back into the common stock of our human knowledge. The effect of the former is to increase tremendously the ratio of things new to things old, both of sheer knowledge as well as of the applications of knowledge. This imbalance between the new and the old is very hard for us to cope with. We have always had to cope with the new, but it tended, or so Oppenheimer implies, to be in relatively low ratio to the old. The effect of the latter, namely the relative impoverishment of the stock of common knowledge as opposed to that known to specialized groups, is also considerable in our day, and unless the universities—at least—can take action, it will get worse, since no other institutions are really equipped.

Why does it matter that novelty predominates in our scientific age and common knowledge is relatively enfeebled while specialized knowledge explodes? Here Leavis and Oppenheimer agree completely. Our vital, living knowledge, our common knowledge of *values* is nearly non-existent in our age, because of the two consequences of the kind of scientifically advancing age this is. One way of putting it is that our knowledge of the good and the beautiful has been incredibly enfeebled.

It is as a centre of this vital, living knowledge, as a centre of common knowledge of the good and the beautiful, that the universities must make a contribution into the twenty-first century and beyond if "Science is Dead" is not to become a slogan in that century. What remedies or schemes for this new form of collaborative research and teaching can we offer to save both science and mankind, at least for the next century? How can this be done in such a way that all the universities of the world can participate?

Some Collaborative Schemes:
A Pocketful of Panaceas

Throughout most of this century in universities in the United States and elsewhere there has been concern for the lost liberal education, based on the classical model. The university education based on the classics, a good approximation to which can still be found at Oxford today, functions as a real centre for a society's culture only when the whole culture looks to classical ideals for inspiration. Britain during its great empiring days did seem to look to such classical ideals for inspiration. If so, then the university education based on classical authors may have had a point, and the university may have had a point – as the centre of such relevant classical learning. Perhaps during that time Britain saw itself as the new Rome or Athens – perhaps it even was the new Rome or Athens.

This illustrates the difficulty of producing a genuine research and teaching centre, the collaborative cultural centre that our universities desperately need today. The centre must be directly related to the onward march of the times. It must also be able to lead in that onward march. In the past twenty or thirty years a number of candidates have been offered as the potential centre for the new university order: a revival of classical studies; historical studies; philosophy (inevitably); literary studies of a crucial, and not too temporally distant, past era; and finally, comparative studies, for example, Athens and America, or the seventeenth century and the present.

A revival of classical studies, however wonderful the Greeks and Romans were, is most unlikely to offer that natural centre to which all the specialist disciplines might turn for cultural and valuational succour in our own age. Universal starvation, genetic control, universal nuclear destruction, and space travel were not part of the deepest thoughts of our Greek and Roman forebears. Nor, it seems to me, are we likely to find any more inspiration in non-European classical models — say, Chinese or Indian — for the same reasons.

Historical studies as the centre of cultural and university studies, a possibility canvassed most seriously by R.G. Collingwood, is a much more interesting candidate. Collingwood's picture was that the science of the West had gotten out of touch with its cultural roots by virtue of an anti-metaphysical streak it had developed in the late nineteenth century. Collingwood's way to salvation was to unite history and philosophy into a new single discipline that would seek out the metaphysical presuppositions of the myriad disciplines we had spawned in the specialist era. In this way we would not mistake our new sciences for things they are not, namely value-free and entirely empirical. If we saw clearly that they were based upon what he called "absolute presuppositions" or "metaphysical presuppositions," and that these differed from discipline to discipline and era to era, we would see what a human and historical enterprise the scientific enterprise is. We would be forced to think deeply and valuationally from the start — not simply when it is too late. Certainly if everyone who were to pass through a university were required also, in collaboration with others, to try to think about the presuppositions of the various specialist disciplines in which they came into contact, they would be the better for it. The one great difficulty with this scheme is that in some sense it requires that the thinkers already be masters of the disciplines whose presuppositions they are to try to wheedle out and contemplate. This tends, therefore, to make the Collingwoodian centre a kind of post-post-graduate study, rather than a collaborative discipline.

F.R. Leavis's notion was that critical literary studies of a great, recent, and relevant era was perhaps the best notion for developing the sensibility and judgement one wished in one's specialists. His own particular favourites were English literature and the seventeenth century (primarily in England, though covering the whole of Europe). I can hardly do Leavis justice in a few hasty lines, but I shall have to try. The rough notion he had was that cultural continuity is connected with the continuity of language, and one's culture is most deeply connected with the language of that culture. Consequently one's collaborative cultural centre in the university must be ultimately literary-critical, although literature here includes more than poetry, plays, and novels. It also includes journalism, scientific writing, and historical thought. Further, it necessarily must be comparative in the international sense that no "culture" stands alone. What the English were thinking in the seventeenth century bore a relation to what, for example, the French and the Italians were thinking. To take an example from science, Newton worked with writings from Galileo, Kepler, Huyghens, and Descartes while working on his system of the world.

Leavis's notion of the centre of culture in the university is a very plausible one for England, but many societies that have universities today have nothing comparable to English literature — indeed, who else does? — and so cannot feel themselves particularly comfortable in its study as the relevant centre of their universities. For most universities, then, the substitution of their own language and relevant cultural achievements would not work in the way in which Leavis's scheme might work for England or, say, Canada. The problem is having a language, a literature, and the cultural achievements directly relevant to the transition to our scientific-technological age. Most cultures have only recently acquired this as a derivative effect of the spread of European and American technology to the world. Consequently, Leavis's scheme for them would, should English or another European language be the centre for study, rather be like a classical study of a distant and alien language. The vitality of the study would almost necessarily suffer.

There are similar difficulties to the variations on the Leavis scheme in which one would study either a crucial past era in detail — and certainly seventeenth-century Europe is the most relevant one in many respects — or the present in one's own country compared with some great classical period. Again, except for the European nations as such — and not all of them — the study takes on the relevance of classics, only a little nearer to hand.

We are left, then, on the horns of a multi-lemma — a classico-modern beast.

Since none of these past studies appears to have the necessary universal appeal or applicability we would ideally like, we are left with a program that dwells either on the immediate present or in some sense on the future. In this sense, too, I think we are increasingly mediaeval. Although the mediaeval period used classical and religious learning, it was always *future* oriented — the life to come was the key notion. Dare I suggest that the cultural centre our universities must become can only be so if it dwells on the future of mankind among the stars? In an age in which the interrogation of nature is dominant, it seems to me that only the question of the future of mankind off this planet, and spreading through the universe, is likely to offer the cultural challenge to our thinking in which the various specialist disciplines, whether historical, scientific, or literary, could crucially come together in a spirit of adventure and research. Our task would not be how to produce a heaven here on earth (although that would be one hoped-for byproduct). Rather, it would be to produce an earth in the heavens fit for the gods.

Just what such a future-oriented centre for research and teaching would look like in detail I cannot yet say. It is, however, a topic to which all universities on this planet may contribute without any special disadvantage, and with the excitement of adventure. In thinking about such a future for our species – and perhaps for our robots – we shall need every glimpse of wisdom, value, and foresight that any culture on earth has heretofore been able to muster.

Notes

1. Abelard, *Historia calamitatum*, in Henry Osborne Taylor, *The Mediaeval Mind*, vol. 2 (Cambridge, Mass.: Harvard University Press, 1962), p. 373.

2. F.R. Leavis, *Education and the University* (New York: Cambridge University Press, 1979), p. 28.

3. Ibid., p. 24.

4. J. Robert Oppenheimer, "Science and the Human Community," in Charles Frankel, ed., *Issues in University Education* (Westport, Conn.: Greenwood, 1979, reprint of 1959 edition).

THE MEMBERS OF THE INSTITUTE

Dr. Blossom Wigdor
Director, Program in Gerontology
University of Toronto

Government Representatives
Herb Clarke, Newfoundland
Joseph H. Clarke, Nova Scotia
Michael Decter, Manitoba
George de Rappard, Alberta
Hershell Ezrin, Ontario
Honourable Lowell Murray, Canada
John H. Parker, Northwest Territories
Henry Phillips, Prince Edward Island
Norman Riddell, Saskatchewan
Jean-K. Samson, Québec
Norman Spector, British Columbia
Eloise Spitzer, Yukon
Barry Toole, New Brunswick

INSTITUTE MANAGEMENT

Rod Dobell	President
Louis Vagianos	Special Assistant
Edgar Gallant	Fellow-in-Residence
Tom Kent	Fellow-in-Residence
Eric Kierans	Fellow-in-Residence
Jean-Luc Pepin	Fellow-in-Residence
Gordon Robertson	Fellow-in-Residence
Yvon Gasse	Director, Small and Medium-Sized Business Program
Barbara L. Hodgins	Director, Western Resources Program
Barry Lesser	Director, Regional Employment Opportunities Program
Frank Stone	A/Director, International Economics Program
Shirley Seward	Director, Co-ordination and Liaison
Parker Staples	Director, Financial Services & Treasurer
Donald Wilson	Director, Communications
Tom Kent	Editor, *Policy Options Politiques*

PUBLICATIONS AVAILABLE - MAY 1986

Order Address:

The Institute for Research on Public Policy
P.O. Box 3670 South
Halifax, Nova Scotia
B3J 3K6

Leroy O. Stone &
Claude Marceau

Canadian Population Trends and Public Policy Through the 1980s. 1977 $4.00

Raymond Breton

The Canadian Condition: A Guide to Research in Public Policy. 1977 $2.95

Raymond Breton

Une orientation de la recherche politique dans le contexte canadien. 1977 $2.95

J.W. Rowley &
W.T. Stanbury (eds.)

Competition Policy in Canada: Stage II, Bill C-13. 1978 $12.95

C.F. Smart &
W.T. Stanbury (eds.)

Studies on Crisis Management. 1978 $9.95

W.T. Stanbury (ed.)

Studies on Regulation in Canada. 1978 $9.95

Michael Hudson

Canada in the New Monetary Order: Borrow? Devalue? Restructure! 1978 $6.95

David K. Foot (ed.)

Public Employment and Compensation in Canada: Myths and Realities. 1978 $10.95

Raymond Breton &
Gail Grant Akian

Urban Institutions and People of Indian Ancestry: Suggestions for Research. 1979 $3.00

Thomas H. Atkinson

Trends in Life Satisfaction Among Canadians, 1968-1977. 1979 $3.00

W.E. Cundiff &
Mado Reid (eds.)

Issues in Canadian/U.S. Transborder Computer Data Flows. 1979 $6.50

Meyer W. Bucovetsky (ed.)

Studies in Public Employment and Compensation in Canada. 1979 $14.95

Richard French &
André Béliveau

The RCMP and the Management of National Security. 1979 $6.95

Richard French &
André Béliveau

La GRC et la gestion de la sécurité nationale. 1979 $6.95

297

G. Bruce Doern & Allan M. Maslove (eds.)	*The Public Evaluation of Government Spending.* 1979 $10.95
Leroy O. Stone & Michael J. MacLean	*Future Income Prospects for Canada's Senior Citizens.* 1979 $7.95
Richard M. Bird	*The Growth of Public Employment in Canada.* 1979 $12.95
Richard J. Schultz	*Federalism and the Regulatory Process.* 1979 $1.50
Richard J. Schultz	*Le fédéralisme et le processus de réglementation.* 1979 $1.50
Lionel D. Feldman & Katherine A. Graham	*Bargaining for Cities, Municipalities and Intergovernmental Relations: An Assessment.* 1979 $10.95
Elliot J. Feldman & Neil Nevitte (eds.)	*The Future of North America: Canada, the United States, and Quebec Nationalism.* 1979 $7.95
David R. Protheroe	*Imports and Politics: Trade Decision Making in Canada, 1968-1979.* 1980 $8.95
G. Bruce Doern	*Government Intervention in the Canadian Nuclear Industry.* 1980 $8.95
G. Bruce Doern & Robert W. Morrison (eds.)	*Canadian Nuclear Policies.* 1980 $14.95
Allan M. Maslove & Gene Swimmer	*Wage Controls in Canada: 1975-78: A Study of Public Decision Making.* 1980 $11.95
T. Gregory Kane	*Consumers and the Regulators: Intervention in the Federal Regulatory Process.* 1980 $10.95
Réjean Lachapelle & Jacques Henripin	*La situation démolinguistique au Canada: évolution passée et prospective.* 1980 $24.95
Albert Breton & Anthony Scott	*The Design of Federations.* 1980 $6.95
A.R. Bailey & D.G. Hull	*The Way Out: A More Revenue-Dependent Public Sector and How It Might Revitalize the Process of Governing.* 1980 $6.95
David R. Harvey	*Christmas Turkey or Prairie Vulture? An Economic Analysis of the Crow's Nest Pass Grain Rates.* 1980 $10.95
Donald G. Cartwright	*Official Language Populations in Canada: Patterns and Contacts.* 1980 $4.95
Richard M. Bird	*Taxing Corporations.* 1980 $6.95
Leroy O. Stone & Susan Fletcher	*A Profile of Canada's Older Population.* 1980 $7.95
Peter N. Nemetz (ed.)	*Resource Policy: International Perspectives.* 1980 $18.95

Keith A.J. Hay (ed.)   *Canadian Perspectives on Economic Relations With Japan.* 1980 $18.95

Dhiru Patel   *Dealing With Interracial Conflict: Policy Alternatives.* 1980 $5.95

Raymond Breton & Gail Grant   *La langue de travail au Québec : synthèse de la recherche sur la rencontre de deux langues.* 1981 $10.95

Diane Vanasse   *L'évolution de la population scolaire du Québec.* 1981 $12.95

David M. Cameron (ed.)   *Regionalism and Supranationalism: Challenges and Alternatives to the Nation-State in Canada and Europe.* 1981 $9.95

Heather Menzies   *Women and the Chip: Case Studies of the Effects of Information on Employment in Canada.* 1981 $8.95

H.V. Kroeker (ed.)   *Sovereign People or Sovereign Governments.* 1981 $12.95

Peter Aucoin (ed.)   *The Politics and Management of Restraint in Government.* 1981 $17.95

Nicole S. Morgan   *Nowhere to Go? Possible Consequences of the Demographic Imbalance in Decision-Making Groups of the Federal Public Service.* 1981 $8.95

Nicole S. Morgan   *Où aller? Les conséquences prévisibles des déséquilibres démographiques chez les groupes de décision de la fonction publique fédérale.* 1981 $8.95

Raymond Breton, Jeffrey G. Reitz & Victor F. Valentine   *Les frontières culturelles et la cohésion du Canada.* 1981 $18.95

Peter N. Nemetz (ed.)   *Energy Crisis: Policy Response.* 1981 $10.95

James Gillies   *Where Business Fails.* 1981 $9.95

Allan Tupper & G. Bruce Doern (eds.)   *Public Corporations and Public Policy in Canada.* 1981 $16.95

Réjean Lachapelle & Jacques Henripin   *The Demolinguistic Situation in Canada: Past Trends and Future Prospects.* 1982 $24.95

Irving Brecher   *Canada's Competition Policy Revisited: Some New Thoughts on an Old Story.* 1982 $3.00

Ian McAllister   *Regional Development and the European Community: A Canadian Perspective.* 1982 $13.95

Donald J. Daly   *Canada in an Uncertain World Economic Environment.* 1982 $3.00

W.T. Stanbury & Fred Thompson   *Regulatory Reform in Canada.* 1982 $7.95

Robert J. Buchan, C. Christopher Johnston, T. Gregory Kane, Barry Lesser, Richard J. Schultz & W.T. Stanbury	*Telecommunications Regulation and the Constitution.* 1982 $18.95
Rodney de C. Grey	*United States Trade Policy Legislation: A Canadian View.* 1982 $7.95
John Quinn & Philip Slayton (eds.)	*Non-Tariff Barriers After the Tokyo Round.* 1982 $17.95
Stanley M. Beck & Ivan Bernier (eds.)	*Canada and the New Constitution: The Unfinished Agenda.* 2 vols. 1983 $10.95 (set)
R. Brian Woodrow & Kenneth B. Woodside (eds.)	*The Introduction of Pay-TV in Canada: Issues and Implications.* 1983 $14.95
E.P. Weeks & L. Mazany	*The Future of the Atlantic Fisheries.* 1983 $5.00
Douglas D. Purvis (ed.), assisted by Frances Chambers	*The Canadian Balance of Payments: Perspectives and Policy Issues.* 1983 $24.95
Roy A. Matthews	*Canada and the "Little Dragons": An Analysis of Economic Developments in Hong Kong, Taiwan, and South Korea and the Challenge/ Opportunity They Present for Canadian Interests in the 1980s.* 1983 $11.95
Charles Pearson & Gerry Salembier	*Trade, Employment, and Adjustment.* 1983 $5.00
Steven Globerman	*Cultural Regulation in Canada.* 1983 $11.95
F.R. Flatters & R.G. Lipsey	*Common Ground for the Canadian Common Market.* 1983 $5.00
Frank Bunn, assisted by U. Domb, D. Huntley, H. Mills, H. Silverstein	*Oceans from Space: Towards the Management of Our Coastal Zones.* 1983 $5.00
C.D. Shearing & P.C. Stenning	*Private Security and Private Justice: The Challenge of the 80s.* 1983 $5.00
Jacob Finkelman & Shirley B. Goldenberg	*Collective Bargaining in the Public Service: The Federal Experience in Canada.* 2 vols. 1983 $29.95 (set)
Gail Grant	*The Concrete Reserve: Corporate Programs for Indians in the Urban Work Place.* 1983 $5.00
Owen Adams & Russell Wilkins	*Healthfulness of Life.* 1983 $8.00
Yoshi Tsurumi with Rebecca R. Tsurumi	*Sogoshosha: Engines of Export-Based Growth.* (Revised Edition). 1984 $10.95
Raymond Breton & Gail Grant (eds.)	*The Dynamics of Government Programs for Urban Indians in the Prairie Provinces.* 1984 $19.95

Frank Stone	*Canada, The GATT and the International Trade System.* 1984 $15.00
Pierre Sauvé	*Private Bank Lending and Developing-Country Debt.* 1984 $10.00
Mark Thompson & Gene Swimmer	*Conflict or Compromise: The Future of Public Sector Industrial Relations.* 1984 $15.00
Samuel Wex	*Instead of FIRA: Autonomy for Canadian Subsidiaries?* 1984 $8.00
R.J. Wonnacott	*Selected New Developments in International Trade Theory.* 1984 $7.00
R.J. Wonnacott	*Aggressive US Reciprocity Evaluated with a New Analytical Approach to Trade Conflicts.* 1984 $8.00
Richard W. Wright	*Japanese Business in Canada: The Elusive Alliance.* 1984 $12.00
Paul K. Gorecki & W.T. Stanbury	*The Objectives of Canadian Competition Policy, 1888-1983.* 1984 $15.00
Michael Hart	*Some Thoughts on Canada-United States Sectoral Free Trade.* 1985 $7.00
J. Peter Meekison Roy J. Romanow & William D. Moull	*Origins and Meaning of Section 92A: The 1982 Constitutional Amendment on Resources.* 1985 $10.00
Conference Papers	*Canada and International Trade. Volume One: Major Issues of Canadian Trade Policy. Volume Two: Canada and the Pacific Rim.* 1985 $25.00 (set)
A.E. Safarian	*Foreign Direct Investment: A Survey of Canadian Research.* 1985 $8.00
Joseph R. D'Cruz & James D. Fleck	*Canada Can Compete! Strategic Management of the Canadian Industrial Portfolio.* 1985 $18.00
Barry Lesser & Louis Vagianos	*Computer Communications and the Mass Market in Canada.* 1985 $10.00
W.R. Hines	*Trade Policy Making in Canada: Are We Doing it Right?* 1985 $10.00
Bertrand Nadeau	*Britain's Entry into the European Economic Community and its Effect on Canada's Agricultural Exports.* 1985 $10.00
Paul B. Huber	*Promoting Timber Cropping: Policies Toward Non-Industrial Forest Owners in New Brunswick.* 1985 $10.00
Gordon Robertson	*Northern Provinces: A Mistaken Goal.* 1985 $8.00

Petr Hanel	*La technologie et les exportations canadiennes du matériel pour la filière bois-papier.* 1985 $20.00
Russel M. Wills, Steven Globerman & Peter J. Booth	*Software Policies for Growth and Export.* 1986 $15.00
Marc Malone	*Une place pour le Québec au Canada.* 1986 $20.00
A. R. Dobell & S. H. Mansbridge	*The Social Policy Process in Canada.* 1986 $8.00
William D. Shipman (ed.)	*Trade and Investment Across the Northeast Boundary: Quebec, the Atlantic Provinces, and New England.* 1986 $20.00
Nicole Morgan	*Implosion: An Analysis of the Growth of the Federal Public Service in Canada (1945-1985).* 1986 $20.00
Nicole Morgan	*Implosion: analyse de la croissance de la Fonction publique fédérale canadienne (1945-1985).* 1986 $20.00
William A.W. Neilson & Chad Gaffield (eds.)	*Universities in Crisis: A Mediaeval Institution in the Twenty-first Century.* 1986 $20.00